2008 B26 W9-BXW-692

12/22

ELMWOOD PARK PUBLIC LIBRARY
1 CONTI PARKWAY
ELMWOOD PARK, IL 60707
(708) 453-7645

1. A fine is charged for each day a book is kept beyond the due date. The Library Board may take legal action if books are not returned within three months

2. Books damaged beyond reasonable wear shall be paid for.

3. Each borrower is responsible for all books charged on this card and for all fines accruing on the same.

THE
PREDATOR
STATE

How Conservatives Abandoned the Free Market
and Why Liberals Should Too

James K. Galbraith

FREE PRESS
New York London Toronto Sydney

FREE PRESS
A Division of Simon & Schuster, Inc.
1230 Avenue of the Americas
New York, NY 10020

First Free Press hardcover edition August 2008

FREE PRESS and colophon are trademarks of Simon & Schuster, Inc.

For information about special discounts for bulk purchases,
please contact Simon & Schuster Special Sales at 1-800-456-6798
or business@simonandschuster.com.

DESIGNED BY ERICH HOBBING

Manufactured in the United States of America

3   5   7   9   10   8   6   4

Library of Congress Cataloging-in-Publication Data
Galbraith, James K.
The predator state: how conservatives abandoned the free market
and why liberals should too / James K. Galbraith.
p. cm.
1. Free enterprise—United States. 2. United States—Economic policy—1981–.
I. Title.
HB95.G35   2008
330.973—dc22   2008006660

ISBN-13: 978-1-4165-6683-0
ISBN-10: 1-4165-6683-X

For C.A.G.
with love
and in memory of
J.K.G.

If liberty of speech is to be untrammeled from the grosser forms of constraint, then uniformity of opinion will be secured by a moral terrorism to which the respectability of society will give its thorough approval.
—Charles Sanders Peirce, *The Fixation of Belief*, 1877

CONTENTS

CONTENTS

PREFACE

This book got under way right after Hurricane Katrina, the destruction of New Orleans, and the dispersion of several hundred thousand refugees across the American South, including to my hometown of Austin, Texas. It seemed clear immediately that Katrina had been the Chernobyl of the American system. That is, beyond the natural calamity and the human tragedy, it was—like that Soviet reactor meltdown nineteen years before—a disaster that exposed and laid bare the fallacies of an entire governing creed.

But where the Soviet creed was of central planning, ours was its polar opposite, a cult of the free market. And as I charted my way through this book, I came to realize that the relationship between actual policy in the United States and the doctrines of policy is not simple. In uncanny ways, this relationship has come to resemble its counterpart in the old Soviet Union: actual policies were (and are) in no principled way governed by official doctrine. Rather, the doctrine serves as a kind of legitimating myth—something to be repeated to schoolchildren but hardly taken seriously by those on the inside.

What is the purpose of the myth? It serves here, as it did there, mainly as a device for corralling the opposition, restricting the flow of thought, shrinking the sphere of admissible debate. Just as even a lapsed believer kneels in church, respectable opposition demonstrates fealty to the system by asserting allegiance to the governing myth. This in turn limits the range of presentable ideas, conveniently setting an entire panoply of reasoned discourse beyond the pale of what can be said, at least in public, by reputable people. There is a process of internalization, of self-censorship. Once the rules and boundaries prescribed by the myth are understood, adherence becomes reflexive, and at the end of the day people come to think only what it is permitted to think. They know when they might be "going too far."

So the first task of this book is to describe the myth, its logical structure, its popular appeal, and especially the set of rules for policy to which it leads. This task is eased by the existence of a clear historical moment when those rules were crystallized and stated most clearly. That moment occurred in 1981 with the inauguration of Ronald Reagan as President of the United States. The early Reaganites performed an important service to intellectual history by distilling their ideas into four major bodies of economic law: monetarism, supply-side economics (including tax cuts and deregulation), balanced budgets, and free trade. The first part of the book describes these more or less in turn.

A governing myth hides an underlying reality, and any attempt to govern through the myth is bound to be short-lived. So it was with Reagan. But what is the essence of that reality in the American case? If we do not actually live in a world made by Reagan, just as the Soviets did not actually live in a world made by Marx, what is the true nature of our actual existing world?

An evolutionary economist knows where to look for the answer to such a question: at institutions. In the American setting, once one starts to do that, it becomes immediately clear that the fundamental public institutions of American economic life were those created by public action in an earlier generation—by Franklin D. Roosevelt in the New Deal and World War II, by Lyndon Johnson in the Great Society, and to a degree by Richard Nixon—and that these institutions have, to a large extent, survived to the present day.

But if they have survived, obviously they have not survived undamaged. The catastrophe of Hurricane Katrina pointed to two types of damage. One was *an erosion of capability*, evinced in this case by the failure by the Army Corps of Engineers to maintain the levees protecting New Orleans to a standard sufficient to withstand a Category Three hurricane, which is all that Katrina actually was by the time it came ashore. This kind of erosion presupposes nothing about intent. It can and does happen simply because of resource constraints, misjudgments, accidents of politics, and history. We see this sort of erosion far and wide in American government, but repairing it is characteristically thought to be mainly a matter of dedication, competence, time, and money.

But Katrina, and especially the aftermath of the disaster, also illustrated a second and more serious sort of rot in the system. This I will call *predation:* the systematic abuse of public institutions for private profit or, equivalently, the systematic undermining of public protections for the benefit of private clients. The deformation of the Federal Emergency Management Agency into a dumping ground for cronies under the government of George W. Bush—"Heckuva job, Brownie"— captured the essence of this phenomenon. But so too does the practice of turning regulatory agencies over to business lobbies, the privatization of national security and the attempted privatization of Social Security, the design of initiatives in Medicare to benefit drug companies, and trade agreements to benefit corporate agriculture at the expense of subsistence farmers in the Third World. In each case, what we see is not, in fact, a principled conservative's drive to minimize the state. It is a predator's drive to divert public resources to clients and friends. This seemed to me to have become the reality underlying the myth, and the second part of the book is devoted to sketching it out.

Finally, in a book like this, there always comes the question of what should be done. I chose to restrict myself to three very basic ideas. Having spent much of my career as a policy adviser, admittedly often to quixotic contenders for high public office, I could have written much more in this part. But I chose these three ideas in part because they struck me as being the most despised, the most dangerous, the hardest to get across, and therefore the most important of all the essential points that might be offered here.

The three ideas are, for all that, quite simple.

First, because markets cannot and do not think ahead, the United States needs a capacity to plan. To build such a capacity, we must, first of all, overcome our taboo against planning. Planning is inherently imperfect, but in the absence of planning, disaster is certain.

Second, the setting of wages and the control of the distribution of pay and incomes is a social, and not a market, decision. It is not the case that technology dictates what people are worth and should be paid. Rather, society decides what the distribution of pay should be, and technology adjusts to that configuration. Standards—for pay but also for product and occupational safety and for the environment—are a device whereby society fashions technology to its needs. And more egalitarian standards—those that lead to a more just society—also promote the most rapid and effective forms of technological change, so that there is no trade-off, in a properly designed economic policy, between efficiency and fairness.

Third, at this juncture in history, the United States needs to come to grips with its position in the global economy and prepare for the day when the unlimited privilege of issuing never-to-be-paid chits to the rest of the world may come to an end. We should not hasten that day; in fact, if possible, we should delay it. We should take reasonable steps to try to keep the current system intact. But given the rot in the system, we should also be prepared for a crisis that could come up very fast. The fate of the country, and indeed the security and prosperity of the entire world, could depend on whether we are able to deal with such a crisis once it starts.

This is a short book, lightly referenced, written for a general audience and not especially for a scholarly one. I have by no means attempted to cover every argument or document every point, and I have deliberately steered clear of numerical data and algebraic equations. Readers who have followed my work will recognize this as a departure from my usual methods; some may be disappointed. A price of accessibility is that the evidence behind some of the strongest factual claims made here cannot be laid out in full; I rely on the reader's trust that while errors are certainly possible, claims are stated in good faith, based on what I believe to be true. For my part, I found the task of writing in plain English and without the habitual load of notes, charts, and tables extremely difficult. It certainly forced me to try to clarify my thought, and I hope that I have, to some degree, succeeded at that.

Austin, Texas
November 25, 2007

PART ONE

Another God
That Failed

CHAPTER ONE

Whatever Happened
to the Conservatives?

Does anyone else recall the days when to be an economic conservative in the United States meant something? As a young liberal on the congressional staff a long time ago, I remember them in vivid frustration. The 1970s saw the rise of two distinct conservative movements, the supply-siders and the monetarists: radical tax cutters and deregulators on one side, apostles of strict control over the money stock on the other. Their rise culminated in the Reagan revolution of 1980, which brought them both into high office. This was personal: the conservative alliance devalued my Keynesian education, obstructed my career, and deprived me and my few comrades on Capitol Hill of purchase on the levers of power. It was difficult politically. As executive director of the Joint Economic Committee in 1981, I organized a largely futile frontline resistance. But intellectually it was even worse. However much one disagreed with them, these were people who *believed*. They were idealists. They had the force of conviction. Worse still, they were setting the agenda. And there was the thought: Suppose they were right?

The Reaganites offered up a famous combination of policies that had grown largely from seeds planted in the academy during the long years of liberal rule. The central element was reduction of taxes on wealth, intended to unlock the productive powers of capital, spurring saving and investment. Tight money was intended to end inflation quickly, brutally if necessary. And with this came a wide-ranging assault on government, regulation, and unions, whose purpose was to let market forces—and private capitalists—rule.

Except among the immediate victims, the great conservative ideas for a time had wide appeal. Some of it was scientific. For each problem, they offered a solution. Each solution was rooted in the attractive vision of free individual economic choice, coordinated only by the marketplace and the gentle persuasions of price. The solutions had scholarly credentials; they were rooted in the economics my generation had imbibed in graduate school. For that reason, President Reagan was able to draw on some of the most prominent economists in the country, not all of them ideologues by any means. Murray Weidenbaum and Martin Feldstein were his first chairs of the Council of Economic Advisers, and even young tyros Lawrence Summers and Paul Krugman, who each came in for a year under Feldstein, would serve in his administration. Nobody of remotely comparable talent would work under George W. Bush.

In addition to intellectual legitimacy, the popularity of the conservative viewpoint in those days had an emotional, even a romantic, aspect. The conservatives promised prosperity without the trouble of planning for it, achieved through a simple three-step program: cut taxes, end inflation, and free the market. At a deeper level, they promised an end to a kind of politics that many in elite circles—frankly in both major parties—had come to loathe: the politics of compromise, redistribution, and catering to the needs and demands of minorities and the poor. America in 1980 had compassion fatigue. The conservative agenda promised, perhaps more than anything else, to make compassion redundant. In addition, it was audacious, radical, flashy—a program with sex appeal. Suddenly it was the conservatives who were the brave and brash bad boys of American culture, while liberals like myself had become the country's killjoys, young fogies hopelessly in the grip of old ideas.

What is left of all this, twenty-five years on? Essentially nothing. The election of November 7, 2006, swept conservative Republicans from their majorities in both houses of Congress and signaled a new skepticism about entrusting government to those who profess to despise it. Plainly the public no longer believes what conservative leaders say about free markets. The death of Milton Friedman ten days later symbolized the era's end. Yet as the *Wall Street Journal*'s own Friedman obituary conceded, policymakers had long previously discarded the practical substance of his ideas.* Central banks do not

---

*Greg Ip and Mark Whitehouse, "How Milton Friedman Changed Economics, Policy and Markets," *Wall Street Journal*, November 17, 2006, p. A1.

attempt to control the money supply. Regulation has been reinstated in finance, and the facts of climate change make a new era of environmental interventions inevitable, sooner or later. Meanwhile, the world has given up waiting for tax cuts to unleash the hidden creativity of the business class.

The issue today is not whether the great conservative ideas once had appeal or a foundation in reputable theory. The issue is whether they have a future. And on that point, there is general agreement today, largely shared even by those who still believe passionately in the conservative cause. The fact is that the Reagan era panoply of ideas has been abandoned as the intellectual basis of a political program. There are almost no monetarists left in power. There are no convinced supply-siders (though the catechism is still occasionally recited). There are no public intellectual leaders in any campaign for "free markets" and against regulation. "Free trade" has been reduced to a label, pasted over trade agreements that are anything but "free." The economic conservative still reigns supreme in the academy and on the talk shows, but in the public realm, he is today practically null and void. He does not exist. And if he were to resurface today in the policy world, offering up the self-confident doctrines of 1980, he would be taken seriously by no one.

Today, in the great policy house of the conservatives, there are only lobbyists and the politicians who do their bidding. There are slogans and sloganeers. There are cronies and careerists. There are occasional fix-it men who are called in when major disasters have to be repaired. There are people who predict disaster, quite routinely, in order to justify the destruction of Social Security and other popular programs, for the transparent purpose of turning them over to friends on Wall Street. Mercifully few believe them, though that does not end the danger, for they represent forces whose power does not rest on persuasion. There are university economists who can be tapped, as ever, for high public office, but they plainly lack convictions. Once in office, they come and go, doing nothing to advance the conservative case. In public view, the conservative house stood for a long time, a mansion visible from all parts of the landscape. But inside, the place was decrepit; its intellectual foundation had collapsed. A few true believers continued to live there, but it was not any great surprise, even to them, when it fell down.

What are the Reagan conservatives doing today? Milton Friedman himself, the father of monetarism, in 2003 repudiated his own old policy doctrine: "The use of quantity of money as a target has not been a success. . . . I'm not sure I would as of today push it as hard as I once did," he told the *Financial Times*.* In the face of the complete collapse of the evidence on which they had based their case linking money growth to price change, the other monetarists have mostly dropped the topic or passed on. Practically everyone today agrees: the Federal Reserve sets the short-term interest rate, and it is interest rates, not the money stock, that drive the economy. Indeed, the Federal Reserve recently quietly ceased to publish certain monetary statistics in which the academic world had lost interest (and no one else ever had any).

Jude Wanniski, the original supply-sider, died at age sixty-nine in late 2005. He never stopped being a supply-sider and, I think, a true believer. But from 2001 onward, he devoted himself to opposing, eloquently, the neoconservative wars; he and I became friends and even coauthored an article on one occasion. It was joint antimonetarist advice—from the "first supply-sider" and the "last Keynesian"—to the Federal Reserve against raising interest rates. George Gilder, who scourged the poor and celebrated wealth in the early 1980s, went on to become a guru of the technology revolution in the 1990s; when the tech boom collapsed, so did the market for his stock-picking skills. Paul Craig Roberts, assistant secretary of the treasury for economic policy in the Reagan administration, later author of *The Supply-Side Revolution* and a columnist for *Business Week*, has become a vehement voice against the Iraq war, the building threat of a war with Iran, and the assault on civil liberties that is part of the "global war on terror." Bruce Bartlett, once an avid young supply-sider and author of *Reaganomics*, remains an old-fashioned advocate of the most forlorn cause in modern history: small government. In 2005 he published a book entitled *Impostor: How George W. Bush Bankrupted America and Betrayed the Reagan Revolution*.

Perhaps the greatest conservative true believer was the Old Objectivist himself, Alan Greenspan, for eighteen years chairman of the board of governors of the Federal Reserve System. Though never a monetarist, Greenspan assiduously favored tax cuts, spending cuts, and deregulation. In office he always deferred to the avatars of free markets, refusing to use his judgment or his soapbox or his regulatory power against speculative bubbles in technology and housing. His

---

*Simon London, "Targeting the Quantity of Money . . . .'Has Not Been a Success,'" *Financial Times*, June 9, 2003.

philosophy on these matters was that markets are like that and the job of government is to clean up the mess after the crash. Yet in his monumental recent confessions, *The Age of Turbulence*, Greenspan delivered his verdict on the Republicans of 2006: "They traded principle for power and ended up with neither. They deserved to lose."*

It is fashionable today to dismiss the Reagan conservatives, including those I have mentioned, as swindlers, the mere tools of the monied interests who backed them. This is the approach taken, for instance, by *New Republic* senior editor Jonathan Chait in his new book, *The Big Con*, while Paul Krugman in his new book, *Conscience of a Liberal*, tends to treat them as either swindlers or fools. I have no objection to the political economy of those books; money does talk. But I do not think the verdict is entirely fair. The fact that money hires ideas is not necessarily a decisive argument against the ideas; it does not make the ideas illegitimate on their face. Nor is it correct to argue that the monetarists, the supply-siders, and the deregulators were fringe-end elements in academic circles. To the contrary, Milton Friedman's followers entirely dominated discussions of monetary policy for a generation. Flat-taxers like Robert Hall and Alvin Rabushka were ensconced in top departments and think tanks; supply-sider Robert Mundell won the economists' version of the Nobel Prize. The fact is, Reagan's radicals had a deep academic bench, including a fair number who did not think his policies went nearly far enough. The disillusionment today of the remaining Reagan policy veterans with the Bush regime goes deeper than the fact that they are not on the payroll. It has to do, rather, with the collapse of their ideas as governing doctrine. Meanwhile, they are now shunned by the theorists in the academy, who would rather not leave fingerprints on the wreckage. But they rightly remember the day when the big professors were happy to be their friends.

There is a reason, in short, that principled conservatives find themselves in the political wilderness once again: they belong there. They are noble savages and the wilderness is their native element. They do not belong in government because, as a practical matter, they have little to contribute to it; they are guilty of taking the myths they helped to create too seriously, and to sophisticated people, that makes them look a bit foolish. They are against deficits, government spending, and the expansion of publicly financed health care coverage. Fine.

*Alan Greenspan, *The Age of Turbulence* (New York: Penguin Press, 2007), p. 244.

What do they propose to do about them? They favor income tax cuts, and cuts in tax rates on all forms of wealth, but do they still argue, as a good conservative needs to believe, that such cuts would be self-financing, that savings, investment, and work effort will bloom? Of course they don't, because the experiment was tried, and it failed. They still favor free markets in broad principle, but do they speak in detail of the fate of the airlines, the national forests, the coal miners, and the savings and loan industry under deregulation? No. We find that for the most part, these are topics that the latter-day divines of the free-market-in-principle would very much prefer to avoid.

Looking forward, one may ask how economic conservatives address our current problems. Do they have an alternative to our oil addiction, to imperial commitment, to global warming? No. Did they have a program of recovery for the city of New Orleans? No. Is there a realistic conservative plan for health care? No. There is merely opposition to everyone else's ideas. Is there a realistic conservative approach to immigration? Not really. Part of the conservative movement favors a brutal and impossible wall, and part of it favors a return to indentured servitude in the form of a guest worker program. Have the conservatives come to grips with the changing global economy, notably the wave of economic crises since 1980 and the rise of the one large country to stay away from the globalized financial system, namely, China? Do they have a vision for the future of the world monetary system should something happen to confidence in the dollar? No. The terms of the policy dialogue have changed, but the terms of reference of the great conservative economic worldview have not.

It is therefore no surprise that George W. Bush failed to make principled use of principled conservatives, thereby earning their embittered rejection. The reality is that no government, no matter how far to the right in political terms, could make any serious use of them. The experience of the past quarter-century and the evolution of practical understanding about economic policy since the Reagan years simply makes it impossible to take the conservative worldview seriously as a constellation of ideas to be applied to policy. And therefore it is fair to say that there will never again be any U.S. government for which a truly principled conservative might work. In the final analysis, Bush is remarkable merely for his lack of interest in hiring committed intellectuals to shill for his policies, and therefore for his willingness to court rejection by the principled conservative crowd. He ran an unapologetic government of businessmen and lobbyists, governing largely without academic cover.

Moreover, not only have the conservatives been cast from power, they have also ceased to evolve. Is there any such thing as a modern conservative economic policy idea? Not only are there no Reaganite intellectuals in Bush's government, the flow of new suggestions from the academic citadels into the policy arena has stopped. To find the main work of today's leading academic conservatives requires reaching back thirty years. All of the ideas that define conservative economic thought in America (and in the rest of the world) were well known a generation ago. They were all tested, in the United States, the United Kingdom, and around the rest of the world, in the cauldron of the 1980s. And they were nearly all abandoned by policymakers long ago—by the end of the 1980s at the latest in the United States, by the early 1990s in Britain, and by the end of the 1990s in most of the rest of the world. Those that were enacted, like charter schools, are in the evaluation phase, and the record is not especially good. Those that remain on the agenda (or are likely to come again), like the privatization of Social Security, have no new justification. The arguments cooked up for that cause are at least twenty years old. Academic economics today is divided largely between a body of pragmatic work that is no longer very conservative (but, rather, apolitical) and a body of conservative doctrine that lacks any connection to the policy world.

These abandonments were not incidental defections, without which we would still live in the world of Reagan and Thatcher. They were experiments that failed. They were lessons learned, often the hard way. They were strategic retreats, sometimes under heavy fire. The reality is that the disciplined application of conservative principles to economic policy leads to disaster. This is particularly true of policies intended to manage or transform the economy as a whole.

Everywhere and always, monetarism leads to financial crisis. Supply-side tax cuts have no detectable effect on work effort, or savings, or investment. Financial deregulation, from the savings and loan debacle to the subprime mortgage fiasco, leads to criminal misdirection of the firm. Cuts in government spending are neither necessary nor sufficient for productivity gain. These are facts now well absorbed by practical policymakers, around whom the vestiges of past conservative verities hang in tatters. Only the dedicated academic economist can pretend to be unaware of them, and the conservative creed economics survives at

9

all not because of a renewable wellspring of success stories, but only because it retains a powerful grip on the academy itself, on the ideas that scholars reproduce for the closed circle of their own journals. That grip will be difficult to dislodge because academics do not face elections. But it is no longer a very important fact for the policy world.

A similar fate has befallen the made-for-export version of the conservative creed, the so-called Washington Consensus of international development strategies, a set of universal precepts of sound money, balanced budgets, deregulation, privatization, and free trade. These too rose in the wake of the Reagan revolution and its international counterpart, the debt crisis of the Third World. They were forced on Latin America, East Europe, Africa, and parts of Asia on the promise that the "magic of the marketplace" would generate growth and prosperity in the wake of failed policies of protectionism, subsidies, and ineffective support for industrial development. It turned out that economic success in the Third World since 1980 has been in negative relation to the consensus. Those that adhered most closely to the Washington Consensus, like Argentina, suffered crisis and collapse, while those that followed their own paths, notably China, prospered. As this became clear, rebellion against the Washington Consensus has spread across Latin America, Africa, and much of Asia, where today the model is universally repudiated in principle and increasingly evaded in practice. In Argentina, once a poster child of neoliberal conformism, economic recovery followed the repudiation of debts both philosophical and financial. In despised places like Venezuela and Russia, high energy prices have fostered financial and philosophical independence, and the International Monetary Fund (IMF) is today in most of the world a spent force, with no remaining programs in Latin America at all, revenues insufficient to cover its spending, and large layoffs in the works. Even managing director Dominique Strauss-Kahn has admitted that the organization is "a factory to produce paper."

These are the facts. But even though as facts they are widely recognized and acted on in practice, our political discourse has its own rituals and does not yet admit them. Indeed, few politicians in either party have yet publicly divorced themselves from the Reagan revolution, in particular from the idea of the free market. Politicians notoriously say what is convenient and act along different lines entirely, causing problems for those who try to write about their views in a careful and serious way. But perhaps on no other issue is this tendency more pronounced than in matters relating to the markets—a word one apparently cannot use in public in the United States without bending a knee and making the sign of the cross.

And here the political world is divided into two groups. There are those who praise the free market because to do so gives cover to themselves and their friends in raiding the public trough. These people call themselves "conservatives," and one of the truly galling things for real conservatives is that they have both usurped the label and spoiled the reputation of the real thing. And there are those who praise the "free market" simply because they fear that, otherwise, they will be exposed as heretics, accused of being socialists, perhaps even driven from public life. This is the case of many liberals. Reflexive invocations of the power of markets, the "magic" of markets, and the virtues of a "free enterprise system" therefore remain staples of political speech on both sides of the political aisle. However, they have been emptied of practical content, and the speakers know it.

Yet this is not another book about the insincerity of the group of conservative impostors in power; that case has been sufficiently made, and I have already delivered my own views on George Bush, Dick Cheney, and Alan Greenspan in another book.* This book is mainly about the rise and fall of authentically conservative ideas, about the inadequacy of their central metaphor, the free market. My purpose is not to denigrate those who took up the conservative cause a generation ago; many have become my friends and I respect them. My plan here is to take the conservative project seriously, on the premise that it was offered in good faith. The principled conservatives were, in my view, naive; I obviously believe they were wrong, and they have been abandoned by history, but none of this proves that they were dishonest. And if some really were cranks and charlatans, they had plenty of company among the most respectable and prestigious academic economists in the land.

My aim, in this exercise, is to try to free up the liberal mind. For while the right wing in power has abandoned the deeper philosophical foundations of its cause, liberals remain largely mesmerized by those foundations. Outside the area of trade policy, where an enduring populism reflexively opposes "free trade" agreements, liberals have largely

---

*Unbearable Cost: Bush, Greenspan and the Economics of Empire (London: Palgrave Macmillan, 2006).

accepted the basic conservative principles: monetary control, balanced budgets, regulation only where it can be shown that "markets fail." And until they break the spell, they will not be able to think or talk about the world in terms that relate effectively to its actual condition. Nor will they be able to advance a policy program that might actually work. And since liberals may well, at some point in the near future, seize the keys to the realm, what they think and (more important) *how* they think has come to matter, once again, as it has not really mattered for nearly half a century.

To take an example, Senator Hillary Rodham Clinton has, in the past, shown an admirable willingness to criticize the "free market." According to the radically conservative journal *Human Events*, in 1996 she said on C-Span that "the unfettered free market has been the most radically destructive force in American life in the last generation."* Yet in 2007 her presidential campaign program on the economy promises to "reward savings" and "balance the federal budget"—classic conservative themes. She calls for measures to "make health care affordable," which implies that she believes health care should still be bought and sold on the market. While calling for stronger protections for the middle class, she is careful to declare her faith: "Now, there is no greater force for economic growth than free markets, but markets work best with rules that promote our values, protect our workers and give all people a chance to succeed."†

Senator Clinton is, many believe, a liberal. And as an example of the type, she is typical. Liberals continue to behave as though they face a philosophically coherent adversary and as though the politics of the day require formulating a program that responds to that adversary. In their economic policy efforts, many liberals thus engage in a dialogue with themselves, starting from doctrines, such as monetarism or balanced budgets, that have practically no ongoing defenders outside of the pure theorists hidden away in academic life. This leads to a paralysis of thought and action and to programs doomed to futility and failure from the beginning.

Partly in consequence of their enthrallment with the frame created for them by the conservative worldview, the Left has been doing too

---

*Thomas D. Kuiper, "Quote Wars: Milton Friedman vs. Hillary Clinton," *Human Events*, April 13, 2007. http://www.humanevents.com/article.php?id=20237.
†http://www.hillaryclinton.com/news/speech/view/?id=1839.

little thinking of its own. Liberals have yet to develop a coherent post-Reagan theory of the world, let alone a policy program informed by the political revelations, world policy changes, and scientific realities emerging from the Age of Bush. For the most part, they do not analyze, and do not engage with, the actual program of the right wing in power today. It is emblematic of this that the leading Democratic idea of the 2008 campaign has been health care coverage, an idea that has been a lead item on the progressive agenda since 1948—sixty years!—and that Democrats take today as essentially unchanged since the defeat of President Bill Clinton's health care plan in 1993. It is not to minimize the importance of universal health insurance to say that the preeminence of the issue in national policy dialogue reflects the stasis of the liberal mind much more than it reflects a considered strategy to counter the powerful forces that have lately shaped our age.

In consequence, new economic issues emerging under the influence of pressing events are dangerously underexamined. These issues include war, climate change, energy supply, corruption and fraud including election fraud, the collapse of public governing capacity, the perilous position of the international dollar, and the position of immigrants in American society. These issues form the crux of the future of economic policy, and against them the achievement of universal health insurance seems relatively straightforward. But none of these issues is getting more than passing development as yet from those to whom liberals look for ideas.

The Iraq war has, in particular, driven home to everyone involved the bankruptcy not merely of the Bush administration's management but of the larger strategy of global military dominance built up in the Reagan era and still run largely by the personnel of that time. The military officers know this. But where is the liberal political voice who has dared speak of it in public?* Hurricane Katrina stripped away the illusion that the federal government retains the capacity to move quickly to serve the needs of ordinary citizens in time of crisis and peril. Katrina illustrates exactly what to expect in the event of further natural disaster or cataclysmic attack. But where, again, is the liberal political organization that places this issue at the center of a program? Nor have we yet come to grips with the growing crisis in housing and housing

---

*An honorable exception is former senator Gary Hart, in the political wilderness for many years.

finance: a crisis that as I finish this book is generating foreclosure notices every month nearly equal to the numbers displaced by Katrina. As for international finance, an esoteric and complex issue to most people except when they travel to Europe and experience the precipitous decline of the dollar at first hand, the liberal response is to leave all this in the hands of friendly bankers, a gift to the leaders of Wall Street whose expertise is supposedly keen, and who are happy to act as the mediums of market discipline, delivering the message that nothing much can be done. There is no way effectively to address any of these issues within the straitjacket dictated by the "magic of markets."

It remains for us to step outside this deadly framework, first to examine the tenets of the old conservative worldview one by one, and then to develop an alternative within which the problems we actually face can be addressed as we go forward.

CHAPTER TWO

The Freedom to Shop

To explain the appeal of conservative economics to the wealthy is no great challenge. These ideas have always enjoyed a firm foundation of support among the rich who want low taxes, among business leaders desiring minimal public oversight (and risk that they might be sent to jail), and among bankers who generally prefer high interest rates on their loans, if not their deposits. Indeed the confluence and harmony among these constituencies and their allies in academic life is so great that lines of causation are sometimes suspected, by the deeply cynical, to run from the money to the ideas and not the other way around.

But what about the appeal to everyone else? How did the Reagan revolution become, even briefly, almost a mass movement? How did the material interests of the very rich come to seem to be appealing to so many who were not, and who knew—or should have known—that under the conditions being created, they would never themselves become rich?* Reagan was in fact never quite as popular as the media incessantly argued at the time, but in no sense did he represent a pure plutocracy; his movement and even his economic policies did indeed have the makings of a mass base. It was (and always is) the purpose of an ideology—of a set of ideas—to reach out beyond those who were buying and those who were bought, to convince a much larger group with no direct financial stake in policy outcomes. For this purpose, the conservative movement had a secret weapon, and that was the link between markets and "freedom." This they called the concept of "economic freedom."

What is "economic freedom"? One might think that such a concept

---

*Thomas Frank, *What's the Matter with Kansas?* (New York: Henry Holt and Company, 2004), memorably explores this issue.

15

would refer to freedom from the compulsions of economic life: from the necessity of working in order to eat, for example, or the choice between paying for medicine and paying the rent. But this is not the case. Nor is economic freedom akin in any way to what we normally consider to be political freedom: it is not closely related to the freedoms of speech, the press, or assembly—freedoms related to the right to participate in political life and to influence public policy. It does not consist, for instance, of meeting basic needs so that cultural and political expression can thrive. The great proponents of economic freedom are not Deweyan democrats; they are not interested in promoting mass participation in political decision making.

Indeed, the conservative concept of economic freedom actually stands opposed to any measures that commit the state to raising the standard of living of the broad population. It opposes such ideas as universal health care, free public education, and public subsidies to the arts, and it particularly opposes these measures if they are to be financed by redistributive and progressive taxation. Social welfare implemented by democratic decision, as in Roosevelt's New Deal, Lyndon Johnson's Great Society, let alone the Chile of Salvador Allende or the Venezuela of Hugo Chavez, is to this way of thinking intrinsically unfree.* Meanwhile, the "free market" regime of Augusto Pinochet, in this conception, brought "economic freedom" to Chile. People can be free economically without having any voice in politics at all, indeed while living (or, for that matter, dying) under the jackboots of a military junta.

Economic freedom thus consists in the ability to live one's economic life—and that alone—in a sphere separated from state control and therefore reserved to the interaction of private forces. As Milton Friedman would define it in the title of his 1980 best seller,† economic freedom to conservatives means being *free to choose*. It is a freedom *to spend*. To put this idea into perspective, we should call it what it is: the freedom to shop.

One tends to look past this idea on the grounds that it is palpably

---

*Conservatives routinely refer to Chavez as a dictator, as they did to Allende, even though both were democratically elected in fair and free elections and ruled according to law.

†Milton and Rose Friedman, *Free to Choose*, 1st ed. (New York: Harcourt Brace Jovanovich, 1980).

absurd, a perversion of language, to treat shopping as freedom. Is China therefore a free country simply because it has great shopping? Was the problem with the Soviet Union that it did not? Is the freedom to seek a wide variety of goods and services at wildly varying prices, from the upscale boutique to the mall to the factory outlet, really on a par with any other meaning of freedom? It is easy to scoff at the very idea, so remote from our liberal conception of freedom as bearing the lofty realms of political and social decision taking. But to scoff is a mistake. What's surprising is *how many people think so*, how instinctively correct the conservative notion of economic freedom seems, and how deeply this concept has penetrated modern life. A great many Americans actually do define themselves by the kind of shopping they do, as they fill their homes with the shopping that they have done. Similarly a great many people loathed the Soviet Union and the countries of Eastern Europe not because they were repressive but because they were drab. A great many Westerners saw a yearning for "freedom" in what was, for many, not much more than the wish for a better diet and stylish clothing.

In consequence, the freedom to shop has become, after a fashion, a political right. Wal-Mart's access to cheap goods from China depends on the availability of those goods but also on the U.S. government's willingness to let them in. Correspondingly, efforts to reverse the globalization of world trade, should they lead to rising prices and a reduced diversity of consumer goods, will threaten a way of life. They will be seen by much of the population as a fundamental attack on established freedom. And the populists who would protect jobs by restricting imports will come to be seen by many as the enemies of "freedom." Similarly, no one has written a right to cheap motor fuel into the Constitution. Nevertheless, as Jimmy Carter discovered in 1979 and as no American President has since forgotten, woe betide the government that lets the tanks go dry. The same has surely also become true of many items in the cornucopia of the American shopping mall; it is interesting to reflect on how the American people would react to a shortage economy, should they ever have to live in one. From a political standpoint, it seems that freedom became not what the Constitution or the laws protect, but simply what people think it is at any given time.

The concept of a freedom to shop has been extended, insidiously, from its origins in the realm of goods. It has reached, for instance, the realm of careers, where it plays even greater havoc with the normal use

17

of words. In a "free" capitalist society, with private schools and universities able to admit whom they please and charge what the market will bear, the freedom to choose one's profession becomes in part the freedom to become what one can afford to become. It is not the calling that does the choosing, in other words, but the person who chooses the calling he or she can pay for. The choice is "free"—because it's mainly a matter of money. It depends only partly on talent, training, discipline, or accomplishment of any kind; it does not depend on membership in any cultural elite. Money is, in this respect and from this perspective, a leveler—not a source of class distinctions but a way of breaking them down. The college dropout can become the country's richest person, and any charlatan a banker, business leader, or President of the United States. These are therefore the democratic professions, while those like mathematics or physical science that continue to govern themselves, to impose reasonably strict professional standards, are elitist. Money cannot buy an appointment in a physics department, and for this reason, physicists constitute a group whose public values are not entirely to be trusted.

By a logic of this kind—the triumph of the sensibility of the late George Wallace, but now so prevalent in our politics that we barely take note of it—Milton Friedman and Ronald Reagan, and later even George W. Bush, could present themselves as the democratic and even egalitarian, "regular guy" forces in the American society of their day. They did this through an inversion of perception that economic progressives and political liberals never got, but that resonated powerfully with at least part of the American public.

And then, even stranger, we have extended the concept of a freedom to shop from the markets for goods and labor to the market for capital itself. Thus, market freedom comes to include the freedom to buy and sell the livelihoods of other people. This is what makes the capital market—Wall Street—the ultimate judge in America of whether companies live or die, by whom they are run, and in what strategic direction they evolve. In this philosophy, government has no role except to protect investors from fraud. The strategic direction of the country plays no role, as that would be "industrial policy." Labor, consumers, and the environmentalists have no legitimate voice at all, but that of Goldman, Sachs or Kohlberg Kravis Roberts and Co. is not to be questioned. Freedom rules when money talks, and no one has the will or the wherewithal to talk back.

A great many people, not merely the rich, accept these ideas: a freedom to shop, a freedom to buy the career that you want, the freedom to merge and to acquire. They do so in part because it completely liberates them from any standard other than wealth and also from the political process. In this world, any policy that reorganizes or constrains the allocation of money beyond the minimum policing required to keep markets honest is in essence and by definition an assault on freedom. Even elections are not "free," unless those who have money are free to buy them. In our legal doctrines, written into the Constitution by latter-day zealots, the right of a big company to drown out public speech is itself "freedom of speech." Bush put it very simply in the 2000 campaign: the point of tax cuts was to return to people money that was already theirs.

Presiding over the choices one is free to make, mediating between the chooser and the chosen in the world of buy and sell, is a vaporous but omnipresent institution: the *market*. The market is the necessary counterpart to economic freedom; it is the broker, the means of detached and dispassionate interaction between parties with opposed interests. The market ensures that one person's freedom interferes with no other. Buyers want a low price; sellers want a high price. The market works out the price that exactly balances these desires, a price that is fair because it is the market price.

But this raises the question: What exactly is a market? What does it do? How does it work? The "market" in modern usage is not some physical location. It is no longer a place on the village square, a flea market, a supermarket, or a Wal-Mart. It is not a place to which one can go. It is not a person, a judge before whom one can appear, a jury before whom one must argue. Unlike the government, or a business enterprise, or a court, the market has no specific legal or procedural properties. Is it really an institution at all? Or is it something else, something more general? What, in other words, is the social and political function of this word?

When you come down to it, the word market is a *negation*. It is a word to be applied to the context of any transaction so long as that transaction is not directly dictated by the state. The word has no content of its own because it is defined simply, and for reasons of politics, by what it is not. The market is the nonstate, and thus it can do everything the state can do but with none of the procedures or rules or limitations. It is a cosmic and ethereal space, a disembodied decision maker—a Maxwell's Demon—that, somehow and without effort, balances and reflects the preferences of everyone participating in economic decisions.* It is a magic dance hall where Supply meets Demand, flirts and courts; a magic bedroom where the fraternal twins Quantity and Price are conceived. It can be these things precisely because it is nothing at all.

Because the word lacks any observable, regular, consistent meaning, marvelous powers can be assigned. The market establishes Value. It resolves conflict. It ensures Efficiency in the assignment of each factor of production to its most Valued use, and of each consumable good or service to the customer who wants it most, provided, always, he or she can pay. From each according to Supply, to each according to Demand. The market is thus truly a type of God, "wiser and more powerful than the largest computer," its enthusiasts say—somehow resolving the inchoate mass of differing individual preferences into a common best outcome. Markets achieve effortlessly exactly what governments fail to achieve by directed effort. No fuss, no muss, no budget, no time wasted in discussions, no voting, and no appeal. No wonder that conservatives and all who fall under their spell prefer markets to governments.

Of course, economics would not exist at all if the economist did not make some effort to study the organization of markets—their conduct, structure, and performance. And this study leads to doubts and questions. To achieve everything of which they are supposed to be capable under ideal conditions, markets must "work." And if they do not? If monopoly, oligopoly, duopoly, monopsony, asymmetric information, or externalities or the fundamental irrationalities of the behavior of real people stand in the way? These problems fill economics textbooks and journals, and academic economists have been preoccupied with them for decades. For this reason many academic economists are not in fact the enthusiasts of leaving everything to markets that their public image supposes them to be. But such issues have to be minimized in political discussions because they open the door to intervention. For the purposes of conservative economics in the policy realm, an imperfect market is as impermissible as a tolerable government, for once one admits imperfections, something has to be called to rescue, and, alas, only government is available for that purpose. And at that point, "freedom" is sunk. A market process that is directed or controlled by government is, by definition, no longer a market process at all.

*The reference is to a famous thought experiment in classical thermodynamics.

Thus, the profession of an immutable and pristine faith in markets is the hallmark of conservative idealism. The market is the guarantor of freedom, while the state is its nemesis: markets good, government bad. And this perspective is more than just the position held by a handful of zealots. The achievement of the conservative economics, as we have already seen, has been to make it the ticket of entry into reputable political discussion, a rite of passage for anyone who wants to be taken seriously on the public stage.

Those who do not wish trouble swallow the liturgy whole. Thus the 2008 Republican presidential candidate Mitt Romney described himself: "Romney believes a strong economy depends on free people and free markets. He supports low tax rates, minimal government regulation, free trade, and policies that encourage savings and investment."*

Can anyone in modern American politics actually oppose the market? Of course not. Can anyone deny its relevance, or even its existence? To do so would be political suicide—precisely like denying the existence of God, and for the same reasons. Though there are many private doubters, the private doubts are edited out of the public sphere. In politics the atheist makes a show of going to church. Can one seriously claim that government—a tangible decision-making process that actually exists—does a better job than the market, a hypothetical entity that for many practical purposes and problems does not exist at all? No. You cannot do that; it would be unthinkable. To profess skepticism or disbelief is to disqualify oneself on the face of it. Thus, we see the grip of "free-market economics" on the public stage: to be taken seriously, one must be able to profess a belief in magic with a straight face.

What, then, is a reality-based person to do? Many people appear to believe that the best they can do under the circumstances is to hedge and qualify, at the margins. That is, they can aver that the market *may* be imperfect, that *under certain conditions* it may fail, that it *might* function better given the aid of fuller information or certain constraints on behavior. And this position, deeply rooted in academic economics and therefore at least somewhat defensible on the public stage, has become the "liberal" position in debates over markets, linked to the slogan "Making markets work."

The problem with this compromise is that it depends on a misreading of the academic economics on which it is based. The underlying

*http://www.mittromney.com/News/In-The-News/Mitt_Romneys_Strength.

idea appears to be that markets exist but sometimes have problems: a bit of monopoly power, some kinks in the flow of information, a few side effects, maybe a little difficulty predicting the future. But in fact, the modern currents of academic economics are far more devastating than that. Each of the problems just mentioned is not incidental; rather, they are pervasive. Taken together, they raise serious doubts about the idea that markets can work at all. To state that again: taken together, they form an overwhelming critique of the very concept of the market.

In the purest version of the theory that underlies the conservative vision of the perfect market, economic man is a machine to whom whimsy and evolution are unknown. In practice, man is inconsistent; changeable; sometimes, though not consistently, irrational; his judgments biased and distorted and influenced by his peers. Modern behavioral economics has begun—but only begun—to notice this, seeking by experimental methods to show whether the actual behavior of presumptively competent people corresponds to the predictions of the rationalist theory. The findings, associated with the Nobel Prize–winning work of the Princeton psychologist Daniel Kahneman, are that they are not. Ordinary, intelligent people appear consistently unwilling, or unable, to calculate the consequences of their decisions in a manner predicted by the view that they are responding purely to the market. Instead, they act as social beings, concerned about their standing with their peers, about the fairness of the deal they are being offered, and other matters quite irrelevant to the utility of the object or money on offer. These are remarkably subversive findings, for they suggest that even if there were no monopoly, no externalities, perfect information, and perfect foresight, markets composed of real people would still not perform as the conservative vision requires.

But of course there are easier ways to reach the same conclusions, and behavioral economics is of interest mainly because it speaks to market-obsessed academics from within all the mind-boggling restrictions that they habitually impose on their analyses in order to make the problems appear capable of solution. The real world is a different place altogether. And as my father, John Kenneth Galbraith, argued throughout his long career, an economics of the real world requires an altogether different point of departure. In the real world, the autonomous individual is not the active agent who matters most. The business enterprise, the company, the corporation is. And companies do everything they can to take advantage of human changeability. They seek to control markets, even to replace them altogether. And often they succeed.

Control of markets entails measures available only to large organizations, including (1) the capacity to design and develop new products, (2) the capacity to adjust the presentation of such products to what research and experience indicate the public will actually buy, (3) the capacity to influence the public's buying preferences through advertising, and (4) the capacity to coordinate with one's competitors to ensure that the market is not glutted, so that the possibility of profit is open. Needless to say, under such a system, the "free" market is actually a threat, a source of uncertainty and risk. To the greatest extent possible, therefore, it is made to disappear. Only the fiction that the company operates in a market is maintained, for the obvious benefit of shielding the corporation from close scrutiny of its actual business methods.

The actual world therefore cannot be what a conservative means by a "free-market system." In the actual world, the "freedom to choose" among a menu of items set out for sale—however vast—does *not* give to the consumer an equal weight in the decisions over what is produced. Instead, it merely reproduces, in conditions of comparative but far from complete disorder, the phenomena of planning, rationing, queuing, indoctrination, and control that characterize *unfree* systems. Advertising is propaganda. Research and development is planning. The call from the Wall Street analyst and the visit from the ministerial inspector are the same. Lines form, under capitalism, every day. A little competition helps, but it does not wash this away.

So who is "market freedom" for? It is the freedom of what my father called "The Planning System." It is a real, practical, secure, and highly valued form of freedom. But it is a freedom for business alone, and even less than that: it is a freedom for stable large corporations with substantial political power, for only such businesses can muster the power to exercise that freedom in the fullest: from disposition of the resources and command over labor, to the design of its products, to the pricing and the distribution and the planned obsolescence, and to the management of all the consequences, including environmental and political ones. The freedom to shop, for the rest of us, is an incident to this freedom.

In this context, the freedom to shop is a good thing—a bit of competition is better than none at all. The fate of societies that have neglected this freedom has been historical defeat, despite remarkable accomplishments in other realms, including science, culture, and the living standards of the poor. But the freedom to shop remains a terribly limited thing, compared to political freedom and democratic process, on the one hand, and to human needs, on the other. What is amazing, of course, is that the meaning of freedom in every normal sense—of speech, association, faith, assembly, and the press—should be replaced in the conservative view by "market freedom." It is amazing that the freedom from fear and from want are also replaced by it. It is amazing that the public role in art and culture and science should be subordinated to and suppressed by it. It is amazing that the association of markets and freedom should have taken such firm root in so many minds. Amazing that such nonsense could go so deep, and last so long.

CHAPTER THREE

Tax Cuts and the Marvelous Market
of the Mind

Americans do not save enough! That is an unchallenged principle, conservative in origin but shared across the political spectrum. Conversely, those who *do* save occupy a special place in the pantheon of market heroes, as they do in a popular culture that they themselves lovingly finance. They make possible investment, capital formation, and economic growth. They empower the inventor and enable the entrepreneur, building for a future in which all can enjoy more, later on. They are also the rich. But this is practically incidental; their wealth is not just for themselves, but part and parcel of the prosperity all enjoy.

The special virtue of the savers has an important policy implication: *savings should not be taxed*. What the savers do is, after all, vital to the future prosperity of us all. It is the secret formula behind the growth of the whole cake. To tax it for current consumption—to support the lifestyles of the indolent and the poor—is socially destructive and practically sacrilegious. The consumption of the poor is, after all, only for themselves: except as a matter of compassion, it makes no difference to anyone else whether the people at the bottom of the economic ladder, who contribute nothing more than easily replaced labor to the economic system, are fully clothed, decently fed, properly housed, or able to live a dignified life. That is their problem. The saving of the rich is, in contrast, something that they do for us all. It is a gift, and a blessing. This is the doctrine of supply-side economics, the underpinning of conservative tax policy since the late 1970s.

In the 1970s the phrase *supply-side economics* came into political fashion, associated with men like Art Laffer, Jude Wanniski, Paul Craig Roberts, and others connected with the editorial page of the *Wall*

Street Journal; later, with the congressional office of Jack Kemp; and, finally, with Ronald Reagan's 1981 tax bill. Their purpose was to eliminate, so far as possible, taxes on saving—that is, taxes on capital income—and the progressive rate structure of the income tax. Bright, aggressive, unscrupulous, and politically effective, they seized the supply-side label for their own. But contrary to the claims made by many critics, I do not consider that they misused it. Rather, they saw the potential that an academic movement had for policy and exploited that potential far more effectively than its original authors ever could have done. Later, when things went badly, the academics sought to protect their reputations in the usual way, pointing to caveats and to fine distinctions that were not voiced very loudly when the issues were hot.

Supply-side economics relies in every important respect on the correct, efficient, and predictable functioning of markets. And these markets must function perfectly, in areas where markets as institutions do not actually exist, in domains where their presence can only be inferred or assumed but not observed. Of these areas, the most important is the interior of the individual human brain. The first idea of supply-side economics is, in a word, that tax rates strongly affect human behavior, that there is a tax price associated with individual saving, and that cutting that price will produce a conditioned response. If saving is cheaper, the theory holds, more will be done. On this point, supply-side economics is deeply rooted in academic economics—just as its most impassioned advocates claim. It is nothing more, and little less, than the economics of rational choice.

But is it right? Is there any reason to believe that total private saving in the actual American economy does in fact respond materially to the marginal rate of taxation? Breaking this question down into two parts, is there a good theoretical reason to believe this, and is there any actual evidence that it is true? The answer, it turns out, is no, on both counts. Simply put, the conservative faith in tax cuts is based on a mirage.

In the first place, one must ask: To whom is the incentive to save, implied by a reduction of taxes on saving, directed? The answer is obvious: to that group whose taxes are actually cut. But this answer is obvious only on the surface. Determining whose taxes are actually cut by any particular proposal requires detailed empirical knowledge. The precise direction of the incentive depends on the precut structure of the tax code, on the distribution of taxable income, and also on the specific details of the tax cut.

For reasons that seem obvious but were rarely made clear, supply-side tax cuts from the late 1970s to the 2000s have always focused on the reduction of income taxes at the top of the income scale: on the marginal rates paid not by ordinary working Americans but by the extremely rich. The characteristic cut contained small sums for those in the lower orders, permitting the authors to state, correctly, that most who paid income taxes would receive a cut. But the largest cuts were always for the biggest players—those with the highest incomes and therefore exposed to the highest marginal tax rates. And given the structure of incomes, the numbers of people affected by large cuts were always smaller—much, much smaller—than those affected by the peanuts passed out to the working population.

Point Number One about supply-side economics: it always was, and always will be, a doctrine that rests on the effect of an incentive directed at an extremely small group of people. For this reason, talk about the effect of tax cuts on "work effort" was never a persuasive part of the campaign. Part of the supply-side propaganda was a slogan about "increasing incentives to work, save, and invest." But the numbers affected by a changing incentive to work were never going to be large enough to make a material difference; rich people are in any event not paid by the hour. The only relevant issue is whether that small group of people would control a large enough part of total income and whether they could be induced, by changing the structure of taxes, to save *and* invest it.

The supply-side contention, in a nutshell, was that by reducing the top rate of tax on personal income from (say) 70 percent to (say) 30 percent, a large increase in total saving could be obtained. What is the logic of this statement? Since saving is remunerated by payment of interest, the incentive relates basically to the difference between the pretax and posttax rate of interest. The idea was that if the pretax interest rate was (say) 7 percent, a reduction in taxes on that order would raise the after-tax rate of interest for a very rich person from just over 2 percent to just under 5 percent (from 30 to 70 percent of the pretax interest rate). This more than doubling of the rate of return would, it was argued, bring forth a new flood of thrift, shifting resources from consumption to savings and thence to investment.

The problems with the argument start with the fact that people do not face a simple choice between "savings" and "consumption." Rather, they face a spectrum of choices between the financial uses of funds we call savings, very short-term consumption items (such as food and drink), and longer-term consumption goods (such as housing or land). The longer-term consumption goods already have, built in, an internal rate of return: they are consumption goods that yield benefits (including but not limited to expected capital gains) over long periods of time into the future. That rate of return is largely untaxed, and it could easily exceed (say) 5 percent per year. And so the actual choice facing the wealthy taxpayer given a tax cut windfall is not between a more expensive bottle of wine to be drunk at dinner and putting cash in the bank. Along with some nice wine, this taxpayer chooses between a new house, more land, art, bonds, and financial investments. Some of those alternatives to the bottle of wine may be very highly valued. Cut taxes, and there is no reason to think that the shift into purely financial savings will be large.

Here is a second problem: even if you believe that interest rates affect saving, the difference that tax cuts can make to the after-tax rate of return is small compared to the differences in pretax interest rates changes in monetary policy bring on a routine basis. In the period immediately after Reagan took office, short-term interest rates touched 20 percent. In the period immediately after George Bush took office in 2001, they were 1 percent. These changes dwarf the effects of tax cuts on realized returns. But in fact they too made very little difference to the volume of savings. Savings plummeted in the Reagan recession when rates were high, and they were very low again in the late 1990s and early 2000s, when rates were much lower. If changes in monetary policy affecting interest rates themselves did not matter to savings, it is hard to believe that changes in tax rates on interest rates would.

In the real world, the volume of savings has very little to do with the interest rate, because people do not make economic decisions with savings targets prominently in mind. Instead, they set consumption goals, or rather habits, and enter into long-term contracts for certain consumption services, such as mortgage and tuition payments, car loans, and utility contracts. Savings is whatever is left over. If income is higher than expected, that will be a lot, and consumption will eventually be adjusted upward. If income slips, there will not be very much. But the interest rate has little to do with it, except insofar as interest rates affect income. Savings slumped in the Reagan recession because high interest rates wrecked jobs and destroyed incomes; this effect overwhelmed any shift from consumption to saving among the beneficiaries of the Reagan tax cuts.

And here is the third problem. Recall that the entire supply-side argument rests on perfectly functioning markets, including a "rational" response to tax cuts experienced by a handful of very rich people—the marvelous marketplace that is supposed to operate in their minds. But *if* the markets do indeed work perfectly, we are compelled toward the following conclusion: public policy should not care at all about the supply of saving.

To see this, consider how the market for savings is supposed to work. To whom do our noble wealthy supply their saving? In the accepted story, they supply it to something we call the "capital market." To put it in concrete terms, let us say a bank, or a broker, or perhaps a mutual fund. The capital market is an efficient mechanism for the allocation of resources: it transfers the funds from the saver to the investment project with the highest achievable rate of return (after taking account of risk)—that is, from the capitalist to the entrepreneur. In a seamless process, there is first a necessary reward to the risk taker—the big prize for seeing and taking a chance. And after that, the saver is rewarded: she earns the return associated with the investment and justified by her thrift.

But if a market is "efficient," it must allocate returns exactly. It must allocate them in full in relation to the quality of effort expended, the risk assumed, and the astuteness of investment judgment. The private saver—the capitalist—must get the entire return that is due to capital provided. Meanwhile the person executing the project—the entrepreneur—gets the entire return to risk. Between the two, they must get the entire return. That is what market efficiency means, if it means anything at all.

So what is left over for society? What do workers, or anyone else, get out of the process of accumulation? In the simplest, clearest, purest form of the market model, there can be only one answer to this question. *Nothing.* The acts of saving and investment are purely private. The benefits are therefore purely private. Any benefit accruing to anyone other than the original saver or capitalist would have to be counted an inefficiency. It would have to be viewed not as a success but as a failure of the market system. In an efficient market economy, society should get nothing out of the actions of saving and investment.

And correspondingly, in a true "free-market" system, there could hardly be any shortage of savings. The amount that individuals choose to supply, based on their preferences between consumption now and later, would have to be the optimal amount.

But this obviously is not what devotees of the gospel of savings shortage would have you believe. To be a desired object of public policy, saving must be in some important respects a *public* act, with *public* benefits. It cannot be purely private. If it were, there would be no point in directing public policy toward increasing the total amount of savings and investment undertaken. You cannot argue simultaneously that markets are efficient *and* that savings are scarce. That is trying to have it both ways.

Well, one might say, the tax system already imposes a distortion on these private decisions. To the extent that savings are taxed, the after-tax rate return on savings departs from the market rate of interest. In that case, savings (in theory) will be lower than they would be if untaxed. And therefore investment will be lower, accumulation will be lower, and so forth. But so what? If the benefits of saving and investment are entirely private, entirely reserved to the savers themselves, why should public policy care whether gross saving is high or low? The point of public policy is public welfare, not to make rich people as rich as they might possibly be.

It follows from this that any argument favoring saving as a goal for public policy must assume that there are public benefits. There must be benefits that do not flow to those doing the saving in the first place. There must be a contribution to the foundation of rising living standards for other participants in the economy, potentially including workers and others with comparatively low incomes who do not themselves engage in private saving.

But how can this happen? *Only by market failure.* In the fable of the grasshopper and the ants, the ants survive the winter and the grasshopper does not, an object lesson to future generations of grasshoppers. But now we find that some of the ants' hard-won savings go to feed the grasshopper as well, and not just through the winter: they raise the grasshopper's standard of living all year round. By any standard of efficiency, they shouldn't do this! Among other things, the effect must discourage the grasshopper from saving. That the ants' savings help the grasshopper is a failure of the market mechanism. Yet without that failure, there is no reason to regard the ant as an insect of special virtue, or savings as a fit object for public encouragement.

This argument is an application of a well-known body of economics: the theory of externalities and public goods. This is a body of theory that deals with cases like pollution, where a private transaction has effects on those not directly involved, and with cases like national defense, where a good has benefits shared by the entire population whether they pay for it or not. For any economist who takes externalities and public goods seriously, a shortage of savings is conceptually unproblematic. But such an economist cannot also believe simultaneously in the perfect efficiency of the market.

The problem has yet another aspect. If saving is in part a public good, then the economic theory of public goods* tells us that the private market will provide too little saving. Even at a zero tax rate, savers will ignore the marginal social benefit, which is that part of the return to saving that benefits the larger society and not the individual saver. This suggests on impeccable grounds a vital role for public saving and investment, or at the least for forcing the saving rate to levels higher than individuals would choose on their own. If saving is, even in part, a public good, then the government should make up the difference between the investment that savers choose and the optimal social amount.

But of course, among pro-saving conservatives, this argument is never heard.[†] Instead, conservatives focus solely on a deficiency of *private* savings; they restrict their attention to that part of the supposed deficiency that could supposedly be remedied by cutting taxes. This has nothing to do with the deficiency that would remain, on account of an external social benefit. Should the government attempt to raise the overall volume of saving, filling the gap left by the failure of the market to account for marginal social benefits in excess of marginal social costs? Conservative thinking recoils from the thought, even though it is a plain implication of the economic theory to which it claims to sub-

*Paul A. Samuelson, "The Pure Theory of Public Expenditure," *Review of Economics and Statistics*, November 1954.

†It *is* heard among economists associated with the center-left in American politics, notably the "old Keynesians" such as Robert Solow of MIT and his intellectual allies and descendants.

scribe. Once again, if saving is a public good, it is hard to see what disadvantage there is to having the government provide it. But if saving is not a public good, then it is impossible to argue that the market does not provide enough.

Conservatives are on a cleft stick. If they hold to the perfect efficiency of markets, there is no ground for arguing for an insufficiency of saving and also no ground for arguing that lower taxes on capital income are desirable on account of larger social benefits, such as growth or higher living standards for the population at large. On the other hand, if one argues that the overall economy is made larger and richer by saving, then markets are not efficient. In that case, there is also no ground in the conservative case against redistributing the benefits of saving after they have been earned, through taxes and transfers. Thus if one could design a tax that encouraged saving in the first place but wholly redistributed the gains after the fact, the truly principled conservative would have, so far, no economic ground to oppose it.

So when the incoherence is stripped away, what is the conservative case against taxes on saving? Basically it is, after a fashion, ethical. The concern is with infringing a natural right of individuals to profit from their own accumulations, combined with a view that saving is virtuous per se. In this view, government redistribution is per se pernicious: to take from the rich and give to the poor is to confiscate by taxation the gains of the saver and to pass them along to . . . consumers. If it is a tax on savings, it must diminish the quantity of savings offered. If a constant volume of public services or income redistribution must be supported, then it is easy to conjure a downward spiral, in which ever-higher tax rates must be imposed, with each increment to the rate further suppressing the base, until all the geese with golden eggs are cooked. But to the pure conservative, such a loss to "society" is beside the point, since it is a loss only to the individuals who held the capital taxed away. Rather, there is simply something offensive about the redistribution from a moral point of view, since it robs a person of a property to which the market has assigned a natural claim.

This is the argument that now forms the intellectual underpinning (such as it is) of the evolving U.S. and global tax regime. It seeks to foster savings, minimize redistribution, flatten tax burdens, and place as much as possible of the burden of taxes on consumption. Every major tax bill from 1981 forward has moved in this direction or accommodated itself to such movement, so that capital gains and dividends (which were once taxed at 70 percent at the margin) now face a tax rate of 15 percent. Beyond this, it has become easy to move capital income offshore, altogether beyond reach.

If this policy has any foundational justification, it cannot lie in the idea that public benefits flow from private savings. It must therefore lie in the claim that property has a natural right not to be taxed. But since taxes have to fall somewhere, this implies a corresponding claim about labor: that labor has no similar natural right. Why the right of property should stand over the right of labor is left as a puzzle—an unstated puzzle, since if it were stated clearly, it would be no puzzle at all; it would simply be a power relation.

What then is the right amount of saving, and how can we judge that it should be any different from what it is?

The moment you admit this to be a reasonable question, the choice of a "correct" or "optimal" savings investment share becomes a public policy decision. And this is something on which the market, in principle, provides no guidance. In fact, the theory does not even tell us for sure that the free-market level of savings and investment must be too low. Externalities can in principle be positive or negative; the decision whether savings and investment should be higher or lower than in an untaxed, free-market, zero-government system is necessarily a matter of economic theory, taken in combination with empirical public policy judgments.

But within the framework handed down to us by the greater conservative economics, no mechanism exists for making such judgments. Instead, the conservative economics gives us a declaration ex cathedra. Savings rates are too low. They are shockingly low. How do we know this? By introspection, by dictation, and perhaps by comparison with China (in former times, Korea, Japan, France, and the Soviet Union all stood in). Savings must therefore be encouraged. Why? So that investment will rise, so that we can compete with the selected objects of comparison. No reason is given why their savings rates are better than ours, or why it would be appropriate for us to adopt policies giving us their savings rate. One never hears about the policies of industrial development, capital control, and what conservative economists call "financial repression" that invariably accompanied the high savings rates in those cases. And one never hears of a possible downside. One never hears that savings rates might be too high, that the fruit of excess savings might be excess investment and capital waste. In these comparisons, one never hears that the saving and investment rates of the Soviet Union were in the range of 40 percent—similar to those of present-day China—right up to that country's economic collapse.

Finally, there is an empirical question. Does it work? In the ostensible pursuit of higher savings, we have enacted since the late 1970s innumerable tax reductions and other incentives to save instead of to spend. Is there any evidence that stimulating the incentive to save actually raises the overall rate of saving?

There is a clear answer to this question: What is the measurable impact of tax incentives to encourage savings? None. Personal savings rates, capital formation, and economic growth have not increased. Average rates of gross investment fluctuated between 15 and 16 percent of gross domestic product (GDP) in the 1950s and are at exactly those same levels at current writing. Of this, personal domestic saving covers less than 1 percent of GDP. Practically all gross investment is accounted for by the capital consumption allowances and retained earnings of corporations—and by the savings of those who sell to us from overseas.

Thus, the entire thirty-year exercise in promoting saving in order to increase investment has been a bust. The experiment has been made repeatedly, and no effects have been observed. Indeed, from 1997 onward, for the first time in recorded history, the acquisition of financial assets by American households fell below zero, staying there through the end of the decade. I shall argue later that this was not the disaster it is sometimes portrayed as being. Indeed it was an integral feature of the boom experience in those years, and it was replicated at the peak of the Bush expansion in 2006 and 2007. But it is entirely fatal to the idea that tax incentives for private saving actually increase the overall supply of saving or that these govern the rate of private investment. In fact, the rate of private investment rose quite happily even though the rate of private saving fell; the balance of the financial "burden" was divided between a smaller budget deficit and larger deficit on the current account.

So what do tax cuts on capital income actually accomplish, apart from the obvious fact that they shift the burden of taxes per se—and on the surface—from the wealthy and toward the middle and working classes? From an economic standpoint, the main effect seems to have been to shift the locus of post-tax income from firms to households. By reducing, or even eliminating, the tax advantage of retained earnings, tax cuts on capital encourage firms to pay out a larger share of net income, in part to shareholders but especially to managers themselves. This accounts in part for the explosion of chief executive pay; intercorporate competition that formerly took the form of flamboyant headquarters or expensive company emoluments (the corporate apartment of 1950s films) can now be passed directly to the CEO as private income without catastrophic tax implications.

And so the decision-making power passes from the corporation to the person—a return to the nineteenth century's locus of control over the capital stock. The consequence has been a shift in the composition of investment—roughly from factories and other corporate forms of investment to residential housing and other private forms, fueling an exceptional boom in high-end home construction, visible across the American landscape. In the years following the information technology bubble, the housing boom took on the role of a principal driver of total American investment, contributing heavily to the growth of investment from 2004 to 2006.* This collapsed in 2007, writing a final note in the saga of supply-side failure.

Oddly, within the framework of the argument made earlier, the changes in the tax code favored by conservatives have indeed rendered the markets more efficient. That is, they have concentrated the benefits of saving more strictly in the hands of those who carry it out and cut off the corresponding flow of benefits to organizations—notably business firms—in which many others have a stake. The richest Americans have seen their private incomes rise. They have responded by dotting the landscape with mansions. These they consume on their own: a purely private good. To a greater extent than before, the benefits of tax cuts flow strictly to the individuals who receive them, and in this way, the markets more effectively exclude

---

*As an aside, this does not mean, necessarily, that the rich got richer during the early Bush years, in consequence of their favored tax treatment. For, during at least the early phase of the Bush administration, the new rich of the stock-bubble decade grew markedly *less rich*, in consequence of the deflated value of their capital holdings. The tax cuts served only in part to compensate them for their losses. From a political point of view, Bush's discovery was that the elites have an asymmetric view of gains and losses. They credit an administration much more for loss-compensating favors done on the tax side than they do for the sequence of policies that generate inflated incomes in the first place. Thus they favored Bush over Clinton, even though under Clinton they were richer, on balance, than under Bush.

those who do not have money to save from enjoying the rewards accruing to those who do.

But if that is the case, then they have surely also robbed the act of saving of the cachet of virtue, the very feature that justified its favored treatment in the tax code! What, after all, is the social benefit of the construction of all those mansions? No one among the beneficiary population was badly housed to begin with. And while jobs were surely created in the mansion boom, the same jobs could surely have been created in other ways.

In sum, vesting investment decisions in the hands of purely private parties leads to decisions that reflect, in a large degree, purely private interests. Where these parties are private business organizations, the market operates inefficiently, but business investment gets made, with benefits that accrue to parties other than the owner-shareholders. There is, therefore, a social argument for policies that support private investment in the business sector. But where these are for expansive housing and other luxury objects, the market operates very efficiently to reserve the whole of the benefit to those who carried out the act of saving. There is—by the exact same argument—no social justification for investment directed along these lines. And therefore there is also no justification for the favorable tax treatment of capital income, which increasingly permits the wealthy to retain full control over the allocation of their wealth.

And if for any reason one favors capital investment of a collective sort—the creation of physical capital assets that cannot be privately consumed—then it follows that a different tax regime is called for. In particular, a *progressive* tax on high incomes and capital gains, deferred until those gains are realized, and on gifts and estates is the efficient method. Such a system, which strongly penalizes financial speculation, encourages wealthy individuals to keep their savings locked up in corporate stock, where they will be used actively by the business firm, and discourages firms from increasing their dividend payout or the grant of stock options to their top management. It is a system, in other words, that favors business enterprises rather than the individuals who are in a position to control them. And it is a system that discourages—through the estate tax—the excess saving that leads to dynastic accumulation, giving a strong incentive to those who do accumulate to place their wealth in the hands of a nonprofit institution before their death rather than let it revert entirely into government hands.

That was the old American tax system—the system we used to have until the supply-side revolution. Under that system, when we had it, companies rather than persons controlled the flow of investments. The overall volume of saving and investment was more or less exactly the same as it is today. As a dispassionate view of theoretical considerations would lead us to expect, individual tax rates do not affect the gross rates of saving or investment, so long as the option of deferring tax is available by retaining income within the corporation. But they do affect the composition or use of funds. And the result was considerably more investment in factories and office buildings, and considerably less in palatial private real estate, relative to the total flow of investment, than we experience today. Markets were indeed less efficient. But cities were built, jobs created, art and architecture fostered, and the conditions for a shared prosperity more effectively met. People still go to New York and San Francisco and Chicago to gaze on the surviving fruits of that particular time. In Cleveland and St. Louis they can, if they choose, tour the ruins.

Did supply-side economics bring all of this to an end, putting the rich individual back in charge of American capital and taking the American corporation down? Perhaps, in substantial part, it did. Perhaps this was the real supply-side revolution: not so much of the rich against the poor as of the rich individual against the corporation. Physical investment in business assets now occurs where the tax codes encourage it, by keeping income in corporate hands. (That is notably true, in particular, in China these days.) In the United States, thanks to Reaganomics and its Bush successor, this is no longer the case.

Something could be learned—perhaps even by conservatives—from the theory and history of this matter. But perhaps the lesson ought to be taken up by liberals. The reason for action is not that the flow of income to the very rich is by itself an immoral thing, but that the resources are needed, and could be used, for larger pressing purposes that meet greater needs. The purposes and needs have changed, of course, since the 1940s and 1950s. But the need for a system that meets needs has not changed, and will not change. It's just that we do not have one today.

CHAPTER FOUR

Uncle Milton's War

Liberals once had their own reputation for being tough on inflation. It was a great liberal triumph of World War II that the war was conducted with nearly stable prices, especially given the scale of the mobilization and the combat. The job was done with controls—rigid controls—over prices, wages, and rents.* And in the decades that followed—until the Reagan era—wage-price guideposts, specific interventions against inflationary price shocks, and periods of comprehensive control were kept in use. But by the late 1970s, this system had met its match. And the inflation that it could not control destroyed the economic reputation of the liberal generation that took power under John F. Kennedy and lost it with Jimmy Carter.

Ever since, liberals have avoided the topic. The idea that there might be some distinctly liberal way to prevent or control inflation has simply disappeared. For an economist, next only to fealty to market principles in general, vigilance against inflation became the equivalent of being "tough on defense," a prerequisite for credibility, for being taken seriously in policy discussions. And vigilance against inflation came to mean: support the Federal Reserve when it tightens money and credit.

The doctrine underlying this shift was monetarism—the idea that the Federal Reserve should fight inflation, above all else, by controlling the growth of money and credit. In policy circles this doctrine triumphed completely, though, as we shall see, only for a brief moment, for it proved far more destructive than its architects had imagined. And yet, even so, the essence of monetarism remains influential to this

---

* In 1942–1943, they were administered, very aggressively, by my father.

day—a kind of doctrinal touchstone, a needle's eye through which any economist has to pass to be admitted to the kingdom of influence and power. When inflation threatens, free markets and supply-side economics provide glimpses of the promised land to come. But monetarism arms the shock troops in the actual, nasty war.

The mobilizing idea came from Milton Friedman. "Inflation," Friedman famously wrote, "is always and everywhere a monetary phenomenon."[*] Central banks controlled the supply of money, and so they too were free to choose: to turn inflation on or turn it off. Monetarists assumed a simple cause and effect from money emissions to changes in the average level of prices. Moreover, fighting inflation by controlling money had no downside, except perhaps in the very short run. Free markets would adjust the supply and demand for labor, thus ensuring full employment only if wages were allowed to adjust fully. Yes, the war on inflation might be brutal for a while, but it would not last long. There was at most a temporary cost of higher unemployment, for a permanent gain of stable prices.

Control over money became the official policy of the Federal Reserve in late 1979, and the Federal Reserve embarked on a sustained campaign to end inflation in early 1981. Unemployment soared, and bankruptcies toppled companies throughout the country, especially in the industrial Midwest, but the Federal Reserve did not relent. Finally, in August 1982, Mexico defaulted, exposing the weakness of the New York banks. U.S. unemployment stood at 11 percent. Then, after two and a half years of pain with disaster looming, monetarism was abandoned. It would never again serve as the official guide to policy. Interest rates fell, the economy began to recover, and within a few years the Federal Reserve was no longer even pretending to be concerned when measures of money and credit started growing very rapidly.

And yet in this brief period, the monetarist solution seemingly did its job. Inflation did disappear. What had been a chronic and seemingly intractable problem in 1979 had vanished by 1984. And the high unemployment of 1982 was largely erased by the recovery of 1983–1984. A permanent benefit was achieved at what appears to have been a severe,

---

[*]Milton Friedman and Anna J. Schwartz, *A Monetary History of the United States* (Princeton, N.J.: Princeton University Press, 1971).

but only temporary, cost. On this elementary evidence, monetarists could (and did) claim victory, cementing the hold of the basic monetarist principle—that the Federal Reserve was responsible for preventing inflation—over policy discussion. This occurred even though the stable relationship between money growth and price change disappeared from the data, and so their doctrine disappeared from academic economics. Unlike the exponents of balanced budgets, free trade, and supply-side economics, the monetarists had made a tactical error: rooting their argument in a precise numerical relationship. The relationship between money and prices could be tested, it was tested, and it failed the test.

But this raises a question. If monetarism worked as anti-inflation policy in the early 1980s, which unquestionably it did, did it work in the way that had been predicted or advertised? The facts suggest it did not. In particular, if the monetarist doctrine were correct, then a single, brief period of anti-inflation rigor should not have killed inflation. When monetarism was abandoned and money and credit growth were allowed to run riot, as they were in the mid-1980s and again with even more exuberance in the late 1990s, inflation should have revived. It did not. Money and credit soared after 1983, the stock market and the housing market soared (leading eventually to the asset bubbles of the 1990s and the present decade)—but there was no inflation as the term is technically defined. A housing boom certainly raises costs for some, and a stock boom certainly changes the distribution of income. But monetarism spoke to general effects on prices and living costs, and of these there were none. Inflation was not just controlled. It was dead—at least for the time being.

And if inflation could be killed, rather than merely caged or subdued, that raises a follow-on question: Of what did it consist when it was living? If monetarism incorrectly forecast inflation for the 1980s and 1990s, did it also misdiagnose the inflation of the 1960s and 1970s? Was that inflation really due to "easy money"? Was it really a matter merely of central bank irresponsibility, entirely avoidable had monetarists been in control at that time?

Here again, as with taxes, there is an older, now largely forgotten view, which holds that inflation is primarily the consequence of the exercise and abuse of market power. It occurs, in this view, when circumstances contrive to give particular institutions inordinate, unchecked control over a major national or a global price. That could be the price of labor—the wage rate—but it could also be the price of oil. Or it could be the price of capital: the rate of interest. In any of these cases, concerted increase in a key price can push up prices generally because the reflexive response of business to a rise in costs is to raise product prices to cover. Inflation is a matter, in this view, of cost push. Most of the time, cost push is difficult, because it is hard to organize and maintain a sufficiently broad-based cartel and therefore difficult to deliver a large shock to costs in the whole system. But sometimes it does happen. Labor unions in the United Kingdom in the early 1970s had that power, as did (on a small scale) the municipal unions in New York City. In wartime, when every demand is critical, this sort of power comes into existence on a larger scale, and has to be curbed directly. The signal historical fact behind the inflation explosion of the 1970s was, of course, the explosion of oil prices in 1973. Was that "caused," in any direct sense, by U.S. domestic monetary policy in 1972? No. There is no direct link. But it was caused, very plausibly, by the changes in the international financial regime that happened just a few months earlier.

For a quarter-century following World War II, the noncommunist world had operated under financial rules established at Bretton Woods, New Hampshire, in 1944. Exchange rates for all countries but the United States were set in dollars; that for the United States was set in gold. Rates were fixed, but they could be adjusted from time to time. Fixed exchange rates and U.S. dominance meant that major commodity prices for the entire world were geared to the American market. In particular, the oil price was set largely by the Texas Railroad Commission, which controlled the utilization rate of American oil wells, at that time the swing oil producers in the largest oil-producing country in the world.

The Bretton Woods rules provided that if the United States ran a trade deficit, other central banks could demand gold in payment, drawing on the formidable gold hoard that the United States had accumulated mainly during the two world wars. This proved to be the Achilles' heel of the arrangement. Through the 1960s, as the United States reached full employment and the war in Vietnam grew more costly, increasing U.S. trade deficits generated an increasing gold outflow. Eventually it became clear that the system, which had been designed for a world in which the United States was running trade surpluses, could not be sustained.

The Bretton Woods system started to collapse on August 15, 1971, when Richard Nixon closed the gold window and devalued the dollar.

This was an unprecedented step for the United States, which immediately raised the price, measured in dollars, of commodities traded around the world. Nixon imposed price controls to prevent this price surge from showing up in the American inflation reports, and he imposed export curbs to prevent U.S. producers from diverting supplies to the more profitable external markets.

So from 1971 onward, a worldwide inflation (of dollar prices) was under way, not directly because of U.S. money growth but mainly because of the collapse of fixed exchange rates. Initially oil prices, which were set by a cartel in dollars, stayed out of this and held steady. But that meant that oil producers were suffering from inflation in the prices of everything they consumed. And in 1973, following the Yom Kippur War, the Organization of Petroleum-Exporting Countries (OPEC) struck back, abruptly quadrupling the oil price. And by then, domestic price controls had been largely lifted, so the shock could not be kept away from American consumers. Oil and commodity prices fed back into the U.S. economy through cost-of-living escalators built into wage bargains. Inflation was the result of this process. It did not originate with the central bank, and the central bank could not have prevented it.

Once inflation got into the system, it was not easy to get rid of it. Wage contracts with cost-of-living escalators tended to pass inflation along from one part of the economy to another. The Nixon, Ford, and Carter administrations tried to grapple with this problem with pay and price boards. These efforts were not wholly unsuccessful. Inflation did slow in the face of controls and guidelines, and the cost to workers—in lost output, higher unemployment, and declining real wages—from checking inflation by these measures was much less than one would observe later. But they were deeply aggravating to free-market conservatives. They were an irritating reminder that government was not obliged to concede to private industry the right, in principle, to set prices. And they accorded to organized labor a policy role, a place at the table, at a moment when conservatives around the world had come to the conclusion that it would be easier, and more effective, to destroy the union movement than to work with it in cooperation.

The opportunity came in 1979 when the eclectic anti-inflation policy of the 1960s and 1970s hit a second crisis due to the Iranian revolution, the second oil shock, and further declines in the value of the dollar. By this time, the liberals charged with intervening to help keep prices under control were simply tired, and major fractures in the liberal coalition were evident. Important forces in Jimmy Carter's administration were unwilling to make concessions to organized labor that might have ensured labor's cooperation, and labor, for its part, was not satisfied with the bargain that it was offered. There was, in particular, little prospect of a genuine policy of full employment. Quite to the contrary, Carter's advisers were practically panicked by the size of the budget deficit and determined to cut back on social spending, including employment programs.

In this situation, the monetarists had an opening. By blaming the problem entirely on monetary policy, they cut through the political complexities and eliminated organized labor from its role in the politics of fighting inflation. They offered a simple solution: reform the central bank. Give it an unequivocal mandate. This hard-line position was backed by the rising academic prestige of the monetarists, and it also had the effect of off-loading responsibility for inflation control from larger and politically vulnerable actors, such as the President and the Congress. That was irresistible. Paul Volcker, who was not a convinced ideologue of any known stripe but a dedicated servant of the interests of the financial system, assumed the chair of the Federal Reserve system in June 1979 with a mandate and a sense of urgency that none of his predecessors had ever enjoyed.

Volcker soon threw the Federal Reserve into the front lines of the inflation battle. This decision came in early October 1979. Volcker's first sharp rise in interest rates led to the short recession of 1980, which paved the way for Jimmy Carter's defeat in November.

As noted earlier, in 1981, with Reagan's backing, Volcker launched his main offensive. Short-term interest rates shot up to near 20 percent. The machinery industries of the upper Midwest, citadels of union power, went bankrupt. The campaign against inflation was swift, brutal, and effective. But it did not work primarily through monetary control. Rather, the growth rates of the money supply slid to zero, not because the Federal Reserve prevented banks from making new loans, but because the slump in activity was so dramatic that demand for additional credit practically disappeared.

Thus, the application of monetarism succeeded, but at a cost that no one, not even the Federal Reserve under Volcker, was prepared to pay on an ongoing basis. And yet, it is also true, and it soon enough emerged, that monetarism was no longer necessary. Inflation was gone.

Two institutional changes ensured this: the collapse of labor union power and pattern bargaining in industrial wages, and globalization: the increased reliance of American consumers on manufactured imports produced in low-wage countries. Together these facts transformed the structural environment of American price setting. Together they created a low-inflation, postindustrial, deunionized economy, much more unequal than before but nevertheless with a reasonably high living standard ensured by cheap imports. And while later central bankers spilled oceans of ink describing their steadfast commitment to price stability, in fact the issue of inflation did not arise again, even once, between 1982 and 2005.

Support for this view now emerges in the memoirs of Alan Greenspan. After eighteen years at the helm of the Federal Reserve, during which time Greenspan was amply praised for keeping inflation under control, in retirement he writes that this accomplishment was not his doing. Rather, he benefited from the collapse of the Soviet Union and the rise of China. And Greenspan is right. The collapse of the Soviet Union dumped huge supplies of industrial materials and of fuel—oil and natural gas—onto world markets, which depressed commodity prices. The rise of China, for its part, created a labor reserve at low dollar wages, against which no other low-skilled labor pool could effectively compete. With global commodity prices held down by one phenomenon and global labor costs by the other, global inflation was doomed.

Greenspan's argument is certainly correct, but the timing as he gives it leaves out an important fact. The death of inflation did not follow the collapse of the Soviet Union or the rise of China; rather, the death of inflation preceded these events. Inflation was finished by 1984. The Soviet Union lasted until 1991, and the rise of China to the status of world trading power became evident only in the 1990s. It was the rise of the dollar that came first, bringing the crushing competition of low import prices to bear against price increases originating on American soil.

In an important sense, one can even say that the worldwide debt crisis, which was precipitated by Volcker's anti-inflation campaign, precipitated both the fall of the Soviet Union and the rise of China. It hit the Soviet Union because that country was heavily indebted to the West and relied on its natural resources exports—oil, gas, nickel, and gold—to pay its bills. When the Volcker deflation succeeded in bringing down the oil price in 1985–1986, the Soviet Union was certain to feel the consequences. But for China, the situation was different. China was an oil consumer. It was also financially autarkic: it never became involved with commercial bank loans in the 1970s. Thus, in the 1980s, the People's Republic was ideally positioned to take advantage of the troubles that oil producers and dollar debtors were suffering in the world economy and to build up its infrastructure and its exporting base.

Meanwhile, on the home front, the statistical arguments that the monetarists had used to build their academic case for a simple relationship between money creation and price increases broke down. New financial technologies brought a proliferation of different forms of credit and close substitutes for money (such as credit card balances). It became difficult, and in the end impossible, to draw distinctions between what was money and these forms of "near money." For a doctrine based on the concept of a "quantity of money," this was very bad news.

The proliferation of "near money" showed something else about credit capitalism—something that was profoundly subversive of conservative economics. It showed that in the real world, the central bank does not actually control the quantity of money at all. Rather, the central bank does something conservatives think government should not do at all: it fixes a price. That price is the interest rate—specifically the interest rate that banks charge each other on short-term loans. That interest rate governs all of the others, and banks decide how much credit to extend, not what price to charge. Indeed, banks generally do even less than that: the total amount of credit is determined, most of the time, by the volume of economic activity and the preferences of the public, not the other way around.

Monetarism as such did not survive in the academy, but a key policy implication, that the Federal Reserve should not try to promote full employment, lived on. This was a doctrine first introduced in 1968, once again by Milton Friedman, as a corollary of monetarism. The doctrine held that efforts to push the unemployment rate below a critical threshold (the "natural rate," or NAIRU*) would generate *accelerating* inflation, essentially because the money printing required to induce

---

* "Non-accelerating Inflation Rate of Unemployment," in the jargon.

higher employment would be translated, by a rapid process of labor and product market adjustment, into higher money wages and higher prices. The model imagined that the economy existed on a knife edge, in which even a small deviation toward low unemployment would generate the ultimate social catastrophe of hyperinflation. And so, faced with unemployment of one in ten or one in twenty, nothing should be done.

The idea that low unemployment generates runaway inflation was an absurdity on its face. If it had been true, runaway hyperinflations should have been common in history, whereas in fact they are very rare. Yet the natural rate model served the self-importance of central bankers and the perpetuation of conservative rule in monetary policy. If the capitalist economy were truly tumultuous and unstable, teetering forever on the brink of an inflationary abyss, then the eternal vigilance of the central bankers could never be dispensed with, and every year that passed with no inflation would be just another testament to their wisdom and their public spirit.

Over time, central bankers managed to persuade themselves, and many economists, of their indispensability to the anti-inflation struggle. A new idea was advanced: that the "credibility" of central bankers would discourage workers from demanding wage increases that they might otherwise seek, for fear of retribution in the form of high interest rates and unemployment. Of course, if this were true, it would be true at any level of unemployment and there would be no natural rate, but this contradiction was never fully explained. But even apart from that, two things were wrong with this argument. First, even faced with an adamantly anti-inflationary central bank, no worker who had the opportunity to demand a higher wage would rationally refuse to do so, because the consequences would fall in any event more heavily on workers who did not get the raise than on those who did. And second, the initial impetus of pressure for inflation almost never came from workers anyway. Yet no oil company was ever invented that refused to raise the price of gas, when the opportunity presented itself, for fear that a central bank might later raise the rate of interest in response.

Empirical estimates of the natural rate settled in the mid-1980s at around 6 percent, at a time when unemployment rates persistently hovered near 7 percent. Thus the mainstream view of economists concerned with monetary policy was that there was very little running room; the best we could hope for was a very modest improvement in labor markets before the Federal Reserve would have to step in and slow the economy down. This was the state of the debate by the time Alan Greenspan became chairman of the Federal Reserve in 1987.

Greenspan was a very conservative, very cautious man, and he had some early learning to do. Fearful of inflation and anxious to assert his credibility, his first instinct was to raise interest rates. But this set in motion the stock market crash of October 1987, during which the Dow Jones lost a third of its value in a single day. Under the pressure of events, Greenspan shifted course, but he did not shift enough and soon was tightening again. This brought on the prolonged credit slump from 1989 through 1994, during which time he first cut interest rates relatively cautiously and failed, for the most part, to get the economy moving again. Only in late 1991 did Greenspan begin to take the strong measures that were really required, and only in 1994 did growth get back under way.

Later on, in the 1990s, Greenspan found himself riding the crest of a prolonged credit boom. Again he reacted at first with caution, warning famously though obliquely of "irrational exuberance" in the stock market, long before the either Dow or the NASDAQ reached peak values. Yet for a time, he also resisted the provocation of economists who demanded that policy rest on professional fears of transgressing the natural rate.

And so as unemployment gradually fell, the Federal Reserve did nothing. And as unemployment fell, nothing bad happened. Inflation did not rise. Instead, productivity growth increased—quite understandably, since as businesses have difficulty finding labor, they look for ways to get the same output with less of it. Greenspan became increasingly confident that he was on the right track, and except for the fact that it could not be sustained, he was.

For a period from 1996 through 1999, economists reacted to the declining unemployment rate first with dire warnings that sapped the credibility of the profession. Then came a wave of articles explaining that the natural rate must be lower than anyone had realized. Ultimately the articles more or less stopped coming, and silence settled over the grave of the natural rate. For years, conservative economists had argued that low unemployment rates were dangerous, and most of Washington had believed them. Greenspan, by the simple act of doing nothing, blew all of that away. We had full employment; it did not cause inflation. Monetarism, the natural rate doctrine, and the idea that the Federal Reserve must be eternally vigilant against inflation—all of that was wrong! Who knew?*

*Unfortunately, Ben Bernanke, who replaced Greenspan in 2005, did not know, and the Federal Reserve went through a phase of tightening policy to fight essentially non-existent wage inflation in 2005 and 2006. Inflation was rising for the same reason as in the early 1970s, which was a destabilization in the worldwide valuation of the dollar and a rise in the price of oil incident to the war in Iraq. Wages had nothing to do with it. And, as in 1987, rising interest rates produced a financial meltdown rather than a soft landing with inflation control. In the 2007 case, it was the housing market that collapsed under the strain, and Bernanke ultimately learned the first rule of central banking: when the ship starts to sink, central bankers must bail like hell. Whether the lesson was learned soon enough and whether it will stick are matters still to be seen.

CHAPTER FIVE

The Impossible Dream
of Budget Balance

A re there no simple verities left? If the market is not freedom, if savings are not virtue, and if the Federal Reserve does not control inflation, what's left? What about balancing budgets? Here we have a conservative principle with bipartisan support. Surely Democrats should take pride in the great achievement of the Clinton years, which was to bring about not only budget balance but an actual surplus in the federal accounts, and for two years in a row. Surely liberals should flay the odious government of George W. Bush for "irresponsible tax cuts" leading to "unsustainable deficits," which "threaten the prosperity of the country" by "passing the bills to our children." Surely if all other forms of economic conservatism, embraced by Republicans, are fit for the dustbins of history, then this one, embraced by Democrats, must be worth preserving.

Alas, no. In fact, budget balancing was the very first conservative pillar to collapse; its demise was the most successful compromise with reality in the Reagan years. Reagan's tax cuts were supply side in name—but they were also tax cuts. Their largest effect was simply to add money to private pockets. Combined with the tax cuts, Reagan's spending programs—on the military in the first instance and then in his failure to make fully offsetting cuts in domestic programs—ensured an enormous swing toward budget deficits from 1980 through 1983. And this in turn fueled the strong economic expansion that began in that year and continued through the end of the decade.

This was a conservative form of Keynesian policy that dissolved the historical obstacle to Keynesianism: the truculent opposition of the very rich. The American oligarchs of the 1930s had loathed FDR, not because he was bringing economic recovery, but because in so doing, he upended the existing social order: henceforward they would have to deal with trade unions, big government, and regulatory agencies. However prosperous the society might be, their own role in it would be diminished. Reaganomics sidestepped this issue by aiming the tax cuts at the rich and running budget deficits through rather than around the existing wealthy. Under Reagan's Keynesianism, the price of prosperity became not the overthrow of established social relations but their perpetuation.

The Democratic response to Reagan's success was, naturally enough, to ignore the economy and complain about the deficits. As politics, this had a certain logic: it helped the Democrats play against type, shedding their image as "big spenders" and winning support on Wall Street. It was, however, a weak reed with the larger public, who were disinclined to look the gift horse of "morning in America" in the mouth, and tended not to concern themselves with whether the return to economic prosperity had been delivered by illegitimate means. It also worked to hamstring Democratic policy initiatives going forward as the party tied itself up with budgetary restrictions—such as the notorious "pay-go" rules—intended to demonstrate "fiscal responsibility" to a skeptical public. The assertion of the primacy and importance of these rules, however, would merely confirm for the public what conservatives had earlier charged: that the Democrats were not to be trusted with public money.

Democrats worked with Republicans in the 1980s to undo Reagan's tax cuts, passing tax increases in 1982 and 1984 and the Tax Reform Act of 1986. And the drama of the Democrats' search for reputability in the eyes of the fiscally righteous would play on through the 1990s in the budget negotiations of the first Bush presidency and the deficit reduction package of the early Clinton term. The promise of these packages was that interest rates would fall. In fact, right after the Clinton package passed in late 1993, the opposite happened: interest rates started to rise. Ultimately President Bill Clinton did balance the budget, in the last three years of his term. However, this was not by design but by accident—an unexpected, unpredicted consequence of the information technology boom, fed in part by capital flowing into the United States after the Asian crisis in 1997 and the Russian crisis in 1998. As the stock market rose, federal revenues shot up, in large part through capital gains and stock options realizations. At the peak of this rush of tax money, giddy federal officials predicted that the entire federal debt would be retired within fifteen years. It was another illusion.

They were forgetting Keynes, who had tried to teach them that the budget surpluses of the late 1990s would be a serious economic policy mistake. By draining funds from the spending stream, their effect was to doom the durability of the expansion. The combination of an unsustainable stock bubble with a super-tight fiscal policy would ensure that the next administration would face an economic slump. And exactly this happened: the bubble collapsed, the expansion ended, and the dream of eliminating the federal debt faded away as though it had never been. Yet by and large, the Democrats still did not learn. As late as the end of 2007, one of their leading candidates for the presidency, Senator Hillary Clinton, was still issuing campaign documents calling for "fiscal responsibility" and a "balanced budget."

The position of Democrats on deficits has a tortured history, long suspended between realism and respectability. A tour of this history demonstrates why budget deficits are built into the global financial system, starting in the 1970s, why balancing the budget on a sustained basis is impossible so long as that system endures, why the attempt to do so is actually harmful, and—sadly—why liberals have largely failed to understand this.

Campaigning against Herbert Hoover in 1932, Franklin Roosevelt called for a balanced budget; only after the election did he sacrifice fiscal probity to fight the Depression, which required public spending far above the capacity to tax. Eight years later, the war multiplied this necessity. When FDR died in 1945, the federal debt was over 100 percent of national product, itself double the prewar value, and yet— or, rather, therefore—the United States was the strongest economy in the world. Then, throughout the 1950s, except in years of recession, the ratio of public debt to gross national product (GNP) declined. As this happened, the old canons of fiscal propriety were gradually reasserted, and the lessons of depression and wartime began to seem less relevant to a period of growth and creeping inflation. Among the more progressive business leaders, the conventional view became that budgets should be in surplus in good times to offset the deficits that were inevitable in downturns. Still, only a few purists in the academy favored balanced budgets on all occasions; they were taken seriously by no one.

In John F. Kennedy's administration, a rare period of Democratic realism, the key debates were between Keynesians of different stripes.

One such was between those (led by my father) who favored increased public expenditure and a creative leadership role for government, financed mainly, if not wholly, by taxes, and those (including Paul Samuelson, James Tobin, and Robert Solow) who argued that government should mainly manage the aggregate flows of expenditure and demand. My father, speaking from the Left, favored balancing the budget over the cycle: he wanted the tax revenue in order to make possible more spending. Samuelson, Tobin, and Solow favored deficits, relying on Keynes's multiplier mechanism to raise income and therefore tax revenue. They did not believe that tax cuts entirely financed themselves, but it was widely understood that higher growth would push deficits back down as the economy approached full employment. Kennedy's proposed tax cut of 1963, enacted under Lyndon Johnson in 1964, was the great victory for their view. My father foresaw that it would someday prove fatally seductive to conservatives, generating a new form of reactionary Keynesianism; he would live to see this prophecy validated in two reactionary administrations.* Henceforward, demands for growth and employment could be met by tax reduction, while public investment would be checked by the budget deficits that would become the chronic result. Tax cuts indeed had two decisive advantages: they helped the vocal rich, and they worked quickly. One could always argue that a spending-led recovery would come too late, and the opponents of that course could also always hold things up long enough to make their predictions come true.

The Kennedy-Johnson tax cut, together with the growth in government associated with Great Society programs and the Vietnam War, did work: it moved the economy toward full employment, which was reached by 1966 and sustained through the end of Johnson's term. It also worked equally well to balance expenditures with revenues eventually: the budget for fiscal year 1969 was balanced, for the last time until the late 1990s. Budget balance gave pride to the fiscal engineers, but rising tax revenues acted as a drag on activity, helping to precipitate the recession that greeted Richard Nixon's administration in late 1969.

Richard Nixon, it is probably fair to say, was entirely free of constraining economic ideas. On taking office, he famously declared him-

*This historical point has been developed recently by Bruce Bartlett, "Starve the Beast: The Origins and Development of a Budgetary Metaphor," *Independent Review* 12 (Summer 2007): 5–26.

self a Keynesian convert, prepared to run deficits if they were needed. And they would be, as the recession of 1970 stretched on and threatened his reelection prospects. Though surrounded by routine conservatives, he reached out in time of crisis to men of wholly political instinct and few inhibitions, notably the former Democratic governor John B. Connally of Texas. Nixon's 1972 election year program, combining price control, accelerated public spending, and a famously easy monetary policy thoughtfully provided by Arthur F. Burns at the Federal Reserve, was a classic of short-term Keynesianism. Once again, deficit spending worked. It yielded a year of real growth near 6 percent, a rapid decline in unemployment and surge in real wages, and a monumental reelection victory over the antiwar Democrat, George McGovern. Thanks to price controls, there was also little increase in inflation, at least at first.

But just as what Nixon did on the international economic policy front in 1971 and 1973 was to kick off the inflationary 1970s, so too it would have profound and long-lasting effects on the budget. These effects took many years to enter the textbooks, and politicians still do not understand them. They were to make balancing the budget an obsolete policy goal, and actual budget balance something that could be achieved only on a very short-term basis, under conditions of exceptional financial imbalance in the private sector—conditions that would not be seen until the late 1990s and may not be seen again for a very long time to come.

As we have seen, when Nixon abandoned the Bretton Woods system, he devalued the dollar; he slapped on export controls, so that price-controlled wheat and soybeans would not leave the country for more profitable markets in (especially) Japan. He also closed the gold window, depriving foreign central banks of their right to gold at the fixed rate. Gold prices were freed, and they soared. In 1973, Nixon completed the demolition job. Following the advice of international monetarists such as George Shultz, he declined to restore a managed global exchange rate regime, inaugurating the era of floating exchange rates. Henceforward commercial banks, and not central bankers or the IMF, would be the line of first resort for countries requiring cash. Now, too, countries could choose for themselves how to hold their reserves; the exorbitant privilege previously accorded the dollar was no longer guaranteed; a new winner in the contest to serve as reserve currency for the world economy might in principle emerge. (This was in a sense the ultimate test of the superfluity of government.) Advocates of the floating-rate regime spoke in soothing terms of the wisdom, self-adjustment, and smooth approach to equilibrium in the market for foreign exchange.

The reality was quite different. Foreign exchange markets became speculative and erratic. Rich and powerful countries contrived, by various mechanisms (leading ultimately in Europe to the common currency, the euro), to protect themselves, creating new systems of exchange rate management to replace what had been lost. Sometimes these worked, and sometimes they failed, as the UK would discover when speculators busted the pound in 1992. Poorer countries suffered and made do as best they could. Their wealthier citizens availed themselves of the simplest effective expedient, which was to move assets out of the unstable national currency and into dollars, British pounds, or Swiss francs. Banks offered private banking services aimed at assisting the wealthiest in getting their assets out of countries that attempted capital control. Meanwhile the same banks offered new loans to developing countries at floating rates and high fees.

Faced with a declining dollar and a growing world economy, commodity producers could and did raise their dollar prices, a process that culminated with the OPEC oil shock in 1973. The resulting inflation threw U.S. macro policy into reverse gear, and the tight policies that followed drained purchasing power and depressed business profits, generating recession and unemployment. Meanwhile, the dollar continued to fall, a process that was widely interpreted as reflecting the eroding competitiveness of American manufactures. International problems and domestic problems went hand in hand. Gerald Ford and then Jimmy Carter inherited from Nixon an economy in which international financial actors had little faith and that could ill afford to have faith in itself. The mood of the period, which gave rise ultimately to Ronald Reagan, was one of national economic decline. The federal budget deficit was an increasingly intractable headline indicator of this decline. But the rising U.S. deficit in international trade was also a large part of this perception, for after 1974, the American economy was almost never again to be in surplus with respect to the rest of the world.

What few understood was that the budget deficit and the trade deficit were closely linked, and each was closely related to the evolving character of the global financial system. They were so closely related, in fact, that they usually amounted to two aspects of the same thing. And as the new global monetary system developed, the growing need for dollars—for monetary reserves—held outside the United States would come to guarantee that the United States would necessarily experience both trade deficits and budget deficits almost all of the time. The deficits were not so much a symptom of a declining position as the tribute paid to the United States for its position atop the world financial order. The falling dollar in the 1970s stemmed from the threat to that position, following the Nixon shocks, the triumph of international monetarism, and the destruction of Bretton Woods.*

There is a basic relationship in macroeconomics, as fundamental as it is poorly understood, that links the internal and the international financial position of any country. A country's internal deficit, that is, its "public" deficit and its "private" deficit—the annual borrowing by companies and households—will together equal its international deficit. In the early postwar United States, the typical pattern of the private sector, which consists of companies and households, was to run a small net surplus each year, of around 2 percent of GDP. Thus, the private sector accumulated financial assets, while the public sector built up a corresponding stock of debts. Overall, the country enjoyed a situation in which approximate external balance could be (and was) maintained, so long as the public sector deficit did not exceed 2 percent of GDP. If households and companies were depositing money in the banks every year, government could borrow that money without having to look for it abroad. To put it another way, government did not borrow abroad, and so the government's deficit, which is the amount by which public spending put into the economy exceeds taxes taken out, created an exactly offsetting private surplus.

This situation came under strain in the 1960s as trade deficits rose with the Vietnam War. Part of the U.S. debt began to be held abroad. And under the financial rules then prevailing, it was possible for foreign countries running trade surpluses with us to demand settlement of the balances in gold. Since the gold stock underpinned the financial architecture, its loss could not be tolerated. This was the limiting factor on U.S. growth, and therefore the system that Richard Nixon felt obliged to terminate in 1971 in order to make possible his highly expansionary reelection campaign.

---

*And this is why—once the United States restored its grip on the top of the financial pecking order in the 1980s—the Reagan deficits, for all the horror they provoked in political circles, did not cause financial problems.

The final end of Bretton Woods followed in 1973. Now, nothing except the market itself prevented us, in principle, from running large external deficits all of the time. But it was necessary for someone to be willing to hold the corresponding debts, and this, foreigners in the 1970s were collectively unwilling to do. And so those with more dollars than they wanted sold them, and the price went down. The falling dollar should in theory have worked to close the trade deficit but it did not; instead it fueled even more inflation in the United States, and the trade deficits did not go away. Meanwhile, the anchor that had also tied the U.S. federal budget position to one of approximate balance had been broken—without anyone in high policy positions taking note. The old wisdom, which held that budgets should be balanced or perhaps balanced over the business cycle, continued to be spoken, but it was obsolete.

Congress was oblivious. Nixon had faced a liberal Democratic Congress and a showdown over the intrinsic powers of the executive branch. When Congress appropriated funds, in line with the Constitution, for certain social programs, Nixon asserted the right not to spend the money. He wanted to starve the spending programs he did not approve of. Congress refused to go along. One of the results was a major reform in 1974 of the budget process. This gave us the system of budget resolutions and Congressional Budget Office review of spending and tax proposals that we have today.

Those reforms locked into place an obsession with the budget deficit and an implicit priority for balanced budgets. Thereafter, all legislative proposals would be judged against their effect on the deficit— and on the completely artificial assumption that they would have no effect on the underlying economy. The rules simply assumed that neither the volume nor the content of the spending would affect the total volume of GDP, despite the accounting reality that government purchases of goods and services are actually part of GDP, so that GDP goes up at least dollar for dollar when this form of government spending does. Official Washington ruled out by fiat the possibility that any legislative program would affect economic behavior in such a way as to stimulate growth, a fact that would also infuriate the supply-siders a few years later. A system designed by Democrats embraced the old Republican fiscal ideal, the balanced budget, on no better ground than the atavistic appeal of the number zero. Baby and bathwater were discarded alike; the entire criterion of budget policy would become the level of the bathtub ring.

That was bad enough, but the events that followed made things worse. As the 1970s proceeded, stagnation and unemployment cut into tax revenues, while the cost of Medicare and Medicaid (among other things) grew rapidly. The deficit rose, in spite of the new budget systems, giving the impression of policy failure, and to reduce the deficit became the single great economic policy priority. The Carter administration, which had started on a Keynesian note, became obsessed with deficit reduction. The budget process became a morality play, divorced from economics, in which the goal of the players was to present themselves as favoring virtue and opposing vice. In 1980, President Carter actually withdrew his budget and briefly proposed a "balanced budget" instead; had it been enacted, the effects would have been disastrous. But Carter was defeated for reelection, and the Senate went Republican for the first time since the early 1950s.

When Ronald Reagan took office in January 1981, unemployment stood at 7.1 percent, inflation at 13.6 percent. With talk of a "misery index" (inflation plus unemployment) exceeding 20 percent, Reagan declared the "worst economic mess since the Great Depression."* Within a few weeks, the new president's economists had cobbled together his "economic recovery program" combining his tax cuts, increases in defense spending, cuts in all other types of spending, and monetarism. Together these were projected to yield rapid growth, leading to budget balance by 1984.

But of course the budget projections were impossible. The economic assumptions of the Reagan team were unjustifiably optimistic in the short run, since—following the logic of budget forecasts—they ignored the actual effects on the economy of the plan. Because the plan, which included the brutal monetarist assault on inflation, produced a recession, the unavoidable result was an exploding budget deficit. (At the Joint Economic Committee in 1981, our staff was the first to publicize projections showing that budget deficits would shortly top the then-impressive figure of $100 billion per year.) And in the recovery that followed, the high interest rates that had been invoked to quell inflation produced a gigantic increase in the value of the dollar on

*Ronald Reagan, "Address to the Nation on the Economy," February 5, 1981.

international markets. Correspondingly, imports were cheap while U.S. export markets collapsed. The U.S. trade deficit consequently exploded. Given the normal relationship between the two deficits, this ensured that the budget deficit would not go away.

Of course, from an economic point of view this was hardly all bad news. On the contrary, Reagan rode to reelection on the strength of his tax cuts, the deficits, and the boom they generated in 1984. Why did it prove possible for Reagan to do what Carter could not, namely run large deficits, without a fall in the dollar and consequent inflation? Because the Federal Reserve's policy of super-high interest rates and a super-strong dollar helped Reagan out. By attracting a flood of investment capital back into the United States, the strong dollar policy reconciled fiscal stimulus, recovering employment, and a rapid end to inflation. The dollar now became the unchallenged world reserve currency, which meant the United States not only could, but had to, run trade deficits to the extent of the demand for reserves. So long as the domestic private sector remained of a mind to accumulate financial assets, which it did through the Reagan term, the trade deficits had to be translated, as a matter of accounting, into federal budget deficits of a similar size. The doctrine of "twin deficits" did gain official notice— Paul Volcker spoke and wrote about it in the mid-1980s—but the interpretation then given held that budget deficits were to blame for the trade deficit.* The role of the world financial system in making the trade deficit inevitable was overlooked.

And the ideology of balanced budgets endured. Reagan's successor, George H. W. Bush, could not escape the fixation on deficits that Reagan had so blithely dismissed, in part because Bush felt a need to soften Reagan's partisan image by meeting the "fiscal responsibility" Democrats halfway on this issue. Beset by deficits caused by yet another recession, Bush sat down with the Democrats at Andrews Air Force Base in 1990, and there they hammered out a bipartisan deficit-reduction plan. As is well known, this included tax concessions that infuriated the Republican base, helping to ensure its lack of enthusiasm

---

*A more formally correct, but no less misleading, interpretation holds that the culprit is the savings-investment balance: too much investment and too little saving. But so long as foreigners wish to hold dollar assets, and so long as we permit them—indeed, encourage them—to do so, a domestic savings-investment imbalance is both inevitable and desirable.

for Bush and his defeat in the election of 1992. So the politics of bipartisan reconciliation was for him a bust—a fact that one suspects was not entirely lost on his son.

But despite the high reputation of the Andrews Air Force Base accords among historians devoted to the virtues of bipartisan agreement, the deficit reductions of 1990 also did not work as economics. The economy plainly needed a bigger deficit, not a smaller one, at that time. Though economic growth resumed at an anemic pace, there was no new job creation, and no decline in unemployment, until the credit boom got started in 1994. Bush had relied on the power of monetary policy to generate a strong recovery, and it did not work for him. Of Greenspan, the hapless ex-President said, "I reappointed him, and he disappointed me." In fact, it was hardly Greenspan's fault that the moribund banking industry of the late 1980s could not finance a strong recovery in 1991. A robust fiscal expansion, involving bigger deficits, would have been necessary. And this, in a search for virtue and bipartisan agreement, he denied to himself.

Then came Bill Clinton. Clinton too took the bipartisan line on budget deficits and started his administration with yet another big push to reduce them. The great budget myth of the 1990s was that Clinton, by some miracle of economic prestidigitation that had escaped his immediate predecessor, did succeed in launching an economic recovery on the strength of a deficit reduction package, including major tax increases, enacted in the last gasp of the Democratic Congress in 1993. This is nonsense. Whatever the merits of the Clinton tax program, which was on the whole progressive, it did not generate either the recovery that began in 1994 or the boom that took hold in the late 1990s. The sources of growth and then of boom came from other places.

Congress passed the deficit-reduction package in the late fall of 1993. Given the supposed importance of this action to the climate of expectations, long-term interest rates should have fallen when the one-vote margin to make the bill law was secured. Instead they rose. The policy sequence of cutting budget deficits in order to reassure credit markets and lower long-term interest rates was tried. It did not work.

The recovery took root anyway, and one can pinpoint the date it really began—precisely—to February 4, 1994. On that date, Alan Greenspan *raised* the short-term interest rate, allowing short rates to begin to catch up to the rise in long-term rates that had been under way for some months by that time. Normally, raising short-term interest rates is a contractionary measure, with negative consequences for growth. But the circumstances in 1994 were special. The nation's large banks by that point had been in a state of near-insolvency for half a decade and had been slowly rebuilding their balance sheets by a simple device: milking the government for high interest rates on long-term bonds while paying out very low rates to their depositors. The very steep yield curve then prevailing (the difference between short-run and long-run interest rates) meant that a bank could do this, and make at least a modest profit, without lending to businesses at all. The rise in short rates squeezed the banks' costs, which had the effect of forcing them to cover their costs with riskier commercial and industrial loans, which up to that moment they had not been willing to make. Whether the Federal Reserve itself understood that this would be the consequence of its actions remains unclear, but expansionary it was. The "credit crunch," widely discussed in the press for weeks leading up to this action, abruptly disappeared. Money suddenly became available for risk-taking firms. Job growth almost immediately resumed. This was an important development that actually saved the Clinton administration down the road, but it had almost no connection to the deficit-reduction package of late 1993.

For the next three years, the recovery gathered force. Unemployment fell, the budget deficit began to diminish, and inflation did not rise. The 1997 Asian crisis brought a flood of capital back into the safe haven of U.S. Treasury bonds, strengthening the dollar. The trade deficit rose.

But now the budget deficit did not. Indeed it fell—all the way to zero and into actual surplus, for the first time since 1969. How could this happen? How could our foreign deficits go up while our budget deficit went down? If the money sent abroad did not come from the government, where did it come from? This fact caused many who had been exposed to the "twin deficits" view of budgets and trade to deny that the view was accurate. But they were forgetting the third element in the equation. There is one possible way (and only one) for budget deficits to go down while the trade deficit goes up: for the *private* sector of the American economy to "take over" the budget deficits previously run by the state. And that is what happened. Private businesses and households in the late 1990s chose, for the first time in postwar history, to move massively into deficit. Credit cards, mortgages, and home equity loans suddenly became the drivers of American economic growth. For a time, the American household took over the job of running deficits from the American government. This was the Keynesian *devolution*.

Why did private companies and private households act as they did? There is no mystery to it: the stock market and the housing boom were making many people feel rich. They could afford to borrow, whether on margin against their stocks, or by mortgage against the equity in their homes. And they did, driving the ratio of debt to income to unprecedented levels. At the very good interest rates available, there was nothing to stand in the way, and the loans taken out were for the most part perfectly serviceable so long as the stock market and housing values remained high. In 1999 and 2000, capital gains and stock options realizations boosted personal incomes, especially of the very rich, who then paid income tax at the 1994 rates. Tax revenues spiked upward. For years, both Republicans and Democrats had claimed to want a balanced budget. Now they had one—but it was a problem, not a virtue.

The surpluses did what all surpluses do: a government running a surplus necessarily subtracts in taxes from private spending more than it injects in payments to private incomes. This forced the private economy to finance its expansion with a buildup of debt. But unlike government debt, private debt has limits. It could not last indefinitely, and it did not. The technology boom ended in April 2000 with the crash of the NASDAQ. Tax revenues plummeted—not only for the federal government but also for key states like California, which entered a deep fiscal crisis. The economy tipped over into recession in early 2001, and the budget deficit returned.

All this happened just in time for the arrival of George W. Bush and the return of Reaganism in political perspectives. Though actually only some of Bush's economic initiatives resembled Reagan's (Bush was certainly never attracted to monetarism), his tax policy emulated Reagan's so faithfully that it brings to mind Marx's dictum that the great events of history happen once as tragedy and later as farce.

Like Reagan's, Bush's tax cut had been designed at first for the politics of the moment. The appeal was, of course, to the wealthy financial base of the Republican Party. (Bush's proposal was actually a device crafted for the primary campaign, to draw voters and donors from the ardent Reaganite tax cutter Steve Forbes.) For both Bush and Reagan, the major objective was the reduction of relatively high tax rates on the highest incomes: in the case of Reagan, the high marginal tax rates on earned income and capital gains; in the case of Bush, the high rates on the largest estates, income, and, later, dividends. In Reagan's case, this motivation could be dressed up in the supply-side rhetoric of work, savings, and investment. Bush's emphasis on cutting the estate tax had no such justification; it is hard to argue that the greatest plutocrats need a tax break to accumulate even more than they already have simply for the purpose of leaving bequests to their children. Bush did not try; he simply argued that it was their money, and they should get to keep it. A clever public relations campaign stigmatized the tax by relabeling it the "death tax." It was an argument from the strictest first principles, from a philosophical worldview and in defense of a particular class order. It did not depend on economic conditions.

But as it happened, from the standpoint of the great God who judges fiscal policy in the sweet hereafter, Bush's tax program taken as a whole was about the right size for that moment in time. Economic conditions swung radically in favor of fiscal stimulus as 2001 went on. As the economy slumped and jobs disappeared, Bush at least had a program. The Democrats, locked into their commitment to the Clintonian fantasy of a sustainably balanced budget, had no alternative, although they did offer the modest addition of a short-term tax rebate to the Bush package. Bush lost nothing, and gained everything, by accepting the deal.

September 11 then permitted the rollout of the other side of a fiscal strategy: a massive increase in the military budget, adding about 1 percent of GDP to these expenditures even before the Iraq war. After 2003, Iraq doubled that increase, and Bush proved open to every other new expenditure program, including the Medicare drug benefit, that Congress cared to enact. Here, suddenly, was a president who never saw a congressional appropriation he could not sign. Indeed as the Bush presidency developed, an even more aggressive Keynesianism became its macroeconomic signature. By 2003, logic and circumstance dictated that a stronger economic recovery would require more federal spending. (Not expecting to enjoy any influence, I published a paper to this effect that very year.*) The administration followed the prescription,

---

*"The Big Fix: The Case for Public Spending," Levy Economics Institute Policy Note, January 2003.

raising federal spending just enough in the run-up to the elections of 2004 to keep the economy on a growth track. Having done this over the complaints of conservatives, Bush and Cheney were able to defeat their fiscally conservative challenger, John Kerry, in the 2004 election. Kerry's campaign had been marked by a discussion of tax increases and a lack of imagination-grabbing proposals that might have required new spending. Credit should be given: the Republicans learned to live with the fiscal world as it is. Many Democrats still have not and continue to take positions that will have to be abandoned sooner or later if they wish to succeed when their turn in the presidency comes around again.

And Bush's insouciance paid off. Under the impetus of federal spending, combined with the tax cuts, the economy eventually did recover, turning in a decent growth performance (though a poor record of employment gain) in the run-up to the 2004 election. In 2005 a private investment spending boom began to take hold, partly fueled by the rise of the junk or "subprime" mortgage, which would start to backfire on many households within a couple of years. But the boom had a remarkable (though temporary) consequence: the budget deficit declined sharply in defiance of official projections. By early 2007 the unemployment rate was below 4.5 percent, and the ratio of employment to population was approaching the territory of the late 1990s.

The great irony in this history is that the cherished ideal of a balanced budget, once a key talking point of the conservatives, was proven to be pointless precisely as it was embraced by Democrats. Most Republicans, as a practical matter, understand; once in office, they no longer pretend that the federal government is just like a household. It's the Democrats who do not get it. Self-styled progressives who call for balanced budgets are not merely parroting conservatives; they are parroting dead conservatives, with no living descendants and no practical application in the modern world.

Deficit hawks—Democrats and Republicans alike—have never understood the effects of financial globalization on the budget. The international dimension of the budget deficit enters neither their minds nor their calculations. The Washington discussion circuit, fueled by a vocal lobby of doomsayers, continues to treat deficits as it had before, as though they were the product purely of domestic policy decisions taken in the context of balanced trade and full employment. In consequence, the public discussion of fiscal policy lost contact with reality altogether; it became instead a pantomime of vice and virtue, each achieved without any relation to actual merit or wisdom in the setting of economic policy.

In sum, and to put the matter bluntly, balancing the budget is a mission impossible and a fool's errand. For practical purposes, the realized budget deficit no longer depends on federal budget policy decisions, but rather on international trade and the financial position of the private sector. So long as American foreign trade remains in a permanent state of deficit—which it has to do, so long as a growing and unstable world economy requires dollar reserves—the federal budget deficit is basically permanent. Policymakers and pundits can say what they like about budget deficits. Nothing sustainable can or will or even should be done about them, except through a change in the world's financial system. That may come eventually. It may, for that matter, be in its early stages at this writing. But whatever the future holds, it is in the global financial system, and not in the halls of Congress, that the future fiscal balance of the U.S. government—and whether it really matters to the well-being of Americans—will be decided.

CHAPTER SIX

There Is No Such Thing
as Free Trade

The last verity in the conservative canon is free trade. It was also the first verity in that canon: before budgets, before monetarism, and long before supply-side economics. In the conservative iconography, Adam Smith was, first and foremost, a free trader. So were David Ricardo, John Stuart Mill, and Alfred Marshall. The dissenters—Friedrich List, Karl Marx, John Maynard Keynes—are in order forgotten, dismissed, or remembered for other things. In policy discussion, free trade is so closely synonymous with virtue that its detractors are automatically identified with narrow or "special" interests, such as that of the unions. "Protectionist" is an all-purpose epithet, deployed to defeat argument and stop conversation. Free trade has in this way gained the status of a god, second only to the free market itself.

Adam Smith put the case for trade in simple and enduring terms: "The division of labor is limited by the extent of the market." The larger the market, the greater the division of labor. The greater the division of labor, the more efficient the process of production. The more efficient the production, the higher the achievable standard of living. The Scottish highlands in Smith's day were poor not because they lacked resources (though they did) or talent (also in doubtful supply), but because they were isolated: no ports, no rails (they did not exist yet), bad roads. Without trade, production could not hope to rise to the standards that technology made possible; indeed without trade, technology itself would not rise to its potential.

Smith was right about this, and his argument remains true. The great globalized industries such as aviation, telecommunications, and energy require global markets for efficient operation. These endeavors cannot be replicated at national scale; the effort to do so inside protected national frontiers is virtually doomed to fail, for the internal market is too small and insufficiently demanding. Prices would be too high, quality too low, innovation too slow. No great technical industry restricted to the boundaries of a single state can fully compete with a rival accustomed to winning out in global trade. The Soviets tried it with civil aviation and the Brazilians with computers: it did not work. There may be justifiable reasons, such as national security, for restricting trade in such sectors, but achieving global dominance and maximal technical advance are not among them.

But when Smith wrote of trade between (say) London and Calcutta, he was not writing about free and unfettered trade between nations. He was writing about commerce between two parts of a nascent empire. Certain common conditions applied: the rate of exchange was fixed, the means of payment were relatively secure, trading relations would not be disrupted immediately in wartime. And there was also no question which partner was in the primary and which in the secondary role. Free trade with India was good for Britain because it provided markets for British goods that helped keep British commerce (and, later, British industry) in a class of its own on the world stage. There was no immediate prospect that the colonial partner would surpass the colonizer, reversing the direction of commerce between manufactures and resources. Whether it was good for the Indians depended on whom you asked. Their textile industry would soon be destroyed by cheap British imports.

Outside the imperial or colonial setting, Smith did not oppose foreign trade, for instance, between rivals and frequent enemies Britain and France, but he was conscious of its risks. With France there was the risk that the other country would steal a march on the division of labor, that trade would redound to the superior benefit of the French merchants and, ultimately, of the French state. The immortal passage about the "invisible hand" is usually cited nowadays in support of an unfettered market, but that was not Smith's own point. Quite the contrary: in drafting that passage, Smith was giving an argument *against* gratuitous foreign trade. He wrote, "By *preferring the support of domestic to that of foreign industry* [the individual] intends only his own security"—and so he is "led by an invisible hand to promote an end which was no part of his intention." Something similar could be said for a "Buy America" campaign.

So even Adam Smith was not an unqualified "free trader." His policy concern was, rather, with the balance of trade, specifically the obsessive preoccupation with trade surpluses that had been the touchstone of the Elizabethan mercantilists. Smith sought to dispel the illusion that the accumulation of "treasure," through the pursuit of a surplus, should be the principal objective of a trading nation. For the mercantilists, trade was, like war, merely a means of public finance. A successful war paid for itself with pillage; a successful trading regime paid for itself by running a profit, which is to say an excess of exports over imports. Smith thought this "fruitless." For it, he substituted the idea that a nation's true wealth lay in its productive capacity, and especially in its capacity to exploit the division of labor. For this, a vast trading empire, defended as necessary by military force, was the prescription. The larger the empire, the greater the market, and the further the division of labor could be made to go.

But for Smith, trade nevertheless remained a sphere of competition. The purpose of trade was not the benign satisfaction of consumer wants or the accumulation of personal capital: the wealth sought was the wealth "of nations." A nation traded to accumulate wealth because that was the effective strategy and because wealth, "as Mr. Hobbes says, is power." Smith was a political realist in a world of ever-present or ever-threatening war; he differed from his predecessors in seeing the path to power in new and enlightened terms.

It was David Ricardo who promoted the doctrine of free trade as such, as an end toward maximum production, achieved by specialization. Ricardo's contribution was the doctrine of *comparative advantage*, presented through the exchange of wool and wine between England and Portugal. And the Ricardian doctrine of comparative advantage conquered economics, "as completely as the Holy Inquisition conquered Spain"—so Keynes was to say a century on, though of a different aspect of Ricardo's thinking.

Comparative advantage is an argument based on a highly simplified paper-and-pencil calculation. Ricardo showed that if you had two countries and two commodities, with constant costs of production in both, then unless the conditions of production are exactly the same in both places, both can benefit from specialization, and therefore from trade. This is a textbook exercise, just difficult enough so that the beginning student, having mastered it, will experience the thrill of having learned something. In particular, the charm of comparative advantage lies in the fact that it does not require that there be an absolute cost advantage on either side: trade is advantageous even when one country can produce both goods at absolutely lower cost than the other.

Unlike Smith's argument about the division of labor, comparative advantage makes no use of technical efficiency. Comparative advantage operates on the assumption of unchanged technology and constant returns to scale. There are no economies of scale, no learning curve, no improvements in productivity as output increases. The only require- ment is that conditions of production differ, so that one good—in terms of the other—is relatively more expensive in one country and rel- atively less so in the other. The only efficiency gained from trade stems from the reorganization of production and the reallocation of fac- tors—labor, capital, land—to their best uses in the new, larger, common market. Comparative advantage is thus simpler and more general than Smith's argument in favor of trade: it works with all pairs of countries, all pairs of commodities. For Ricardo, this was powerfully in its favor.

But the argument does not generalize to the actual world. Given three countries and three commodities, it is not obvious that each country will always be the relatively most efficient producer of exactly one good. And then what? Does the country that has no comparative advantage produce nothing? Does it refuse to trade? If its "comparative advantage" lies in exporting labor and closing up shop, is this accept- able? The textbooks do not say. The actual world has some 220 coun- tries and thousands of distinct commodities. In this world—the one where we actually live—the calculation of comparative advantage is intractable, and the doctrine says nothing about who should specialize in what, still less that specialization will exactly reproduce full employ- ment in each place. Actual patterns of specialization are therefore highly path dependent, meaning that what a country will do next depends on what it has learned to do in the past, and on what it is able to learn, given what it already knows, from elsewhere.

Further, comparative advantage is based on the concept of con- stant returns: the idea that you can double or triple the output of any good simply by doubling or tripling the inputs. But this is not generally the case. For manufactured products, increasing returns, learning, and technical change are the rule, not the exception: the cost of production falls with experience. With increasing returns, the lowest cost will be incurred by the country that starts earliest and moves fastest on any particular product line. Potential competitors have to protect their own industries if they wish them to survive long enough to achieve competitive scale.

For most other commodities, where land or ecology places limits on the expansion of capacity, the opposite condition—diminishing returns—is the rule. In this situation, there can be no guarantee that an advantage of relative cost will persist once specialization and the resulting expansion of production take place. A classic and tragic example, studied by Erik Reinert, is transitional Mongolia, a vast grassland with a tiny population and no industry that could compete on world markets. To the World Bank, Mongolia seemed a classic case of comparative advantage in animal husbandry, which in Mongolia consisted of vast herds of cattle, camels, sheep, and goats. Opening of industrial markets collapsed domestic industry, while privatization of the herds prompted the herders to increase their size. This led, within just a few years in the early 1990s, to overgrazing and permanent desertification of the subarctic steppe and, with a slightly colder than normal winter, a massive famine in the herds.*

Some variations on the theme of comparative advantage hold that countries will adjust their inputs—capital, labor, and land—to make best use of the factors in which they are most abundantly endowed. But while there is no doubt some of this, for products incorporating advanced technologies, the product and the process of production are inseparable: you cannot make a modern jet aircraft except by following the rules prescribed by Boeing or Airbus. Therefore, production conditions do not differ materially across potential factory sites, and the fact that labor is cheap and abundant in China does not induce Boeing to produce the MD-80 passenger aircraft, which it assembles there, with more labor and less capital or different materials than in the United States. Rather, Boeing follows the same blueprint in both countries, using the same or similar machinery, to produce a final product to the same exact specifications. The difference between them lies merely in the wage bill: in China, this is lower, and the aircraft either sells more cheaply or earns a higher profit.

In practical reality, "comparative advantage" is more of a slogan than an analysis, and economists tend to use it in two disconnected ways. One is for purely theoretical discussion, unmarried to data. The other is to

---

*Erik S. Reinert (ed.), *Globalization, Economic Development and Inequality: An Alternative Perspective* (Cheltenham: Edward Elgar, 2004).

describe some emergent pattern of trade after the fact. There is no evident need actually to check on the underlying relative costs: if a country has specialized in something, it must have a comparative advantage. Unlike Smith's doctrine of efficiency gains through the expansion of markets, Ricardo's doctrine is mainly a rhetorical device—so much hot air—with very little purchase on the modern trading world. And its key implication, that countries should pick a narrow bundle of products and specialize in them, is absolutely unwise as policy. This is obvious once one considers the time dimension and the problem of risk.

Countries doomed by climate and history to produce bananas, coffee, or cocoa and little else are invariably poor. Why? First, the demand for their products is inelastic: when supply increases worldwide, the price falls, and with it national income. Second, they suffer from diminishing returns. Contrary to Ricardo, it is generally impossible to expand agriculture indefinitely at a constant unit cost: good land and water are in limited supply. Third, a country with just one major cash export will lack a cushion in other products when fashion or technology turns against their specialty. Conversely, diversification pays. Countries with the capacity to diversify across multiple industries are far more likely to weather export demand shocks or insurgent competition from (say) China than those that commit themselves to a single industry or product line. Diversifiers are also better placed to take advantage of new technical opportunities, since by diversification they develop expertise in a range of products and processes.

I can say it flatly: Ricardo was wrong. Comparative advantage has very little practical use for trade strategy. Diversification, not specialization, is the main path out of underdevelopment, and effective diversification requires a strategic approach to trade policy. It cannot mean walling off the outside world, but it is also a goal not easily pursued under a dogmatic commitment to free trade. Indeed none of the world's most successful trading regions, including Japan, Korea, Taiwan, and now mainland China, reached their current status by adopting neoliberal trading rules.

At the same time, it remains beyond dispute that *Smith*, at least, was right. Japan, Korea, Taiwan, and China have prospered in part because they can trade. Under correct conditions, trade is desirable; having a large, unimpeded market is a great advantage. Large, unimpeded markets exist inside large political entities governed by common and stable systems of law. No part of the United States would benefit from repeal of the commerce clause and the imposition of customs houses on the inter-state highways. Europe is greatly richer than it ever could have been with-out the Common Market; small countries (admittedly with exceptions, such as Switzerland) wishing to be rich (or to stay rich) attach themselves to the European Union. Scandinavia got rich by open trade, combined with an aggressive pursuit of high-end manufacturing and design.

The converse also applies. The collapse of the East bloc trading union Comecon, followed especially by the collapse of the Soviet Union, was an economic disaster for those regions—not because they were efficient before (they were not) but because each part relied on trade with the others to keep the industrial structure of the whole community functioning. On a smaller but no less tragic scale, the breakup of Yugoslavia shattered an industrial system that had previ-ously yielded the highest living standard of any country ruled by a com-munist party. Conversely, in modern China, a vast country historically separated into isolated economic regions, integrating the domestic market has been a high priority for national policy reform.* The pur-pose is to break down the inefficient scale and shoddy quality associated with internal protectionist practices, especially in the interior regions. Part of China's progress in the age of reforms has been due to gains (and increased competition, and therefore quality improvement) from internal trade. Similar gains were not possible in the postcommunist Soviet Union due to the excessively integrated, monopolistic character of Soviet industrial production and the fact that the Soviet collapse cre-ated trade barriers instead of removing them.

What's the difference between intranational and international trade? Basically two things: tariffs and exchange rates. Low tariffs reduce the cost of passing frontiers, and so expand the range of the market. A common currency eliminates the uncertainty otherwise associated with working in multiple currency units; fixed exchange rates simulate, to a degree, the security of operating with a single unit of account. And only when fixed exchange rates and low tariffs operate together do the conditions of international trade approach those of the domestic pro-ducer. Without both, the trading corporation faces a much higher risk and, correspondingly, requires more insurance—insurance that may have to be purchased in very costly ways, such as by hedging in the

*As a technical adviser to the Chinese State Planning Commission in the 1990s, I observed this firsthand.

foreign exchange markets. The trading corporation needs, therefore, more lucrative fields of endeavor than the domestic firm. This is why transnational corporations concentrate (for the most part) on high-value-added activities.

The Bretton Woods agreement of 1944, establishing the IMF, the World Bank, and the General Agreement on Tariffs and Trade (GATT; later to become the World Trade Organization), effectively recognized the need for action to make international trade more like trade within countries, that is, to provide stability and security on tariffs and exchange rates alike.

The GATT was to work toward the reduction of tariffs on the trade of manufactured goods, encouraging all countries to exchange their differentiated products, designs, and surplus goods. The IMF was charged with maintaining the general stability of exchange rates, thus reducing the arbitrary and capricious elements of business risk associated with the threat of devaluation in a target market or revaluation in a cost center. IMF member states retained the explicit right to impose controls over capital flow, to prevent speculators from disrupting these arrangements. In this way, the original Bretton Woods agreements internationalized the New Deal. The New Deal system in domestic economic policy was built on the idea of regulating speculative asset markets (banks and the commodity, stock, and bond exchanges) in order to permit goods and labor markets to flourish. Bretton Woods had the same understanding: one regulated speculative foreign exchange markets in order to permit the flow of traded goods to grow and flourish. And it worked: from 1945 to 1971, the growth of trade was roughly double the growth of income, while capital controls remained in place even in the rich countries. But after 1973 the conceptual understanding behind this system disappeared. It was replaced by another, emphasizing the primacy and virtue of all markets in theological terms. The distinction between markets for capital assets and markets for goods and services disappeared. The new view became that markets of all types always produced the most desirable outcome. With that, unfortunately, the conditions for stable growth of international trade also disappeared.

The international monetarist perspective of the early 1970s held that the new regime of floating exchange rates would conveniently isolate, and render autonomous, the monetary policies of the different countries of the world. The markets would judge. Should a central bank print money at too rapid a rate, that country would experience inflation, domestic prices would rise, and the exchange rate would fall. In this way, international prices would remain in equilibrium. Since employment, and therefore output, was held to be set in domestic labor markets, the ebb and flow of monetary stimulus and restriction would have no lasting effect on these "real" considerations. Every central bank would therefore run a monetary policy oriented toward stable prices, leaving all other macroeconomic outcomes to the independent power of the market.

This fairy tale was very far from how international financial markets really worked, for it completely ignored the actual role of capital markets, the flow of lending and the burden of repayment, the speculative nature of markets dealing in foreign exchange, the distinction between "hard currencies" that savers generally were happy to hold and "soft currencies" that could easily lose large shares of their value overnight. And it ignored the part that the large commercial banks, now freed of regulations and capital control, would come to play in the fate of the world economy.

The essence of Bretton Woods had been that each country (except for the United States, which was in the special position of supplying liquidity to the world) would balance its trading accounts over the medium term. A period of deficits would have to be followed by a period of surplus, brought on by changing terms of trade or currency devaluation. A period of capital inflow, reflecting the expected profitability of new investments, would be followed by a period of debt service and profit remittance as the investments paid off. (If they did not, accounts would have to be settled by retrenchment or renegotiation.) The architects of the system were aware that the country supplying reserves to the system—the United States in the Bretton Woods arrangement—would have a privileged position against all of the others. But the discipline of the gold window was meant to ensure that this privilege could not be indefinitely abused. The architects of Bretton Woods knew the perils of financial collapse, and the whole of their system was geared toward ensuring that countries did not go unmanageably into debt.

After 1973 all of this went away; the "market discipline" that succeeded Bretton Woods proved to be no discipline at all. Instead, as a practical matter, all now depended on the judgment of the banks. If they deemed a country worthy, it could borrow, and if it could borrow, then it could import in excess of exports, industrialize, grow, and live well for a time. If they judged a country adversely, it would languish, left to its own resources unless and until it might find an export market sufficient to pay its international bills. (Oil producers could therefore afford to defy the banks, and did so freely. But a country dependent on garment shops and brake fittings would think twice about it.) And when times were flush, only a very determined and reticent government could resist the temptation to draw tens of billions in credits on easy terms, particularly when some tens of millions might always, with little fear of detection, be turned to private account and stored away in Zurich or Grand Cayman.

When a bank makes a judgment about a country, what criteria does it use? Bankers are not scientists. They are usually not even economists; little independent discipline or dispassionate analysis guides their thought. When bankers do analyze, or hire others to do so for them, the world is complex, data outside the home country are poor and hard to interpret, and the underlying conditions may depend more on what other bankers decide to do than on any particular set of facts about the countries themselves. In these circumstances, bankers do what people of means have always done: they trust their own system of beliefs and their affinities of politics and class.

In practical terms, this means that banks tend to go with the borrowers who come to them and make the most persuasive sales pitch at any given time. A good debtor tells his banker what the banker wants to hear. A creditworthy country therefore, in the first analysis, is above all one that opens itself up to the banks. And, of course, what bankers wanted to hear was the conservative creed: fiscal discipline, monetary control, and free trade. You did not need a Nobel Prize in economics to discover this; the information could be had for the price of a subscription to the *Wall Street Journal* or the *Financial Times*.

In this way the ideology of free trade became dissociated from the practice. From the early 1970s onward, one did not trade in order to pay one's bills; one espoused the doctrine of free trade in order to draw credits that would make it unnecessary, in the short or medium term, to pay one's bills. Indeed, the process worked *against* industrial growth through expanded trade. In the climate of floating exchange rates, the immediate consequence of an infusion of commercial credit was a revaluation of the currency: imports became cheap and manufactured exports uncompetitive. The result would be a consumption binge, concentrated among the upper classes, combined with industrial decay and loss of competitiveness in world markets.

Reflection on this sequence makes clear that foreign bank credit cannot generally fund industrialization when capital markets are free. The very forces that make a country seem creditworthy—its adherence to the policy line favored by the bankers—undermine the competitiveness of industrial investment and drive the proceeds of new lending into consumption. In the 1970s this process greatly weakened the economies of Latin America and Africa, leaving them unable to reverse course and expand exports when Paul Volcker unleashed his storm of high interest rates in 1980 and 1981. When the shock hit, those countries had no choice but to cut public spending, cut private consumption, cut investment, and so try to cut their import bill back to the level of their core commodity exports. Since this course of action also impeded industrial growth, it was a formula for misery over the long term.

The storm of the early 1980s was catastrophic precisely in those countries and regions that had become most dependent, in the 1970s, on commercial credits. It hit first of all in Latin America: Mexico, Brazil, Argentina, Chile, Peru—countries heavily indebted to the banks of the United States. It hit Africa, where many countries were heavily indebted to the banks of Europe, especially France and the UK. It hit the Philippines—another financially open and indebted land.* In all of these places, the general consequences were similar. Debt service soared. Public sector services, including education and health care, were slashed; in much of Africa, they altogether collapsed. Exports were demand inelastic so their prices fell; imports could no longer be financed, and so were cut back. This made private business investment, which was reliant on foreign machinery and technology, virtually impossible to carry out. As investment fell, tax revenues followed, deepening the fiscal crisis. Industries selling to the internal market faced extinction; the urban working class was decimated; inequality and absolute poverty soared.

Faced with these calamities, countries faced two possible courses of

---

*The debt crisis did not hit either China or India, both of which had avoided commercial bank credits in the 1970s; as a result both of these countries were able to embark on their modern growth miracles at the start of the 1980s, and to continue them through the 1990s and on into the present decade.

action. They could default on their debts, or attempt to limit payments as Peru under Alan García did, and face hostility and even retaliation from the IMF, the banks, and the government of the United States. Or they could accept a token lifeline from the IMF in return for further changes in their policies. And what, does one suppose, did the IMF demand? Something called "structural adjustment." This meant, in practice, implementing the same policies that bankers and Northern interests had wanted in the first place: fiscal austerity, credit contraction, deregulation, privatization, free trade, and also free capital movement. The IMF became the enforcer for bankerly opinion; dependency would be cured by more of the same.

In most cases, the prescription could not be resisted, at least at first. Yet as the 1980s wore, on it became apparent that these measures offered no solutions: they did not restore growth or cure inflation, and could not credibly promise to do so. Renegotiation of the debts, sometimes prompted by outright default (as in Brazil in 1989), eventually became the recognized necessity. Complex policies to battle inflation, including de-indexation and other reforms of the internal price-wage structures of major Latin American countries, followed. Ultimately an uneasy and unsatisfactory way forward was generally found, at an overall growth rate far lower than had been the case before the triumph of free trade.

To many, this appeared to be the fault of the low-tariff trading regime, and protests focused heavily on the World Trade Organization. It was rather more the result of a failing financial system, the inadequacy of the world order under the IMF, itself a front for creditors, bankers, and their agents in the U.S. Treasury Department at that time. Lacking an adequate internal tax base, vulnerable to capital outflow, and unable to draw on the external credits that achieving a high rate of growth would require, the liberalized countries of Latin America largely stagnated through the 1980s and the 1990s. In sub-Saharan Africa, conditions were considerably worse, for there the poverty was deeper to begin with, the destruction of state structures more complete, the willingness of private investors to enter the scene nearly nil. Sub-Saharan Africa went from the debt crisis to the human calamities of AIDS, war, and a free market in agricultural production; millions died.

Latin America entered the 1990s facing crushing failure and only two viable courses of action. One was stabilization on one's own terms and a return to the growth that could be afforded largely within the limits of the capacity to export, with that capacity enlarged, insofar as possible, by privatization of previously public assets and the associated one-off importation of capital. This was the path taken by Brazil in 1993 (the Plan Real); by Chile, which had ecological goods (fruit, wine, timber, and salmon, in addition to the traditional copper) to sell; and by Colombia (whose real income was bolstered by the drug trade). Argentina was a variation on the theme: after experimenting for a decade with neoliberal policies combined with a currency board to fix the peso to the dollar, Argentina defaulted on its debts and began to recover only in 2001. In most cases, governments moved left, yet with limited aspirations and financial capacity; although some social programs were expanded and inequality did decline slightly, economic results for the working population were at best mediocre. Ironically, September 11 helped, for the low interest rates that followed reduced debt burdens, and the distraction of U.S. policy made life easier for those who simply stopped paying their debts. There was an escape here from globalization, and the influence as well as the presence of the IMF in Latin America virtually disappeared by the middle of the decade.

The interest rate surge behind the debt crisis of the early 1980s had almost equally profound consequences for the balance of manufacturing activities in the rich countries. The trade-weighted value of the dollar rose some 60 percent from 1981 to 1984, and this helped to deliver the crippling blow to the manufacturing industries of the upper Midwest that until then had competed in domestic and international markets with Japan and Germany. Allis-Chalmers, AM International, Saxon Industries, and others went bankrupt, Caterpillar survived but in weakened and reduced condition. U.S. steel and automobile markets were flooded with the exports of Japan, Korea, and Brazil. For a time, American automakers survived largely on the strength of their truck and van sales; the profitability of American-made passenger sedans collapsed in the face of competition from Honda, Toyota, and Nissan. The "big three" U.S. automakers were set on the path of decline from which they have never emerged.

Was this transformation of the world manufacturing scene the product of comparative advantage? Of course it was not. Japan, lacking iron ore or coal in significant quantity, does not qualify as a natural site for the production of steel or steel products. (Japan also ceased around this time to be a comparatively low-wage country, though these products are in any event not labor intensive.) Thus, the emerging Japanese preeminence in those fields at that time had nothing to do with resources, nothing to do with wages, and everything to do with the scale, efficiency, flexibility, and relatively modern technologies incorporated into Japanese manufacturing facilities by the largest and most capable Japanese transnational corporations. Japan, in short, developed the division of labor to be in position to take advantage of markets extended to global scale. And when—if only for a brief period—the structure of relative prices shifted radically in their favor (thanks to the exchange rate), Japanese corporations were able to move forcefully into the American markets, precipitating severe crises, especially in automobiles and steel.

To all this, the Reagan administration actually responded in a pragmatic vein. It could not, of course, abandon free trade or be seen to abandon it, so long as it was bent on propagating the doctrine to the world outside. But neither could it tolerate the consequences of actual free trade at home. Striking for a middle ground, Reagan's officials negotiated what were euphemistically called "voluntary export restraints" in automobiles and steel with Japan. Tariffs were not imposed. But quotas, in effect, were: the major Japanese auto companies agreed to limits on their sales. If that limit meant the demand exceeded supply in the American market (which it did), the companies could and would raise their prices and enjoy windfall profits on each vehicle sold. They also had every incentive, as a result, to build better, heavier, more luxurious cars and to sell them at higher margins to a more affluent clientele than they had previously been able to reach. The way toward Lexus was opened. Ultimately the Japanese could (and did) end the VER regime by opening final assembly plants in the United States, employing just enough American labor (and therefore "content") to permit a return to unrestricted sales. This content was of cars whose designs and precision components were perfected in Japan. This was protectionism, but of a very particular kind: it protected both the interest of the Japanese producers and the ideological cover of the administration, at the expense of American workers, companies, and (to a degree) consumers.*

*It is little wonder that the Japanese were profoundly grateful, rewarding Reagan with a $2 million speaking fee within days of his departure from the White House in 1989. See Larry Gelbart, "Japan Buys a Used President," *New York Times*, November 6, 1989, p. A19. Reagan's speech inaugurated an age of globalized cashing in by ex-presidents, including George H. W. Bush's enrichment through the Carlyle Group

Reagan's own top economists, notably the libertarian William Niska-nen, have long noted the gulf between the free-trade rhetoric of that administration—indeed the deep commitment to free trade on the part of its major protagonists—and the highly managerial, if not pro-tectionist, practice.* But Niskanen's critique raises a question: What should Reagan have done? The Japanese triumph in the 1980s was not due to comparative advantage. It had no permanent roots in resources. It was a product of organizational innovation and the global financial climate, one of them created by human institutions and the other largely a self-inflicted wound. Nothing under these conditions suggests that free trade would have been the right policy, as then the rout of the American producers might have been even more devastating than it was.

The more serious problem with Reagan's policy—in terms that would have been understood by Adam Smith—was that it did not protect correctly. The system of voluntary restraints conceded profit and market position to the Japanese, which could not later be retrieved when the temporarily high position of the international dollar began to be reversed, as happened following the Plaza Accords among the world's major finance ministers in 1985. The result was a permanent change in the composition of American manufacturing and down-grading of the strategic position of many industries. Whereas for-merly we originated the technology and built and supplied the heavy and the precision machinery, now this function passed substantially in many areas to Japan.[†]

And then, in the late 1980s, Japan entered economic crisis for reasons of its own. Deregulation of the Japanese capital asset markets set off what was, and would remain until the NASDAQ, the largest speculative bubble in human history, combining speculation in stocks and specula-tion in real estate to an astonishing degree. Valuations in both became wholly unhinged. At the peak of the bubble, it was notoriously suggested that the Imperial Palace in Tokyo was worth more than the entire state of California. Given the demand for Japanese assets, the yen revalued;

---

of global arms traders. Bill Clinton's honoraria in the first six years following his presidency topped $40 million. The incentive effects of this system on presidential behavior in the national interest is a topic—similar to that of CEO compensation—that bears investigation.

*William A. Niskanen, *Reaganomics: An Insider's Account of the Policies and the People* (New York: Oxford University Press, 1988), p. 363.

†Karel Von Wolferen, *The Enigma of Japanese Power* (New York: Knopf, 1989).

Japanese manufacturing at the lower end, in textiles and electronics, went into depression and migrated to less expensive shores in China and South Asia. The crash came in 1988, precipitating a deep recession in domestic demand from which the Japanese economy as a whole did not begin to recover for over a decade. This dimmed the luster of the Japanese model for American observers, even as they largely overlooked the obvious point: there is evidently no development path that an unfettered, liberated, free capital asset market cannot screw up.

Mexico chose a different path, following the stolen election of 1988 and the rise to power of the U.S.-oriented business elites headed by Carlos Salinas de Gortari. Following the leadership of Miguel de la Madrid, who took Mexico into the GATT in 1986, Salinas decided to negotiate a treaty of economic integration with the United States and Canada: the result became the North American Free Trade Agreement (NAFTA). The NAFTA's essence was the reduction of Mexican import barriers to manufactured goods and agricultural staples from the United States, combined with a new willingness to accept foreign investment and even foreign domination of the Mexican industrial and financial sector. In return, Mexico hoped for—and in 1995 it got—a measure of financial protection from the United States, a signal that it was too big, and too close, to be permitted entirely to fail. The result was an investment boom in northern Mexico for the last half of the 1990s, bringing to power the right-wing political party, the PAN, which had been created to serve the purposes of the northern business elites. There followed a split in Mexican politics between the North and the Center, a split vividly brought to the light in the stalemated election of 2006. Free capital movement, unlimited multinational investment, and the disruptions of open trade in agricultural goods all combined in effect to divide Mexico into two or perhaps three countries: a borderland wholly affiliated with the United States, and subject to the booms and busts of its northern neighbor; a decayed industrial center preoccupied with social issues; and an abandoned South, simmering in rebellion. Here free trade showed its ultimate consequence: the choice between dissolution and civil war.*

---

*Very similar forces had been at work in Eastern Europe since the late 1980s, with comparable consequences. Three countries actually broke up: Czechoslovakia, the Soviet Union, and Yugoslavia. In each case the relatively richest regions (the Czech Republic, the Baltics, and Slovenia) started the process partly with a view to disburden-

In the United States, NAFTA provoked a bitter debate over the effects of free trade on jobs, but most of it was monumentally beside the point. Well before NAFTA, manufacturing exports from Mexico to the United States were substantially free of trade barriers, under the tariff-free *maquiladora* system in place since 1965;* at the start of the 1990s, average tariffs on manufactures entering the United States from Mexico were 3 percent. Jobs were already migrating from the United States to the border regions, notably in automotive parts, to take advantage of a considerable wage differential. Apart perhaps from ensuring its irreversibility, NAFTA contributed next to nothing to this trend. If there was a significant loss of U.S. jobs to Mexico, it had to do with the rise of a regionally integrated manufacturing economy and next to nothing to do with the enactment of NAFTA. Neither supporters (who foresaw large job gains for the United States) nor opponents (who feared large losses) chose to be entirely candid about this.

NAFTA's main actual effects were on the previously protected sectors of the Mexican economy. Lower tariffs forced a reorganization and modernization of Mexico's automotive sector—at the expense, undoubtedly, of unionized workers in Mexico. Mexico's banking and telecommunications sectors were opened to foreign investment and ownership. And a major effect fell on Mexican agriculture as cheaper U.S. corn displaced protected staple agriculture in Mexico. The predictable result was migration: rural Mexicans headed to the booming northern factory towns, to the slums of Mexico City—and to the United States, where the population of undocumented immigrants grew sharply. Food moved south; people moved north. This was for conservatives the bitter fruit of free trade, for their fealty to the farm belt cost them dearly among racial nativists in their own ranks.

Now a new star rose in the East: the People's Republic of China. China's emergence as a world trading power, as a place where real liv-

---

ing themselves of the poor. In each case, free capital movement generated outflow rather than inflow. In each case, reduction of import barriers brought on not competitive adaptation but industrial collapse. In the Soviet Union and in Yugoslavia, rebellion and civil war erupted; almost nowhere in the areas affected by the greatest economic transformation since 1945 did living standards improve for at least a decade. A considerable nostalgia for communism—hard to imagine as that may be—was a very widespread result, especially in the poorer regions of the former Soviet Union.

*The *maquiladora* system permitted semifinished goods to enter Mexico free of tariff, and the final products to be reexported to the United States, also tariff-free.

ing standards have, on average, risen fourfold in twenty-five years, and as the holder of the second largest bilateral trade surplus with the United States, bears an especially cool-eyed examination. How is it that an ostensibly communist country, practicing the strictest form of capital control in the modern world, could emerge as the most rapidly rising trading partner of the United States, in the era thought most profoundly to symbolize the triumph of free trade?

The answer usually offered to American readers is "low wages." And indeed wages in the Chinese manufacturing sector, when measured in dollars, are very low. But the vision of a country of concentration camps and slave labor is belied by any visit to the exporting regions of China, which are bustling, prosperous, and largely frcc of the human degradation associated with the severe poverty still found in rural China or elsewhere in the world, including in India, which is far less effective as an exporter of manufactured goods. It is also belied by the statistics, which show that manufacturing wages in the coastal regions comfortably exceed those in manufacturing, trade, or agriculture elsewhere in the country. Then there is the mute testimony of the security arrangements surrounding the zones themselves, in places like Zhuhai and Shenzen. Checkpoints exist, but they face outward: there is control on entry but none on the exits.

Allowing for the fact that much of the labor is that of young women on jobs of extremely short tenure, relative wages in Chinese export-oriented manufacturing are not very low by Chinese standards, and real wages in the exporting regions—wages measured in terms of the consumption goods they provide for—are not low at all by the larger standards of working populations in the developing world. The reason is that the food, clothing, transportation, and much of the housing available to workers in China is extremely cheap. Where wages are a tenth or less of American values, the prices of necessities are at least that much lower than in the United States. Working people in Chinese cities are largely fit, literate, and well fed; the difference in living standards consists largely in amenities—living space, cars, boats, plasma televisions, distilled spirits—that the ordinary Chinese household does not consume at all.

How do the Chinese achieve this? Not by planning, and not by avoiding the competitive pressures of the free market in consumer goods. Quite to the contrary: China enjoys the largest number of small producers and the most diverse and competitive consumer marketplace on the planet. Correspondingly, many of these firms perform as the competitive model predicts: they earn profits rarely, losses often.

How then do firms survive? Why does China prosper? How can it continue to grow at reported rates near 10 percent, through the Japanese depression, the Asian crisis, the Russian crisis, the Internet bust? The answer is, once again, not to be found in the trading arrangements so much as in the structure of financial control. For in this area, China benefits from its *underdevelopment*.

A key and unique feature of the Chinese scene is the relative *absence* of a developed market for capital assets. Such markets—for stocks and corporate control—do exist; indeed the Shanghai stock market went on an epic run in the mid-2000s.* But the capital markets have limited scope, limited liquidity, and limited power. Most firms are not publicly valued and not easily traded; in this important sense, "property rights" in the firm are limited. Diverse ownership form and relatively small scale are especially characteristic of the vast array of consumer goods producers that now dominate manufacturing in southern China. Though formerly owned by villages and townships in many cases, they have been recently privatized—sold off to managers or workers' collectives—not because they are profitable but because they are not. Selling them off removes their direct claim on the local budget.

In these circumstances, capital markets do not exercise discipline over the medium-term financial performance of manufacturing firms. Firms can run losses, and their shares do not collapse, they are not subject to hostile takeover, and their managements are not replaced. When they run profits (with difficulty, but it does happen) their managers are not enriched per se; there is graft and there is speculation, but there is relatively little possibility, for most executives, of selling out and retiring on the proceeds. To make money in this situation requires preserving the enterprise as a going concern. And that means passing whatever financial scrutiny would otherwise cause the firm to lose credit and to be shut down. In China, this scrutiny is extremely weak.

---

*The fuel behind the Chinese stock and real estate booms remains open to analysis. One possibility is that after certain financial liberalizations in 2002, firms inflated the value of Chinese exports in order to evade capital controls and bring funds into the country. If true, this would explain several otherwise strange phenomena, including mysteriously high reported profits by some major Chinese firms and the astonishing rises in the reported trade surplus and fixed investment as a share of Chinese GDP.

In China, financial supervision is nominally the province of the banks (as it would be for small businesses in the West), but banks in China do not perform this function well. Being state owned, historically policy oriented, and anyway nominally insolvent owing to a large inventory of nonperforming loans, banks tend to support firms through long periods of low profitability or actual losses. The loans often go bad, but so what? Nonperforming loans of the state-owned banking sector are essentially contingent debt of the state itself, which will not (and cannot) permit the banking sector to fail.

The consequence is, as noted, a proliferation of manufacturing firms and extreme competition in the production of basic consumer goods: clothing, small durable goods, electronics, household items, and food. This competition results in a condition of chronic glut in consumer markets. This is evident in the fact that sidewalks across China are covered with stalls. Price competition is phenomenal, as any casual visitor can find out: with minimal effort, prices will fall to a tenth or less of the original offer. There is little possibility that such prices cover the fixed costs of those who produce the goods on offer.

Is there any way for the Chinese manufacturing firm to turn a profit? Yes: the alternative to selling on the domestic market is to export. And export prices, even those paid at wholesale, must be multiples of those obtained at home. But the export market, however vast, is not unlimited, and it demands standards of quality that are not easily obtained by neophyte producers and would not ordinarily be demanded by Chinese consumers. Only a small fraction of Chinese firms can actually meet the standards. Those standards must be learned and acquired by practice.

Luckily, one does not need to visit the pole in order to find the direction; an ordinary compass will show you the way. For the typical Chinese light-industrial manufacturing firm, the optimal strategy for earning a profit eventually is to aim, at least in some ultimate sense, for exports. It is to produce and produce, gaining practice, improving quality, and demonstrating reliability—in the hope of eventually selling part of production on the export market—perhaps first to some low-income venue such as India, later to middle-income countries such as Turkey or Mexico, and ultimately to the United States and Europe. *For this, labor must be treated as a fixed cost.* That is, production must continue regardless of demand. The strategy will be defeated, from the beginning, if firms must interrupt production and dismiss workers simply because the output they are producing cannot be sold immediately at the Wal-Mart price.

So what to do with the output that cannot be exported? The answer is already stated. *That output is dumped on the domestic market at whatever price it may command.* The imperative to the small shopkeeper inside China is not to earn a profit; it is to unload product, because more will be coming in from the factory soon. And the result is falling prices (deflation) for Chinese consumers. Relative to a fixed money wage, this implies a rising real wage in terms of staples. The result—well-fed, well-clothed citizens and a near-absence of visible human depravity in the cities—is visually evident to any observer.

The role of the banks in this system is vastly different from that of banks in the West. They must cover the losses incurred in the short and medium run in order to permit firms to enjoy the possibility of eventually earning the profits potentially available in the export sector. The portfolio of nonperforming loans in this area, far from being an albatross around the neck of the system, is instead its primary motor force. (We do not speak here of nonperforming loans to state-owned enterprises in the heavy industrial sector, but there one finds another twist to the story: those loans support welfare and legacy payments for firms that, in at least some cases, would be marginally profitable if the welfare benefits were instead paid directly by the state.) Capital control and regulation protect the banks, and the economy, from too much external competition.

The result resolves the puzzle of Chinese wages. They are extraordinarily low when measured in dollar terms, which reflects the fact that the labor of young women in light manufacturing has an extremely low shadow price and also a low status in China. But when measured in real terms and by standards elsewhere in the Third World, wages in China are not low at all. They are also very high by historical Chinese standards, so that every adult citizen in the South and along the urbanized coast has a memory of strong improvement in most material respects. This also accounts for the tolerance most urban Chinese display toward the regime; unrest is much more pronounced in the countryside, where conditions are not as good.

Thus, as China emerges from communism, we have the paradox of shopping, already touched on. China reproduces, more closely than capitalist countries do, both the theoretical dynamics and the public welfare implications of the perfectly competitive market. It does so precisely because it lacks the essential feature of advanced capitalism, a fully developed market for capital assets. Such markets are under development—if China truly lives up to commitments made under its World Trade Organization (WTO) agreements to liberalize its financial sector—and one may confidently predict that if it becomes fully developed, the Chinese model will go into crisis, and progress will stop—as it did in Latin America, Eastern Europe, and elsewhere in Asia. But for the moment, the Chinese appear to have that impulse to self-destruction under control.*

For now, a system of low-cost producers under an evolutionary offshoot of communism has morphed into the matched trading partner for the United States, a country that serves as the leading consumer market and the supplier of liquidity to the world system. Though many do not like it, the system is symbiotic. It serves the immediate interests of large parts of both populations: one experiences high consumption standards with declining manufacturing effort; the other experiences rising living standards from a low base. One may doubt the sustainability of this arrangement (perhaps it will not last), but its efficacy is beyond serious dispute. And this much is certain: the Sino-American marriage of convenience is not the product of comparative advantage, and it did not emerge from free trade. The real free traders, in the actual world economy, are those outside this symbiotic system, and for them, the record has not been nearly so good. But of course, since those countries are not as successful, they do not trade as much, and they cannot be cited as direct threats to American jobs. And so their importance to a fair appreciation of trade policy's consequences tends to be overlooked.

*Perhaps not entirely, for the scale of high-end real estate speculation in Beijing and Shanghai in the run-up to the 2008 Olympics suggests the possibility of a fearsome crash.

PART TWO

The Simple Economics of Predators and Prey

CHAPTER SEVEN

What the Rise of Inequality
Is Really About

Addressing an audience of the flagrantly overpaid, on January 31, 2007, the President said, "The fact is that income inequality is real—it's been rising for more than 25 years."*

But is it a problem? The President thought not, and textbook economics agrees with him. To be sure, rising inequality in America may be regrettable; this even conservatives may concede. But it is the result of a changing pattern of marginal products, of "skill bias" in technological change, a by-product of our information age. It is therefore part of the price we pay for the levels of employment that we enjoy and the prosperity that technology brings. Any effort to change matters would only cost us jobs. In his speech, Bush echoed the talking point: "The reason is clear: We have an economy that increasingly rewards education and skills because of that education."

This point of view dominates the way we are asked to think about rising inequality. It is, we are told, a process mediated by the market. And the market is just, setting each wage in line with the productivity of the person doing the work. This rule then implies that a maximum of welfare and an optimum of efficiency will be achieved. Whatever the resulting distribution is, it must reflect the distribution of underlying skills. It is therefore right, normal, and not to be complained of. By assigning rising inequality to the domain of markets, the issue is removed from political and policy examination. That, of course, was Bush's point: don't blame me.

*"Bush Addresses Income Inequality: Economic Speech Touches on Executive Pay as Senators Move to Rein It In," *Washington Post*, February 1, 2007, p. A4.

Accepting the market outcome also means accepting that trying to change it will have a cost. If the market is doing its job, then by definition anything that interferes artificially with the market will hurt efficiency. Raise my wage above my productivity, and why should my employer wish to keep me on? The pursuit of equality not justified by an underlying change in patterns of productivity therefore *produces* unemployment, if this way of thinking is correct. As such, it reduces output and wealth below what they would otherwise be. In a nutshell, this is the efficiency-equity trade-off, beloved by economists for generations. To be concerned with equity, with inequality, under these conditions is actually damaging, a source of mischief, something that prudent and genuinely well-meaning people should avoid.

This is not the end of the argument, for a moral case against excessive inequality can still be made. When you raise the minimum wage or if workers are allowed to form a trade union and raise wages, the conventional story of labor markets predicts that some people may lose their jobs. But even if that is so, those who do not lose their jobs are better off. You can quite reasonably argue that the distributive gains outweigh the employment losses, especially in the short run, and many economists and others make exactly this argument. But under the assumptions given, both profits and output will be less than they would otherwise be. And so the moral case for a more equal distribution remains a stand against the greater wealth of the whole number. It is a stand, in effect, of charity and compassion. It therefore implicitly concedes that the minimum wage and the trade union and any other interventions to raise wages and reduce inequalities are actually matters of charity and compassion. Since charity and compassion have a price—they impair the efficiency of the whole system—they have at best a limited role.

Given this intellectual structure, the principled conservative has a respectable argument for doing nothing. Less intervention means more output, leading to more capital accumulation, faster technical progress, and a higher rate of economic growth. Given enough time, everyone will be better off, and this is true even of those who might have benefited from compassion and charity in the short run. The only proper remedies for inequality in the short run are those that might increase efficiency even more—for example (if possible), by speeding the acquisition of skills and the adjustment of workers to the demands imposed on them by technological change. Apart from this, the power of compound growth rates always trumps the solace of progressive redistribution.

In the 1990s, mainstream economists did get into a quarrel over the precise causes of rising inequality; those who placed all the responsibility on changing technology were challenged by others who thought it might instead be an effect of trade. Partisans of the technology hypothesis saw a rising demand for highly skilled labor, due mainly to computerization. For this, the appropriate remedy (if any were required at all) would be education, to increase the relative supply of skilled labor and reduce its wage advantage. Partisans of the trade hypothesis saw a shift in the effective supply of unskilled labor due to globalization—partly outsourcing and partly immigration. For this, the remedy would be training, to enable those in the rich countries displaced by trade to seek new and better jobs in a changing world. Since few oppose education or training, and of course nobody opposed technology whether it raised inequality or not, it was a distinction with little real difference. Both positions started from a shared belief in the overarching institution of the labor market. Both led to the view that the rise in inequality was not to be tampered with, except possibly to rearrange the queue of those waiting at the bottom of the greasy pole.

Yet as the decade wore on, both variants of the mainstream hypothesis faded away. On the one hand, the rise in pay inequality was too great to be accounted for by trade; efforts to match the scale of the increase to the measurable effects of trade were obliged to cite such phenomena as "defensive innovation"—in other words, technology itself. On the other hand, the effects of technology never turned up in the right places at the right times: mass computerization, which took off in the late 1980s and early 1990s, in particular came far too late to have driven the sharp rise in wage inequalities of the early 1980s. The phrase *skill-biased technological change* still echoes through the world of economists, journalists, and policymakers, but it is very difficult anymore to discern what the evidence for the proposition actually is. Academic economics, not for the first time, has largely retreated from this area in confusion.*

The issue of inequality is complex, and not only because of the inability of explanations based on labor market process to find clear

---

*My book *Created Unequal* (New York: Free Press, 1998) contains an early and extensive critique of the skill-bias hypothesis.

support in the data. A more basic complexity arises from the fact that the rise in inequality with which most people are concerned—that is, the excessive inequality of incomes—has only a little to do with labor markets. That is, labor markets affect pay, but pay is only part of incomes. The inequality of incomes includes the inequality of pay, but also much more than pay: capital gains, interest, dividends, proprietors' income, and so on. The inequality of pay can, of course, usefully be discussed as being affected by the influences of technology, trade, and other changing economic conditions. It is much harder to discuss the inequality of incomes in quite the same way. And although both concepts are important, it is the inequality of incomes that has the deeper implications for an analysis of the distribution of economic power and the future of a democratic republic.

Let's look at that first concept, inequalities of pay. These we can measure with precision, within and between countries around the world. And this permits us to ask a basic question whose answer bears directly on a core belief of market economics. Does the supposed trade-off between efficiency and equality really exist? Is there really a price, in terms of efficiency, output, and growth, to be paid for creating a society where work is more equally paid? Is the moral argument therefore the only tenable and correct objection to high pay inequality? Or is it perhaps instead the case that more equal societies are also more efficient? If it turns out this is the case, then we have some cause for doubt about the standard story, whose implication is that the work product of the market should always be left alone. Indeed, we may have the makings of an entirely different story in which stable distributions, held in place by institutional, social, and political norms, come to drive the evolution of technology and the patterns of trade.

As it happens, Denmark is a useful place to begin an inquiry into this question. Denmark is a small country, nestled in the north of Europe. Unlike its near neighbors Norway, Great Britain, and Holland, it is not floating on seas of oil or gas. Unlike Belgium, which grew rich on the rape of the Congo, Denmark never had major colonies; St. Croix was a minor enterprise, and Greenland is a dud. Unlike Switzerland, Denmark was occupied in World War II; it did not prosper by laundering German money. Denmark also lacks major industry, and apart from fundamental contributions to twentieth-century theoretical physics and lately a strong position in wind generators, it is not a major technological power.

And yet Denmark today is the third wealthiest country of Europe,* evidence of strong, consistent, stable economic growth over the decades. It is also roughly the most equal country in Europe and perhaps in the world. *And* it enjoys roughly the lowest unemployment rate in Europe, alongside one of the highest ratios of employment to active population. If Denmark's celebrated egalitarianism has forced it to sacrifice prosperity, the evidence for this is quite hard to find. Instead, in this one small case, we seem to observe the opposite: an egalitarian country that is also quite rich by European standards and exceptionally rich by the standards of the wider world.

Is Denmark a special case, somehow blessed with unusually gifted or efficient or altruistic people? No. It is, rather, the end point on a continuum that covers most of the countries of Europe. The rules of this continuum are straightforward. First, lower unemployment means higher income. The high-income countries of Northern Europe systematically enjoy lower rates of unemployment, most of the time, than their less wealthy Southern cousins. Second, lower inequality means lower unemployment. The strong welfare states of North Europe have higher employment rates and lower unemployment rates than the relatively unequal countries of the South. These rules apply across all of Europe. Denmark, which is about the most equal and one of the richest of them all, merely sets the standard from which other countries of Europe may be judged.†

---

*After Norway and Switzerland, judging by per capita gross domestic product. According to the Luxembourg Income Studies, Denmark's inequality of net household income clocks in at about 0.24 on the Gini scale in the early 1990s, compared to a value of 0.34 for the United States at the same time. Unemployment rates in Denmark in recent years have generally been at or below 4 percent.

†In 1998 Denmark had gross domestic product (GDP) per hour of only 92 percent of the average for Organization for Economic Cooperation and Development (OECD) states, well below European norms. Moreover, unlike the Japanese, Danes do not work abnormally long hours. They benefit from a larger working population, a higher participation rate in the population, and low unemployment, and together these factors raise GDP per person to 103 percent of the OECD average. Deplorable performance on the same factors reduces the rankings of the EU-14 ("old Europe") as a group from 103 percent of the OECD average in output per hour to just 90 percent of the average per capita GDP. See Bart van Ark and Robert H. McGuckin, "International Labor Productivity and Per Capita Income," *Monthly Labor Review* 122: 11 (July 1999). The OECD includes most countries of Western Europe, North America, Japan, Korea, Australia, and New Zealand.

Is Denmark perfectly equal? No. Of course it is not. No society that insisted on perfect equality—the same hourly wage and the same working conditions for all types of employment—would function for very long. Work is unpleasant, and the motivation to do it efficiently is, under all normal conditions, associated with some prospect of gain. That must mean hierarchy: differential pay for seniority and responsibility and promotions for performance. Exceptions do occur; in wartime, for example, wage differentials can be made practically to disappear. But the experience of communism showed that the wartime commitment to hard work cannot generally be maintained over long periods of time. Actual communist societies resolved this problem in part with labor camps, but productivity in prisons is always low, and complex production cannot be sustained there. Generally the gulag is not a way to get rich.

The Danish example merely shows that a low degree of inequality can be reconciled with an efficient, advanced, and wealthy system. But how do we explain this? Is the relationship between equality and efficiency we observe here accidental? Is it a fluke? Or is it actually a feature of the way well-run economies actually function in the real world?

Part of the answer to this puzzle is not complicated. Inefficiency in many countries arises from unemployment: people who are not working do not produce, and the loss of their goods and services makes everyone else poorer than they would otherwise be. Moreover, unemployment is in part an expression of discontent with one's existing station in life: people are unemployed when they are looking for a better job. The unemployment rates that we actually measure reflect, in part, the desire, and the ability, of people who would otherwise be peasants or on the dole to seek better employment at better pay.

When a society is very unequal, there are, necessarily, just a few "good" jobs and many "poor" ones. That is what being highly unequal means. And when this situation holds, it is normal for large numbers of people to go hunting for the few available good jobs. Long queues are the inevitable result. That is unemployment. Thus, other things equal, *inequality produces unemployment*, and unemployment produces waste: people who are not working do not contribute to the production from which ultimately everyone consumes.

But in a fairly equal society, those relatively low-skill, low-productivity workers are already being paid pretty well. They are within economic shouting range of their more productive compatriots. They therefore have much less incentive to leave their job, even to migrate, and join the search for a better one. Furthermore, highly equal societies subsidize many of the amenities of life, from education to health care to housing: they indulge in the efficient provision of public goods. That being so, who cares to leave? In a more equal society, more people stay employed where they are. The resulting society may lack excitement. Pushed too far, it can completely lack dynamism: again, the Soviet example comes to mind. But if the right balance is struck, it is capable of producing high levels of output and economic well-being simply because the full use of human resources is efficient. This is the Scandinavian principle, and it is not an accident that Denmark is both egalitarian and rich.

This, let me suggest, is actually an economic law, and so it applies also to the United States. Contrary to what many believe, the United States did not reach full employment in the late 1990s by cutting the wages of the poor. To the contrary, there is in the United States a systematic pattern of rising pay inequality in bad times, and falling pay inequality in good times. Were Americans truly living under an equity-efficiency trade-off, then unemployment in the United States should have fallen when inequality rose in the early years of the 1980s, and pay inequalities should have gone up when unemployment fell in the 1990s. But the exact reverse is the case. In the United States, unemployment and pay inequality rise and fall together, month by month and year by year. (This relationship holds monthly as far back as January 1947* and annually as far back as 1920.†)

Studies of the minimum wage echo the law. If the iron trade-off between efficiency and equity held, rising minimum wages would cause unemployment. But as economists David Card and Alan Krueger demonstrated, they do not. California and New Jersey raised minimum wages in the 1980s, and unemployment fell; the same happened when the national minimum wage was raised in the 1990s.‡ Why did unemployment fall? With better pay, quit rates declined, hence job tenure

*James K. Galbraith and Vidal Garza-Cantú, "Inequality in American Manufacturing Wages, 1920–1998: A Revised Estimate," *Journal of Economic Issues* (Summer 1999): 735–743.

†Thomas Ferguson and James K. Galbraith, "The American Wage Structure, 1920–1947," *Research in Economic History* 19 (1999): 205–257.

‡David Card and Alan Krueger, *Myth and Measurement: The New Economics of the Minimum Wage* (Princeton, N.J.: Princeton University Press, 1995).

increased, and vacancies fell. For the firm, there were also efficiency gains, since less had to be wasted on training. Finally, if we were living in the theoretical world of free-market economics, less skilled workers should be more heavily employed, relatively, in the United States than in Europe. But they are not.* The United States and Europe employ roughly similar proportions of skilled and unskilled workers.

The relationship between pay inequality and unemployment is so close as to raise a question: Are these two phenomena really anything other than different ways of measuring the same thing? Unemployment is a measure of the distress of those at the bottom. Measures of pay inequality reflect the divide among those above them. Anything that increases the distress of those at the bottom, weakening the access of low-wage workers to employment, should in principle also weaken the leverage of those just above them, reducing their weekly hours and weeks worked each year, as well as their average rate of pay for each hour. The data suggest that this is exactly what does happen. There is a continuum, not an opposition, of the experience of those who are least successful at working and those who are out of work altogether.

Inequality produces unemployment. Unemployment produces inequality. Measures that reduce inequality also reduce unemployment, and measures that reduce unemployment also reduce inequality. Equality, then, is good for employment and vice versa. Reductions in both inequality and unemployment reduce waste and therefore increase economic efficiency and improve general living standards. But how does this square with the widely held view that the United States is a low-equality, high-employment country, while Europe has chosen a "high road" of good jobs but high unemployment—the path of "inefficiency" associated with an easy life for insiders?

The key to this puzzle lies in the definition of "Europe." In the economics literature, comparison of pay and income inequality between the United States and Europe has always been done on a country-to-country basis. That is, the United States is compared first to Germany, then to France, then to Spain. And indeed, the United States is more unequal in its distribution of pay than almost any European country— much more so than the Nordic countries or Germany, somewhat more than France or Britain, slightly more than Italy. Thus, a comparison by

---

*Richard Freeman, "The Limits of Wage Flexibility to Curing Unemployment," *Oxford Review of Economic Policy* 11:1 (Spring 1995): 63–72.

countries can lead to a trade-off view that the European countries mostly have less inequality and more unemployment. This leaves only a few cases (such as Denmark, Holland, and Norway) to be explained as anomalies.

But this is all based on an error of perception. The European economy is no longer a collection of separated national systems. Spain, Germany, and France are not independent, mutually isolated national economies. There are no barriers to trade or capital flow, in fact, no formal barriers to the movement of labor throughout Europe. There is now a single currency unit across most of the region. The integration of the European economy in practice—from the standpoint of a large multinational corporate employer, for instance—is nearly complete. From every analytical point of view, it is necessary to start thinking of Europe as a single unit. It is therefore necessary, from a statistical and practical point of view, to measure inequality and employment at the European, and not the national, level.

When this is done, the notion of Europe and the United States at the opposite ends of an employment-equality spectrum disappears. Pay inequality within countries of Europe is relatively low, but inequalities between them are very high: much higher than across comparable distances in the United States. Adding the two components, the inequality within and the inequality between countries, one finds that overall inequalities of pay are actually higher in Europe than in the United States. Thus, the standard perception of a European/American counterpoint is simply incorrect. So far as pay is concerned, Europe now is both more unequal and less fully employed than the United States. It is, by the same token, less efficient, but not for the reasons usually given. Rather, the United States wins the efficiency contest—not because it is less egalitarian but because it is more so than the ungainly ensemble of countries that now make up the European Union.

This point applies to pay; it is relevant to discussions of inequality, employment, and (as we shall see later) productivity growth. These aspects of economic inequality are directly related to the performance of employment and the economic lives of the working population; they are the type that is usually dismissed as being driven by "the market." We have seen that this form of inequality closely tracks, and to some degree actually explains, unemployment. It is therefore not decided by supply and demand for skills in a set of individual separated "labor markets." On the contrary, it is a form of inequality whose genesis in the United States is relatively clear: it depends on overall economic conditions. The crises of the early 1980s, stemming from trade and recession, caused a dramatic increase in both pay inequality and unemployment. Then both recovered in the 1990s as full employment was reached and inequalities in the structure of pay declined.* Prosperity is good for the low end of the American workforce.

At this point, anyone who remembers the op-ed pages of a decade ago will ask, What about the late 1990s? Those years saw dramatic increases in the observed inequality of the distribution of incomes. In this period, employment was full, yet this broader, more comprehensive type of inequality went right through the roof. That is an important issue—but it is also a different issue, having almost nothing to do with the demand for skills, the distribution of education, or the effects of trade.

The rise in *income* inequality reflects something that happened to a very small group of people. It does not go through the whole distribution. It reflects, rather, the rise of a new class—very small and unbelievably rich. And it is easy to see from whence the new wealth came. It did not come from the labor market at all. It came instead from the capital market. Specifically, and most flamboyantly, in the late 1990s it came from the stock market.

The stock market is a way of raising money, and during the great stock boom, income for a small number of the very favored could come substantially from funds invested on the stock market and from the revaluation of funds already there. Capital gains or dividends are part of this, but so also were salaries paid from funds raised on the capital markets, for instance, from venture capitalists or in initial public offerings. Since, for a time, unlimited funds were available, so too nearly unlimited sums could be paid to the boss and a handful of his top associates. This is the source of the rise of the "new class," and it is the source of the rise in income inequality as well.

Who got rich? Mainly it was business leaders in the high-tech sectors, along with their close associates in finance itself—geeks and bankers, in other words. But the demonstration effect of this new wealth had implications throughout corporate America, even in companies in routine lines of business whose revenues and profits were not

---

*I have dealt with these issues at much greater length and detail in *Created Unequal*.

exploding and whose stock valuations were not on a par with Microsoft or Oracle. For these companies, the desire to "keep up with the Gateses" (though no one could) helped lead to a general destabilization of CEO pay. That destabilization, we shall argue below, had dire consequences for the way in which the CEO class would relate to its responsibilities as leaders of the business corporation.

This type of inequality, in short, is not the kind that economists speak of when they refer to the effects of technological change or trade in labor markets. It is something else entirely: a phenomenon of financial markets, of the distribution of wealth, of the valuation of capital assets, and fundamentally of the distribution of power. This is a type of inequality about which very few political leaders, and not that many economists either, wish to speak. Two basic kinds of evidence help demonstrate the narrowness of the phenomenon of rising income inequality. One measures the distribution of income across the 3,150 counties of the United States. This measure, which covers all forms of taxable income, tracks the rise and then the decline of valuations on the technology-heavy NASDAQ stock index almost exactly over thirty years. Both measures rise to the identical peak year of 2000, and both decline thereafter. This is powerful evidence that rising (and later falling) inequality in American incomes was primarily a matter of the boom (and later bust) in the technology sector.

We can pinpoint the actual locations of sharply rising incomes in the United States in the late 1990s, and they hold no surprises. They correspond exactly to the handful of counties where technology firms were concentrated, mainly in the West, but also Suffolk and Middlesex counties in Massachusetts, Travis and Williamson counties in central Texas, the area of the Research Triangle in North Carolina, and similar centers of advanced business development. Still, even the technology satellites are minor in the larger scheme of things. Removing just five counties from the mix—Santa Clara, San Francisco, and San Mateo counties in northern California, and King County, Washington, home of Microsoft, and the financial center of New York City (Manhattan)—causes much of the rise in between-counties income inequality in the last years of the 1990s to disappear. Similarly, remove just a handful of sectors from the mix—mainly computers and finance—and the rise in income inequality calculated between sectors also practically disappears. Thus, in the late 1990s, the whole of the rise of income inequality, practically speaking, was the bubble in the information sectors. The financial markets focused the speculation of the whole world on the American information technology sector.

From an economic performance standpoint, this was quite a good thing. The information technology boom contributed the final ingredient to the concoction that produced the great American prosperity of the late 1990s, driving unemployment below 4 percent for a sustained and happy period of three consecutive years. For most working Americans, whose life experiences are driven by general employment conditions and not by valuations on the NASDAQ, the late 1990s were a time of egalitarian growth in which pay at the bottom of the structure tended to catch up with pay toward the middle and the top. But the money pouring into that sector also created the rise in measured income inequality that was observed at the same time, reflecting the ascendance of a new American elite, richer than rich.

From 1997 to the peak in 2000, business nonresidential fixed investment rose by about $300 billion 1996 dollars, a gain of about 2 percent in relation to GDP, or from 12.3 to 14.4 percent. Most of the gain was technology investment. In the two years after the peak, the falloff was on the order of $150 billion. The entire falloff in business investment was then replaced by the increase in the military budget put in place by the Bush administration following the terrorist attacks on September 11, 2001, and the invasion of Iraq in 2003. As a result the U.S. economy returned to near-full strength by mid-2006, and once again the stock market recovered. And inequality, having dipped in 2001 and 2002, went back up again. By 2006, measured inequality in the distribution of taxable incomes had reached new highs, but the winners were in different economic sectors. Now they were geographically concentrated around Washington, D.C.—the center of government spending and military contracting—and in sectors such as aerospace and oil.

Considered politically, the reality is ironic. The great rise in *income inequality* in America was in part an artifact of the economic policies of a Democratic president, Bill Clinton—policies that fostered and encouraged a technological revival and a capital markets boom. It reflected a new and historic compromise, between the leadership of the Democratic Party and the very rich. It was also mirrored by the divorce between the Democratic leadership and the Democratic base, a battle over the direction of the Democratic Party, that is played out in the presidential nominating process, with usually predictable results, nearly every campaign.

Again, from the standpoint of economic performance, Clinton's bubble was hugely successful, with benefits that did extend down the economic ladder. Indeed it was the most successful economic strategy of a generation while it lasted, fostering at the same time *both* rapid technological change and full employment without inflation *and* a decline in the inequalities of pay and an increase in average living standards that actually matter for most people. These were major achievements, and for a few years in the late 1990s, they transformed the world image of the United States from one of a wounded and declining industrial power back to that of the world center of economic dynamism—outstripping Europe, which enjoyed no similar boom and suffered far higher rates of unemployment, and also outstripping Japan, which spent the same years mired in an intractable recession. This underpinned the strength of the dollar in those years, despite a large and growing deficit in the trade balance.

But it did not continue. By the time the Clinton administration ended, so had the information technology boom. And while Bush governed on behalf of a narrow group of plutocrats, it was a different group: Bush had no particular interest in the (by then rapidly deflating) technology sector. Overnight, official Washington's fascination with the Internet practically disappeared. And as the technology sector slumped, overall income inequality at first declined quite sharply. This was merely the unraveling of the previous boom. When Bush's recovery took hold, so did a new group of winners. Bush ran a Beltway Bubble, the natural result of big government Republicanism; as inequality rose again, the new elites were those who made a living off natural resources, drug and media monopolies, health insurance, housing finance, and the global war on terror.

Thus, much of the mystery surrounding our understanding of "inequality" goes away once we recognize that the word covers two quite different aspects of the economy—and neither of them is well explained by "supply and demand for skills." One of them is the inequality of pay: the major force affecting the larger working population. This form of inequality is substantially tied to employment and unemployment, and while it increased dramatically in the 1970s and early 1980s, it also fell quite dramatically in the late 1990s. Higher demand for labor reduces inequality, while pay compression, aided by unions or by minimum wage laws, also helps to reduce unemployment.

The other process is not about working people at all. It is about funds flowing from the financial markets through banks and brokers into technology and other hot sectors. This is a source, rather than a sink, for demand. In the tech boom, working people benefited because there were more jobs. But income inequality also went up because the incomes generated by the stock bubble flowed to a tiny handful of people, in a tiny handful of places. And the same was true in the next expansion, though driven by entirely different policies and favoring a different group.

Why should we care? An economy that moves from bubble to bubble is unsustainable, and bubbles of this kind create a particular kind of wealth, vastly greater than any other in our society. They generate the billionaires who now dominate the Forbes 400. They therefore foster a particular concentration of economic power in the target companies and in their banks. Economic power naturally translates into political power. And so one has to ask, Are the people most favored by an inflating market also those best suited to govern the country and, by extension, the world? That is, naturally, the view they take. It is a view often reflected in the public media, which they tend to own. But it is not entirely self-evident that this view is actually correct. The deepest issue raised by the inequality of economic incomes is, therefore and as ever, the distribution of *political* power. The term of art, in other countries, for people who control power in this way is *oligarch*. That word, which is not meant to flatter, reflects a general understanding that private persons with such wealth cannot be expected to serve any interest other than their own.

What the information technology boom showed, and what the Bush Beltway Bubble has again shown, is that public policy can move wealth around in spectacular ways. It can create oligarchs, and it can destroy them. That being so, one can only expect that the beneficiaries, and potential beneficiaries, would pay close attention to the behavior of the state. They will even devote themselves to using and abusing the state, turning its instruments to their own purposes if they can. If the state is sufficiently large and sufficiently powerful, it may be that working those levers for the creation and consolidation of wealth is more tempting, and a better investment, than the complicated, tedious work of preparing products for consumption by the public at large, still less that of innovating new technologies for world markets.

It is therefore worth examining what kind of power our modern oligarchs actually wield and over what sort of state and what sort of economy they reign.

CHAPTER EIGHT

The Enduring New Deal

Here's an apparent paradox of American life as of this writing: inequality is at or near historic highs. Plutocrats and their lobbies dominate a corrupt political scene. Manufacturing is said to be hollowed out and transnationalized. Chronic deficits afflict (or is it "adorn"?) the budget and the balance of trade. No governing principles for monetary policy seem to have survived.

And yet for the most part, the country prospers, or at least it still did as this book was being written. Jobs were plentiful, inflation low, real wages among the highest in the world. For reasons we have examined, full employment without inflation was achieved as recently as the late 1990s; clearly no iron law dictates that it cannot be achieved again. In this respect, American economic performance remained superior to that of Europe, mired in chronic mass unemployment. Even George W. Bush was producing an unemployment rate of only 4.4 percent, with low inflation, by the end of his disastrous political year of 2006. And as this number was achieved, median real wages began to rise for the first time in a generation.

How can this be? What accounted for the resilience of the American economic model? How does it happen that the model worked out so well, in general terms and for so long, as it did, surviving the abuse of monetarists, supply-siders, and free-marketeers? The answer, I will urge, lies in very robust institutions created more than a half-century ago by the New Deal and its successors. Those institutions survive. Understanding them—and the symbiotic relation to them that today's political conservatives have adopted—is a key to understanding both our economics and our politics today.

The institutions in question are neither purely private nor wholly public. They are not like the socialist welfare institutions of Europe, but neither are they private enterprise. They are, rather, hybrids, even chameleons: private economic activities supported, leveraged, guaranteed, and regulated by public power; public institutions aided, abetted, and buttressed by private money. They are elements of an American social welfare state but dressed up, in characteristically American fashion, in the guise of a market system. Indeed, it is precisely because the United States does *not* have a "free-market" economy that the campaign to pretend that we do has been as forceful and insistent as it has been over the years. Were the truth made apparent, conservative economics would have folded long ago.

In a somewhat cynical vein, one may usefully apply to our actual system an idea familiar to students of Central and Eastern Europe in the late years of communist rule. This is the concept of the *soft budget constraint*, widely attributed to the free-market Hungarian economist Janos Kornai.* Kornai deployed this concept to describe the incentives facing heavy industry under the East European communist regimes. East bloc regimes in those days had many state-owned companies that could not make profits and could not compete in international markets. They were utterly uneconomic and hopelessly inefficient. Yet they were so central to the social fabric of the system in which they were embedded, including its provision of social services, that they could not be allowed to fail. They became widely deplored, and in many cases they collapsed with the regimes of which they were part. In retrospect, they are mourned by many and missed by many more. To millions, they had provided the rudiments of a comfortable and secure life, the threads of which have not been picked up in the postsocialist orders that have since emerged. In the United States today, we have our own version of such favored institutions, supported by state spending—entitlements—but also by bank credit, credit guarantees, and implicit guarantees, the *expectation* of rescue in the event of trouble. Our state-favored institutions are massive. They have many of the flaws of their counterparts in the failed economies of the formerly socialist East. But there are differences too—in particular over what we subsidize, and how, and who benefits. These differences go a long way toward explaining why America has remained largely prosperous, including the ultraprosperous period of the late 1990s.

*Janos Kornai, "The Soft Budget Constraint," *Kyklos* 39:1 (1986): 3–30.

The military is one—a traditional state sector drawing directly on the government's budget and tax base whose escape from effective fiscal control following September 11, 2001, is one of the most important stories of current American political economy. Agriculture is another: heavy subsidies flow to a small part of the working population for reasons that have to do with the way what are now the rural backwaters of America were assigned political power when they became states, mostly in the nineteenth century. And there are several others, all in sectors providing social amenities to the middle class: mainly health care, higher education, housing, and pensions. These are the sectors created in the New Deal, Fair Deal, New Frontier, and Great Society, and more or less deliberately insulated from both budget and market tests in the intervening decades. They now exist as major poles of economic power, strongly capable of defending their share of economic resources—but also vulnerable to subversion from within.

Health care in the United States produces and consumes some 16 or 17 percent of GDP. A typical figure in Europe is 8 to 11 percent.* Public health expenditures within the direct U.S. government budget consume 6.8 percent of GDP; in dollar terms, average per person government expenditure on health in the United States is greater than average per person total expenditure on health in the UK.† In the United States the direct public commitment is only to the elderly and disabled, to poor families, and to veterans. For the rest of the covered population, medical care is paid out of private insurance, which enjoys tax advantages. Overall, the tax-financed share is just under 60 percent of total health expenditure, or 9 percent of GDP.‡ This is about twice the size of the military budget, even after including the cost of the Iraq war.

The American health care system is a mess. Yet its scandals do not lie in insufficiency of care—quite the reverse!—but in two notorious facts. The first is that some 47 million persons lack insurance. This part includes many Latino immigrants, who tend to avoid contact with the welfare system, as well as younger working people, including many

*World Health Organization, *WHO Statistical Information System: Core Health Indicators* (Geneva: WHO, 2006).

†Organization for Economic Cooperation and Development, *OECD Health Data 2006* (Paris: OECD, 2006).

‡S. Woolhandler and D. U. Himmelstein, "Paying for National Health Insurance—and Not Getting It," *Health Affairs* 21:4 (2002): 88–96.

young women: a problem for prenatal and perinatal care. The second is the rapacity of the private actors in the system—drug producers and insurance companies notably. There is no doubt that a similarly effective quantity of medical care could be provided for much less money. There is no doubt that chronic conditions emerge in middle-aged people without insurance, which make them much sicker and more costly to treat once they reach the age of Medicare. (The complications of diabetes alone account for an amazing 10 percent of U.S. health care costs.) Nevertheless, it is precisely the political power of the key actors that has made the American health care system into the economic powerhouse that it is, and that accounts for its size and economic effects. Health care is, moreover, labor intensive, and its expansion favors employment.

Health care fits the model of a soft budget sector uncomfortably well. It is a producer-driven, science-based, technology-dependent, information-asymmetric industry, where the services provided are almost entirely within the purview of specialists and out of the hands of the consumer, who in many cases may be elderly and infirm in addition to ill, anxious, and uncomfortable. Virtually the only "market" recourse consumers of health care may have is to seek a second opinion, and very few have even that much leeway or discretion. In the not infrequent situation in which the "health care consumer" faces a medical emergency, there is no prospect for choice of any kind. In this situation, the only effective restraints on costs are those imposed by insurance companies and, overseeing them, regulators of one stripe or another. The problem is that the regulatory systems work poorly.

Higher education in the United States consumes about 2.75 percent of GDP. European countries typically spend half this amount. U.S. expenditure on public higher education rivals European total spending—1.22 percent of GDP as compared to 1.14 percent in Germany or 1.37 percent in France. In addition there is the private share, another 1.63 percent of GDP, centered on institutions whose multibillion-dollar endowments are highly motivated by the tax system.* College enrollment for those eighteen to twenty-one years old is much higher in the United States than elsewhere in the OECD; for those ages twenty-two to twenty-five, the United States trails only the Scandina-

---

*Organization for Economic Cooperation and Development, *Education at a Glance* (Paris: OECD, 2006).

vian countries.* Fully public institutions dominate the scene in most of the country; nearly 90 percent of postsecondary enrollments, including community colleges, in (say) Texas are in state institutions. Public and private institutions alike receive federal research grants, contracts, and student loans.

Unlike health care, higher education is theoretically subject to market tests: students can choose, in principle, among competing institutions. But in fact the product on sale is deeply uniform from one place to the next, and differences in instructional quality, though they undoubtedly exist, are extremely hard to observe reliably. What consumers therefore do is substitute status for quality: they generally rate universities not by the unknown and largely unobservable virtues of their instruction but by their place in an elaborate, and very well-known, national and regional system of rankings. This creates a system of "positional goods"—the value of an education depends not on the learning acquired but on the relative stature of the institution attended. And therefore, once again, the market does not control; the institutions do. In particular, high-ranking universities price their services so as to maintain a state of perpetual excess demand and put themselves in the position of choosing among competing applicants. In this way they maintain their reputations by preselecting the students most likely to succeed. The price they can charge is in turn partly a function of this perception, a condition well known to defeat the efficiency of the market.† Conversely, in most cases, a leading sign that a college is going downhill is that it is obliged to admit less desirable students in order to fill its seats.

The transformation of education into a status good creates for the university a market position similar to that of the hospital: in full command of the services offered to the consumer. And as with health care, it is the ability to draw on multiple sources of funding that softens the budget constraint. Since undergraduate colleges do not price to "clear the market"—amazing though it may seem to parents who face the

---

*See Table 388 at http://nces.ed.gov/programs/digest/d05/lt4asp#27. For age groups twenty-two to twenty-five years old and older, it is worth noting that enrollment rates in Europe are inflated by the unavailability of jobs. This problem is much less serious in the United States.

†Joseph E. Stiglitz, "The Causes and Consequences of Dependence of Quality on Price," *Journal of Economic Literature* (March 1987), 1–48.

bills, they price low relative to their amazingly high costs—they must make up the difference by cultivating tax-favored gifts and bequests from grateful and sentimental alumni, who rightly or wrongly attribute their success in life to having been admitted years ago by their schools.

The early-twentieth-century American economic genius Thorstein Veblen identified conspicuous consumption, conspicuous leisure, and conspicuous waste as among the central devices deployed by American plutocrats—the "higher barbarians," Veblen called them—to establish and maintain their status within the leisure class. To this, the late twentieth century has added conspicuous philanthropy, which has three advantages over all other forms of competitive display. First, it is institutionalized and enduring: universities chisel the names of their greatest donors on buildings and leave them there until the buildings are torn down. Second, whereas consumption and leisure are inherently limited by time and imagination, philanthropy is a pure numbers game; the business of outdoing the competition is no more than a matter of adding an additional zero to the check. Third, philanthropy is tax advantaged: it removes resources from the clutches of the income, gift, and estate taxes. And so fierce is the competition among the wealthiest Americans for recognition that a considerable number are prepared to overlook the claims of their own offspring, preferring the glories of charity—with 100 percent tax deductibility—to the obloquy of sharing between the children and the government, neither of whom normally display the gratitude that is made available by one's old school.

Finally, because universities perform a variety of public functions—indeed the largest among them are public institutions—they enjoy direct subventions from the state. These take many forms, including direct budget lines in the case of public institutions, and grants and contracts supporting instruction, administration, and research. Federal, state, and municipal governments all participate, at varying levels and to varying degrees.

The net effect is to put the administrator of the American university, particularly the well-endowed private or large public institution, in a position quite unlike that facing the rectors of public universities in most of the world. Institutions elsewhere, with free tuition and full state support, depend entirely on the funding stream from the public budget. If their budgets are cut, their activities must also be cut. This is not necessarily true in the American case. In the United States, in the event of a shortfall in funding from any one source, the administrator's first reaction is to seek a compensating increase from somewhere else: fees can be raised, efforts to dun the alumni redoubled, a new grant applied for. The essence of a soft budget lies in the internal priority given to programs and spending decisions: these are set, and then funds are sought to support them. Cutting programs is an admission of defeat and occurs only as a last resort. It also sends a signal that the university is in trouble, which is poor public relations.

The contributions that American universities make to the economy go beyond the direct effect of higher education expenditure on GDP, and they are somewhat poorly understood. Preoccupied as always with the metaphor of market process, economists tend to assess the contribution of extra years of schooling in terms of the acquisition of "skills." (This preoccupation tends to revulse Europeans, who abhor the industrial influence on university life and are consequently prone to believe that such influences predominate in America.) While some students do acquire skills in college, or so one hopes, the provision of skills is only in a loose sense the mission of American higher education. The job of the professor is only loosely to "produce" a high-performing citizen from the indifferent raw material provided by the country's high schools.

So, what do universities do? First, there is the neglected effect of higher education on employment and labor force participation. Like the health sector, higher education in the United States is very labor intensive. It employs a great many people, including large numbers of the intelligentsia, who are thus kept contented and busy. More important than that, it provides activities and diversions for many of those who—if they were in Europe—would spend their late teenage years in the ranks of the jobless young. The American young thus reap the psychological benefits of legitimated idleness and the rituals of accomplishment provided by colleges and universities at this stage of life; as a rule, they emerge feeling vindicated rather than depressed. As a solution for youth unemployment, the American college system has to be counted one of the great triumphs of the human imagination—or perhaps of dumb luck.

More important still, at the mass level, college education in America is a certification process for admission to the middle class, and at this task the system has also been successful. Just under 28 percent of the adult population of the United States has a four-year university degree or better. This population is ipso facto qualified to participate in the economic life of our credit economy. Having had education loans, graduates are eligible for mortgages and the entire spectrum of access to private credit. They are presumed competent to navigate the tax and subsidy system, to take advantage of credits, deductions, and guarantees. They are also presumed competent to consume advanced durable consumer goods, from private homes to automobiles to personal computers and telecommunications devices. And they do. Many others may gain access to this system by other routes, but a college degree is one sure way in. Thus, the education system acts as a pillar of support for the credit system, which extends the soft budget constraint to the household.

The United States maintains two other public systems for keeping otherwise difficult-to-employ young people away from unemployment. One is the armed forces, with several million members, which consumes 4.5 percent of GDP and provides competent mechanical training to its members (including to virtually the whole of the population of commercial pilots, for example). Second is the prison system, whose economic function is not altogether dissimilar in some respects: it keeps young people off the streets. A major difference is that these three institutions provide very different levels of access to credit and other participatory mechanisms in later life. Those who serve in the armed forces benefit from a raft of programs designed to produce rough parity with those who go through college; those who do their time behind bars are largely on their own. Whether these institutions do good or ill is not the point here. The point is, rather, that like health care, they help underpin economic activity. And government underpins them all, underwriting in all cases their remarkable growth.

Older Americans are no less provided for by government systems. Consumption of housing services accounts for about 10 percent of U.S. gross domestic product, while residential construction accounts for another 6 percent. The housing sector exists on this scale thanks to a vast network of supporting financial institutions, subject to federal deposit insurance, the secondary mortgage markets provided by quasi-public corporations (Fannie Mae, Ginnie Mae, Freddie Mac), and the tax deductibility of mortgage interest. Since 1986, when the tax deductibility of other forms of interest was eliminated, home ownership rates rose—thanks to the state, not the market. By the first years of the new century, home equity had become the major collateral against which home-owning Americans were able to borrow to support their consumption. This in turn softened the budget constraint that slow-growing incomes would otherwise have imposed on the lifestyles of the middle class.*

Finally, Social Security payments to the elderly and other income security programs finance about 8 percent of U.S. GDP (Social Security alone finances between 4 and 5 percent), on the reasonable assumption that these transfers are substantially spent rather than saved by their recipients. Ninety percent of aged Americans receive a Social Security benefit, which provides the major source of disposable income of 65 percent of American elderly and the *only* source of income for 20 percent.† The typical Social Security payment for an elderly couple in moderate health, when combined with Medicare, is adequate for modest comfort in most of the country. The American elderly live in paid-off homes and pay only a fraction of their medical (as distinct from pharmaceutical) expenses out of pocket. Social Security funds a great deal of their ordinary consumption. Pockets of elderly poverty remain—single women with little work credit can be in trouble—but these are pockets, not reservoirs, of poverty. Poverty among the old in America has fallen dramatically since the early 1970s and is now lower than among the general population.

Then there is the earned income tax credit (EITC), a clever scheme to raise the after-tax incomes of the working poor, effectively providing insurance against flux in hours worked and therefore in the annual value of the real wage. The EITC was created under Ford but greatly expanded under Reagan and represents, after a fashion, that President's

---

*There was a worm in the apple, and it came from the private sector. In the post–9/11 financial climate, mortgage originators realized that low short-term interest rates could be turned into a marketing tool, and that by making the loans adjustable, the low rates in the first few years of the mortgage could be recaptured when short-term rates returned to normal. Thus, millions of seemingly cheap mortgages were made to low-income customers, few of whom realized by how much the contracts they were signing could drive their payments up after two or three years. Families moved into their new homes, time passed, the rates reset, and the foreclosure crisis began. The consequences are now unfolding for millions of households, tens of thousands of investors who bought the doomed paper, and the banking system itself. They illustrate perfectly the key vulnerability of the system, which is not to direct political attack, but to predation. We return to this issue in two chapters.

†Social Security Administration, *Fast Facts and Figures About Social Security* (Washington, D.C.: Social Security Administration Office of Research, Evaluation, and Statistics, 2005).

signal contribution to the American welfare state. Since it had Republican credentials, it could be (and was) expanded further under Clinton and again under George W. Bush. The effects on the disposable incomes of the poorest working Americans—the bottom decile of the wage distribution—appear to have been remarkable, and all the more remarkable for having nearly escaped notice.

Try adding these elements together: health care, higher education, housing, and Social Security. Together they account for nearly 40 percent of total consumption of goods and services in the United States. Moreover we have not yet counted the direct contribution of nonmilitary public expenditure at the federal, state, and local levels, which amounts to another 14 percent of GDP (2 percent federal, 12 percent state and local). Of that, a high fraction goes for public education at the primary and secondary levels. (Over 88 percent of American schoolchildren attend public schools, and that proportion has not fallen notably in recent years.) Taking everything together, we find that the United States is not a "free-market" economy with an underdeveloped or withered state sector. It is, rather, an advanced postindustrial developed country like any other, with a government sector responsible for well over half of economic activity. It is just somewhat less organized and efficient in some respects, and considerably more profligate in others, than the European norm. And it is particularly good at disguising this fact and at cutting parapublic institutions in on the action.

The establishment of a large, stable, publicly guaranteed, steadily growing, and debt-funded parapublic social welfare sector has had a straightforward stabilizing effect on the overall economy. It reduced the effects of investment and inventory cycles, and therefore the extent of unemployment, and the risk that an industrial recession would ever turn into another great Depression. A system of interventions at key moments in life—to support the education of the young, assist the sick, help with the acquisition of a home, and provide for retirement—creates a population that is generally disciplined, hardworking, politically content, and low risk from the standpoint of lenders. In turn, the ability and willingness of private households to accumulate debts, largely against the equity in their homes, made it possible for the public sector to run much smaller deficits than would otherwise be the case. This is not the cradle-to-grave welfare state that emerged in postwar Europe. It is not all inclusive, and the patterns of exclusion (and predation) tend to reproduce historic American race relations. But it has been the mechanism that has made possible what I earlier called the Keynesian devolution in America—the transfer of the power to borrow and to fuel economic growth itself from the public to the private sector. It is from the Keynesian devolution, public borrowing privileges gone private, that the household emerged as the prime motor of American economic growth.

This is something quite new: an economy sustained by institutions providing, in the main, human services and driven, in the main, by the accumulation of personal and household debts and a corresponding rise in asset values. It is a system that can emerge only in a world where the country in question is released from one of the age-old obligations of all countries: the obligation to pay for the goods it consumes with goods it produces, of like value. The growth of imports in such a system will exceed that of exports, barring the discovery of new natural resources to exploit. Therefore, for good or ill, the country will be obliged to issue and accumulate external debt—to borrow from overseas. That is the American case, a topic to which we will be obliged to return. And for the system to continue, two conditions must be met. First, there must be a willing holder of the resulting external national debt. Second, the system cannot be allowed to collapse from within. This means that attacks on it from those who see the opportunity to become very rich in the easiest possible ways, by preying on the public sector, cannot be allowed to get out of hand.

The history of the past three decades has often been written as a struggle between the spirit of Milton Friedman and the ghosts of Keynes and Franklin D. Roosevelt—between the market and the state. The Reagan revolution was successful primarily in forcing changes in the way people thought and spoke: it resurrected Adam Smith and Friedrich von Hayek and established a new church of the free market, giving the right wing of the economics profession unprecedented exposure for its most extreme ideas. And this had consequences, to be sure. Welfare programs, including public housing, aimed at the most vulnerable citizens, the nonworking poor, were severely cut. So were state initiatives in energy; efforts to introduce industrial policy were strangled in the crib.

But with respect to the major New Deal institutions of middle-class social welfare policy, Reagan barely changed the facts on the ground. Social Security came through those years with its benefits mostly intact. Medicare and Medicaid continued to grow. The savings and loan institutions collapsed and had to be bailed out, but the larger system of public support for housing remained. Housing recovered, entering an extended boom that ended only with the subprime mortgage crisis. The universities, the public schools, and of course the military came through in the end. Overall, the New Deal survived Reagan quite intact, and the economy recovered—partly led by housing, partly by technology, partly by military spending. This was not because the conservatives around Reagan succeeded but because they had failed.

Those who describe themselves as political conservatives but who are mainly interested in power rather than in ideas drew the lesson. They adapted. They quietly dropped any serious adherence to their own past ideas. Rather than defeat the system, they decided to join it. And to turn it to their own purposes. Without saying a word.

CHAPTER NINE

The Corporate Crisis

A standard story told round the liberal campfire is of the destruction of the New Deal and the Great Society in the years of Ronald Reagan and George W. Bush. These ogres were, in turn, the instruments of hidden hands and dark forces, the tools of corporate power.

The truth may be nearly the reverse. As we have seen, though each did damage here and there, neither Reagan nor Bush fundamentally undid the American social compact. Those institutions—health care, higher education, housing, and retirement—still largely survive, and so (despite much talk of its disappearance) does the middle class those institutions largely created. Yet compared to its world-dominating position in the 1960s, the American industrial firm is not in such good shape. And both ultraconservative presidents presided over important phases in its decline, fall, and corruption.

When my father published *The New Industrial State* in 1967, the great industrial enterprise seemed a stable, even permanent, and largely self-stabilizing element of the postwar American scene. My father's purpose was to build an entire economics suitable to a world dominated by such organizations, and he saw the corporation as largely a replacement for the market: an entity that planned out future technologies, managed the production of current ones, reduced uncertainty in the supply chain, and attempted to ensure a stable source of "specific demand" for its products. This was an economics of the economy as it was. And what it was, at that time, was a system ruled by large organizations for purposes of their own.

But the system of large organizations as my father described it was far less stable than it seemed. Already in the 1970s, it began to suffer the intrusion, on its home markets, of a competing system: the rising industrial colossus of Japan. The Japanese challenge particularly undermined two major interlocking citadels of midcentury American indus-try, steel and automobiles, each home to a powerful union. Those ris-ing competitors had new designs, lower costs, and new production methods; the famous just-in-time method for cutting inventories in automobile manufacturing, known as the Toyota system, was coming into existence. The Japanese (and the Germans too) were also develop-ing an important presence in industrial machinery, construction equip-ment, agricultural implements—mainstays of manufacturing production, blue-collar employment, and industrial unionism in the Upper Midwest.

Thus, when Reagan took office in 1981 and Paul Volcker launched his assault on inflation, the great American industrial firms built dur-ing the halcyon years from the 1940s to the 1960s were already intrin-sically vulnerable. Monetarism would, in effect, blow them apart, for the double-digit interest rates Volcker and Reagan brought on in 1981 had three catastrophic effects on these sectors. First, it destroyed their export markets, sending Third World economies in Latin America, Africa, and parts of Asia into a tailspin from which they would not recover, in some cases, for twenty years. Second, the recession destroyed (though more briefly) their home markets. And third, they drove up the value of the dollar, by around 60 percent in relation to U.S. trading partners. Suddenly anyone who could still purchase equip-ment could get it much cheaper from Japan or Germany, from Komatsu or Siemens rather than from Caterpillar or International Harvester or Allis-Chalmers. In this way, the great American industrial belt, and the unions it housed, were kicked to pieces once they were already down.

By the midpoint of the Reagan era, the economy of *The New Indus-trial State* was in crisis. Many of the large companies at the center of it were in trouble. Many had been bankrupted by high interest rates, the ensuing recession in 1981 and 1982, and the competitive boost that the high dollar gave to competing industries in Japan and Europe. These were the immediate consequences, and others would follow. In partic-ular, there would come a reorganization of the most advanced sectors in the 1980s, and specifically a migration of technology wizards out of the large integrated firms to their own companies in Silicon Valley and Seattle. Finally, in the 1990s and after, what remained of some of the country's once-great industrial and technical firms would fall victim to new waves of financial fraud. Plainly, the great corporation was neither permanent nor invincible; macroeconomic policy, in particular, could set in motion the forces that would destroy it.

As these developments unfolded, there was an intellectual reaction. Not surprisingly, the vision of an organization-based economics went into eclipse. In sociology the term *postindustrial* came into fashion, suggesting a discipline that was moving on. But the reaction of economics was actually to regress. Rather than analyze the decline of the large corporations, by the early 1980s many economists basically decided to pretend that their rise had never really occurred. They would simply assert that the presence of the Japanese and Germans on the world stage meant that there really was "competition" after all. Among other things, this would permit them to dismiss my father from the fraternity of economists altogether. *The New Industrial State* itself, a huge best seller in its day, fell out of print.

To the economists who now took control of our interpretations, a world of unstable and changing corporations was to be seen as indistinguishable from a world of free and competitive markets, in the textbook sense of a very large number of very small firms, each producing a standard product by standard methods and taking prices as given by the market itself. And the well-developed, highly stylized, utterly irrelevant principles of the latter were to be applied to the former, whatever the violence to the facts. Thus, the way opened to the revival of the conservative myth, the application of a set of aged academic ideas to a world in no way suited to receive them.

And yet my father's vision of an economy dominated by large national corporations as of 1967 was not an error. The midcentury was as he said it was. Nor was it a glance at an interlude between two eras when free markets actually prevailed. It was instead the portrait of a way-station, a stage in the evolution of the world business system. The postwar dominance of the large American industrial corporation counterbalanced by government and organized labor was a fact—just as the Soviet Union had been a fact, whose existence was not disproved by its disintegration. It was simply not a permanent fact; it was followed, more rapidly than my father anticipated that it would be, by the destabilization, decline, and reorganization of that system. Thus, what some interpreted as showing up the failings of a book is more fairly seen as a process of fundamental change, of evolution and of decay, and especially of the redistribution of power in the industrial system itself.

In *The New Industrial State*, power passed into the large organization, and specifically to the technostructure—that group of men and women with specialized skills and knowledge who formed the teams required to make the organization work. The decline of national industrial corporations can be seen in part as a process of dispersion of the technostructure's power. This occurred partly in response to growing global competition, partly following a countercoup from the world of international finance, partly in response to a change in the organization of technology, and partly as the result of the rise of a class of oligarchs— the new CEOs, who would serve as parasites on the firm. Thus, power dispersed in several directions. Some of it went with the technologists, as they set off to California and Washington to establish their own independent companies, transforming the large integrated enterprises from producers to consumers of scientific and technical research. Some of it went to the financiers, concentrated in Manhattan, who came to reassert their own standards of financial performance on large companies, at the risk of a disciplinary raid and hostile acquisition. Some of it was lost overseas, to the encroaching enterprises of Europe or Japan. And some of it devolved onto members of the chief executive officer class, previously subordinate in practice to the technostructure, who now became once again an autonomous force in the life of the companies they oversaw.

These four phenomena—the rise of trade, the reassertion of financial power, the outsourcing of technological development, and the ascendance of an oligarchy in the executive class—have, in this way and over the years, had dramatic effects on American industrial corporations, on the way they are run, and on their broadly declining position in the world. Each is worth a few additional words.

Economists love trade, but the public at large is amazingly hostile to it. Why is this? When economists discuss trade, they see only good things: the efficiencies associated with scale and specialization. Yet these are things that, if they exist at all, are deduced from textbook models and therefore basically from the imagination; they are at best only dimly visible on the ground. But by far the most direct effect of trade is simply to cut into a phenomenon people can see or think they can see: the autonomy and security of the firms they actually work for and the countervailing power of the unions within those firms. Rising trade has dimly defined winners, well-defined losers. Even though the steel corporations and auto companies of Japan in the 1980s also paid relatively high wages, they destabilized the environment for

American corporations and their workers nevertheless. Low-wage competition from rising industrial powers in the Third World would only deepen the crisis.

Countervailing power is the ability of workers, through their union, to raise wages by drawing on the market position of the firm. It depends on the ability of the workers to threaten credible damage if their demands are not met. And that, in turn, depends on the resilience, autonomy, and security of the firm. To put it simply, where competition threatens from Japan, China, or Mexico, the firm is endangered and the union is endangered with it. In this situation, outsourcing is a defensive reaction—a way of throwing out the union in order to save the firm.

Unions have always faced a comparable threat from technology (automation), but the implementation of that threat requires effort, imagination, and expense, and the creation of new technologies generates jobs, often within the firm, which can in their turn be unionized. Unions therefore can live with technological change. To move an ordinary factory to Juarez often requires little more than a truck; the threat to do so has a low threshold of credibility and constitutes an irretrievable breach with labor. The rise of trade is therefore a potent weapon against the status of labor. But trade is such a threat because it is, and especially in the 1980s it was, a threat to companies as well as to their jobs.

In the early 1980s, just as trade was creating a highly visible (and for that reason, substantially overstated) threat to the competitiveness of industry and therefore to wages, another shift in the balance of economic power was under way. This was the financial countercoup: the return of banks—investment banks and commercial banks—to the apex of decision making, from which they had been displaced decades earlier by the crash of 1929.

In *The New Industrial State*, published in an age of low interest rates and easy credit for large corporations, the bank was considered secondary to the large corporation. In my father's judgment, the banker was too remote from the details of corporate operations to control them effectively; the technostructure was fundamentally in charge, and the industrial firm, and not its bankers, had the final word on access to credit markets. It was indeed essential that this should be so, for only the technostructure could manage the technology, whose complexity was the reason for a firm's existence. The high interest rates of the 1980s changed all that. Suddenly, after having been secondary for decades, the cost of funds became a predominant consideration for enterprise survival. Monetarism thus made the industrial firm dependent, once again, on its source of finance. In this way, it reestablished the preeminent power of financial institutions in the United States; Wall Street was back in charge, as it had not been for a generation. The result, much remarked on and much regretted in the business literature, was the rise of "short-termism" at the top of the corporation. Financial targets were set and had to be met, whatever their implications for the long-term viability of the enterprise. A company that failed to do so could be punished by a declining stock price and, ultimately, the "discipline" of a hostile takeover, followed by aggressive disruption of the technostructure. In a world of international competition against rising technological powers, this was a formula for further decline—even for the rapid extermination of the American entrants in the competitive chase.

Who could survive? Clearly those best positioned to survive would be enterprises that were so far to the front of the technology pack that they were, in effect, indispensable and irreplaceable, and therefore competitive even in a world of a high dollar and high interest rates. The situation thus greatly favored the emergence of firms that, unlike the integrated industrial behemoths of the 1950s and 1960s, were purely focused on advanced technology. And thus it is no surprise that high-technology elements tended to separate from the large corporation, leading to the emergence of a separate technology sector in the 1990s.

Under these conditions, for those with exceptional imagination, scientific talent, mechanical wizardry, or the skills to persuade venture finance that they possess these traits, the prospects and outcomes were brilliant. They could raise huge sums, pay themselves high salaries, and start new companies in a hurry. Suddenly there emerged a new business elite: young, mysteriously knowledgeable, independent, fabulously rich.

In the popular imagination, this group appeared to be a long way from my father's vision of salaried, bureaucratic engineers and organization men. In fact they appeared, at first glance, to be a familiar type, much celebrated in the economics of an earlier age. Wasn't there now a new breed of that oldest economic archetype: the ruggedly independent entrepreneur? Many so believed. The identification of the new class of business leaders with the old entrepreneurial archetype was irresistible in an age when the ideas of Friedman and Hayek were being aggressively promoted to justify the triumph of free markets. But in fact there was little similarity between the types. To a large degree, the new technology entrepreneurs were in fact the same people who had formerly worked in the great labs of the large corporations.

There was also a large difference in what they did. The "rugged entrepreneur" of the supposed old days triumphed by building smarter and cheaper and by working harder and by attracting and holding customers and market share. All of that took time, and time was something for which the information technology boom had no time. Instead, in the new age, there was a shortcut: getting rich simply meant getting the approval of the capital market. The right connections, a patent, a trade secret, a business plan: these were the preconditions for raising money. Actual business success would come later, if it came at all; one would find out after the fact who had a brilliant innovation and the capacity to pursue it and who did not. But all the executives were rich, at least for a while, as soon as the money had been raised.

These two ascendant social formations—the investment bankers and the technologists—were closely allied. Innovation in one area— Michael Milken's junk bond market—helped fuel the growth of the other. And the alliance between them made stunning inroads into the previously existing institutional structure of the New Industrial State. It would also lead to new political formations, especially in the Democratic Party. As everyone who lived through the 1990s was able to see, the financiers combined with the technoentrepreneurs to promote a vision of the "New Economy"—a "New Paradigm," as it was also called—that briefly dominated the world stage in those years.

The rise to immense wealth of the chief executives in the technology sector, surpassing in market value that to which anyone else in the world would publicly admit, converted those chiefs into symbols of technological prowess. But the same phenomenon had a corrosive secondary effect on other American corporations. It helped to fuel a general explosion in CEO pay as the stock options of the New Economy came to serve as a competitive standard for much larger firms in much more traditional lines of business. Unfortunately, other and more traditional enterprises were rarely, if ever, in position to realize the returns in the stock market or elsewhere that would justify such pay packets for their chiefs. The attempt to reconcile the norms of hotshot high-technology companies with the operating needs of a large enterprise in a traditional industry was a formula for corporate disaster. Enron, a natural gas pipeline company that sold itself to the capital markets as a high-technology trader of energy supplies, was a textbook example, a company that pretended to be something that it was not, and could not be, and that drove itself beyond the bright lines of fraud and criminality in order to maintain the illusion.

The CEO pay explosion is generally treated as a symptom of rising income inequality in the economy as a whole; the gap between the earnings of Fortune 500 CEOs and that of their average or lowest-paid employee is routinely cited. But the context is fallacious. The important issue is not the income or accumulated wealth of a handful of business leaders. It is, rather, an issue of corporate governance. The explosion in CEO pay packets, especially those rooted in stock options, raises a critical question: Does the chief executive work for the company, or is it the other way around?

The epic tale of Dennis Kozlowski, formerly the CEO of Tyco International and then a federal inmate, is characteristic. Having taken control of a nondescript conglomerate, Kozlowski titillated the press by staging a $12 million birthday party for his wife (at least it was for his wife) that featured an ice statue passing Stolichnaya through its penis. But as a writer for *Forbes* commented on his trial: "It's fair to say that Kozlowski . . . abused many corporate prerogatives and that [he] invented new ones just so they could abuse them. [He] acted like [a pig], as a lot of CEOs act like pigs. Still, the larceny charges at the heart of the case did not depend on whether the defendants took the money—they did—but whether they were authorized to take it."*

This is indeed the issue facing the policymaker. Should *any* CEO of a publicly traded company *ever* be authorized to pay himself $100 million a year? The question is not one of aesthetics or morals. It is rather, Is it possible that a chief executive paid in this way will act in the interest of the company by which he is allegedly employed? Or will the CEO, as a matter of course in this situation, simply view the company as a personal servant? As Karen Kozlowski noted on her invitations to the blowout in Sardinia, "The best present for my birthday is your company so please, no gifts."

So long as the compensation of the top boss was kept within the range of normal bureaucratic decency—so long as the gap between the

---

*Dan Ackman, "Tyco Trial II: Verdict First, Law Second," *Forbes*, June 17, 2005.

CEO and the leading technical staff was not too large—then the CEO and the technostructure were largely identified with each other. Also, the top jobs were such that the best technical experts could reasonably aspire to them at the peak of their careers. But with the cult of shareholder valuation, the escalation in CEO pay, and the decision to link that pay to the stock market rather than to corporate cash flow, the top brass gained an entirely different class orientation. Instead of being company men, top executives became, first and foremost, members of a tiny circle of their own.

The consequences were twofold. First, corporate chiefs began to feel interchangeable; their credential was not as the leaders of a particular enterprise but as a CEO per se; the credential for becoming one became, to an increasing degree, that of having been one somewhere else. Thus the recruitment of new CEOs became in part a game of musical chairs among corporations. Wall Street wanted men (and an occasional woman) with experience in cutting costs and driving up stock prices. CEOs therefore began to identify with one another as a group instead of with the companies with which they were affiliated. Instead of pursuing the committee-driven interests of the company—a process from which by lack of deep immersion they were to a degree foreclosed, and to which they would be, in any event, institutionally hostile— many naturally came to focus on the truly important business: that of moving up in the class rankings of CEO pay. At the same time, those in the technostructure could easily see that the corporate game had changed. What had formerly held together as a collective enterprise would now become, in many instances, a game of everyone for himself.

From this, the step to looting is not large. Looting is merely a crossing of the line, the exercise of inherent powers in violation of the rules. The rise of corporate control fraud—of fraud committed not only by the corporation against the customer but against the corporation by its own leaders—is of a piece with the explosion in CEO pay. And this was particularly true where, as in the case of Enron, an entire company managed to transform itself fraudulently from a run-of-the-mill utility to what many thought was an information age breakthrough—and get away with it in the eyes of the financial markets.

The great corporate scandals that unfolded in the 1990s and in the early 2000s were, in essence, an attack from above on corporate structures already weakened by competition from imports, by the movement of the technologists into their own companies, and by the decline of countervailing power.* But what they most exposed was the complete incapacity of the financial markets to oversee from the outside the inner workings of a complex financial structure. In every case—Enron, Tyco, WorldCom, and the others—financial market pressures encouraged fraud. The firms cooked their books, in part and especially at first, to make the numbers previously projected to outside analysts. In every case, this led to an unchecked subversion of social and legal norms, a collapse of the internal mechanics of discipline and control. Once this happened, the incentive and the capacity to loot the enterprise for personal gain were practically irresistible. What was irresistible was not resisted.

Each such collapse was initially rewarded, not punished, by the financial markets. In no case did the financial markets detect the fraud. Quite to the contrary, the markets converted the fraudulent enterprise into a performance standard by which other corporations in the same field were to be judged. Nor did any large accounting or auditing firm blow the whistle; again to the contrary, all the major frauds had their books cleared by reputable accountants. Nor did the ratings agencies, then or later, intervene. In this way, the financial markets and the institutions that are supposed to foster their reputations actually propagated the pressures for fraud, if not fraudulent conduct itself, from one firm to the next. It would be left to inside whistle-blowers, journalists, and ultimately prosecutors and the courts to unravel the precise nature of the deceptions and to apportion blame.

The economics profession, stuck in its vision of the market as a source of discipline, misinterpreted these phenomena entirely. Just as reputable economists had blamed the savings-and-loan crisis on deposit insurance ("moral hazard" was the term of art for this supposed phenomenon), they blamed the California energy crisis on the design of its deregulated markets—not on the behavior of the perpetrators themselves, and certainly not on the pressures from Wall Street. But the actual failures were not in the particular features of the design of energy markets. They were in the very concept that the market could be relied on to police corpo-

---

*The theory of "control fraud" is developed in William K. Black, *The Best Way to Rob a Bank Is to Own One* (Austin, TX: University of Texas Press, 2005). Black was the whistle-blower on the Keating Five scandal and indeed on the savings and loan crisis itself, and his work provides an analytical lens of fundamental importance for thinking through these issues.

rate activity in such situations. In truth, the influence and hegemony of the financial markets lay at the very root of the problem.

The same problem was also apparent at the end of the Internet boom, when valuations collapsed overnight and the wreckage exposed the fantasies that had taken control of investors' sensibilities while the going was good. Shortly after, it emerged (just for instance) that capital markets had financed fifty times the optical fiber cable that was actually required, a record that would have embarrassed a Hungarian central planner of the 1950s. The scandals, however, raised the issue in unmistakable form, posing a question that cuts to the heart of the system: Can financial markets govern corporations? Are they suited to the power that they actually exercise over the future of business firms?

Indeed not, for the market has a tendency to undermine the law. Where the corporate scandals arose from the subversion of social and legal norms, those norms had been weakened by the pressure placed on firms by Wall Street's demands for a high rate of return combined with its blind eye toward sharp practice and by the constitution of top corporate officers into a predator class. All of this was abetted by the increasing legal and financial complexity emerging from a culture of lawyers, accountants, and speculators. Enron was a complex organization, and it was precisely that complexity that made it possible to conceal or obscure the frauds. Yet this does not mean that the underlying issues are ambiguous. In the final analysis, prosecutors and juries have no difficulty passing judgment. More than one thousand felony convictions followed the savings-and-loan fiasco; after Enron, the top executives were eventually indicted, and all convicted, notwithstanding the close personal and political friendship between the chief executive officer and the President of the United States.

CHAPTER TEN

The Rise of the Predator State

W hat did the new class—endowed with vast personal income, freed from the corporation, and otherwise left to the pursuit of its own social position—set out to do in political terms? The experience of the past decade permits a very simple summary explanation: they set out to take over the state and to run it—not for any ideological project but simply in the way that would bring to them, individually and as a group, the most money, the least disturbed power, and the greatest chance of rescue should something go wrong. That is, they set out to prey on the existing institutions of the American regulatory and welfare system.

As a way of thinking about economic relationships, this idea is not new. The metaphor of predation is evolutionary, and its origins are to be found in evolutionary economics, specifically in Thorstein Veblen's *Theory of the Leisure Class*, first published in 1899 and a classic of American thought. Veblen wrote that predation is a phase in the evolution of culture, "attained only when . . . *the fight has become the dominant note in the current theory of life.*" The relationship between those who work and those who fight was a central distinction of organized society—and one completely absent from the benign ideas of self-organized social harmony that emerge from thinking in terms of markets.

In the "higher barbarian culture," Veblen wrote, the "industrial orders" comprise most of the women, servants, slaves, and other chattel, plus the craftspeople and a smattering of engineers. These people are underlings, and they alone perform what in modern societies is called *work*. Only for them, therefore, is it appropriate to think of wages and salaries as compensation for the drudgery of toil. Those who are higher up in the pecking order take a different view. And while (as Veblen wrote) to an outsider the work of the hunter and that of the

126

herder may seem functionally similar, this is not at all the "barbarian's sense of the matter."

The nonindustrial orders comprise the leisure class: warriors, government, athletes, and priests. Captains of industry are an outgrowth of the warrior caste, which explains the organization of much of business along military lines. The leisure classes do not work. Rather, they hold offices. They perform rituals. They enact deeds of honor and valor. For them, income is not compensation for toil and is not valued mainly for the sustenance it makes possible. Income is, rather, a testament by the community to the prestige it accords the predator classes, to the esteem in which they are held. It is a way, in other words, of keeping score.

The leisure class is predatory as a matter of course: predation is what it does. The relation of overlords to underlings is that of predator to prey. The categories of Veblen's economics include prominently the absentee landlords and the vested interests, who live off the work of others by right and tradition, and not by their functional contribution to the productivity of the system.

The ecology of predator-prey relationships is one of mutual interdependence. Predators rely on prey for their sustenance, but they also require and must motivate their assistance. The normal function of the clan, tribe, family unit, or company is not to enrich the owner or master at the expense of the underlings, but to enrich him at the expense of surrounding clans, tribes, families, or companies. In this contest, the underlings naturally must enjoy some benefit both to motivate their cooperation and illustrate the success of the collective enterprise. The success of the enterprise depends in turn on keeping the predators sufficiently in check. If in their compulsion to fight, they lay waste to the environment, then neither they nor their prey will survive.

Thus, contrary to Marx, in Veblen's scheme of things the industrial orders are not driven to the brink of subsistence. On the contrary: the success of the predators depends in part on healthy prey. And to a degree, their prestige also depends on it. Wives and servants are therefore fed and decorated to reflect the stature of their masters; engineers are kept comfortable with "full lunch buckets" so as to keep the industrial machinery running smoothly. Since the lower orders generally understand this, those who are included within the program also realize that their own position could be worse than it is. For this reason, they are not intrinsically revolutionary or inevitably destined to become so.

At one time, Veblen's depiction of economic society was well known in American intellectual circles and among economists, but it was largely forgotten and dropped from memory over the course of the cold war. That era evidently had room for only two grand visions. One was that of Marx, under which the class structure, divided between bourgeois and proletarians, was intrinsically antagonistic and prerevolutionary; in the Marxian dynamic the proletarian would sooner or later face the choice between revolt and starvation. The other was that of Hayek or Friedman, under which each occupation makes a contribution to the welfare of the whole, precisely valued by the market, so that any existing distribution of income is validated, ipso facto, by its productivity. Veblen's vision of an essentially stable order, yet dominated by a predatory and unproductive class, was plainly too subversive for the marketeers, yet it was also too cynical for the Marxists. And so it was effectively squeezed out of existence between them.

The Marxian dream died out long before the cold war ended; it was clear that capitalism had arranged itself so as not to starve its proletarians or drive them to the barricades. And so we have been left with only the orthodoxy of Friedman and Hayek, by whose lights we must treat every economic outcome and every upward shift in the distribution of income, in Pangloss fashion, as an artifact of the best of all possible worlds. If we cling to the belief that our social arrangements are (for whatever reason) less than ideal, or perhaps not so good as they once were, we are, by the lights of this view of the world, simply nostalgic for a different time. Given technology, given demography, social arrangements governed by the markets cannot be improved on. Supercapitalism, as former labor secretary Robert Reich calls it, has simply given us a new set of lords and rulers.*

Veblen himself had little interest in the processes of social reform. Though he toyed with the prospect of a society ruled by a "soviet of engineers," he never seriously believed that the conditions under which they might be induced to cast off the gilded chains of the leisure class were likely to take effect. And he died, in 1929, before the Great Depression started to give rise to the social transformations of the New Deal.

My father admired Veblen. But he was also formed in the Depression

*Robert B. Reich, *Supercapitalism: The Transformation of Business, Democracy and Everyday Life* (New York: Knopf, 2007).

and by the New Deal and by the great mobilization of World War II. In some ways for his generation, the soviet of engineers was no fantasy at all; it was their experience of the world created during their youth. And as a mature economist, my father saw an economic world dominated by large interlocking organizations; his achievement as an economist was to analyze that world. That world had virtues, including countervailing power and the mastery of advanced technology. Its vices—private affluence and public squalor, environmental decay, the manipulation of consumers—were the consequence of unbalanced power. It was a world in which Veblenian predation was possible, but in which the predatory instinct might come under enduring organizational control. But as we have seen, the project of using private organizations to tame personal power failed: the imperative of technological control over production processes was simply not strong enough, especially in an age of globalization, to keep the system in place. Power was again dispersed: to finance, to the tech firms, and to the CEOs.

This dispersion of power led to the reconnection of power with particular persons, and this, in turn, to a result that would not have surprised Veblen: the reemergence of predation, predatory conduct, and pathologically predatory conduct as a central theme in business life. Once power passes back from organizations to individuals, what are they going to do with it? Organizations may have complex social and technical objectives. Individuals generally do not. As Veblen told, for the leisure class, accumulation is mainly a way of keeping score.

In the age of organizations, and for the generation of which my father was a part, the social and political role of the large corporation was defined as one sometimes of conflict but also of collaboration. There were moments—the U.S. Steel crisis of 1962, pitting John F. Kennedy against Roger Blough, the rogue chief executive of U.S. Steel, was a famous example—when the government and the country's leading companies faced off. But there were other moments, and especially during the long premonetarist struggle against inflation in the 1970s, when public and private power were harnessed together, more or less in collaboration, with the government, not the corporation, in a leadership role. Moreover, the regulatory model that emerged in the 1970s depended on the existence of both an independent public power, setting the agenda, and a collaborating element in the private sector. On the environment, occupational safety, and consumer product safety, the envelope of what is possible is defined, almost always, by what is technically possible to the most advanced firms in the line of business under regulation. The tension in the regulatory process is therefore always going to be between the interests of the state acting with the leading firm or firms, and those firms that would be put at competitive disadvantage by the enforcement of new regulations.

Behind these developments is an underlying, and sometimes unappreciated, reality of American business regulation over the past century. While the causes of occupational safety, consumer product safety, fair competition, living wages, and the environment have all enjoyed the backing of spirited and often effective public interest groups, these groups cannot by themselves account or take credit for the pervasiveness of the late-twentieth-century regulatory system. Regulation emerged, reached its high point in the Nixon administration, and survived thereafter because a large part of the business community was prepared to support it. And this was so because while regulation is a burden for some businesses, it is a competitive blessing for others. A functioning structure of regulation is the competitive instrument of the more progressive part of the business community, which wishes—for its own advantage—to force everyone to play by a common set of rules.

In particular, regulation helps the competitive position of relatively advanced businesses by reducing or even eliminating the competition from backward enterprises that offset higher production costs with less safe factories and products and also with lower wage bills. Regulation thus clears the way for "better" companies to supplant "worse" ones; equally, no regulation can survive unless there is some business capable in principle of meeting the standard. The corporate average fuel economy (CAFE) standards can be used as an example. Such standards can advance only with the support of companies capable of meeting those standards; strict regulation favors those companies that can most readily meet them, while lax regulation tilts the field back to the laggards. Unfortunately in this case, the political identity of the more technically progressive automobile companies (which are Japanese) and the political centrality of the more regressive firms (which are American) stand as major obstacles to tightening the standards, and the alliance of the Bush administration with the American producers has been disastrous for environmental regulation in the automotive sector.

But as power ebbed from the corporation in the late 1970s and 1980s and became vested, once again, in free-acting individuals of the type we have described, the basis for collaboration between comparatively progressive elements within business and a broadly progressive state tended to disappear. Instead, business leadership saw the possibility of something far more satisfactory from their point of view: complete control of the apparatus of the state. In particular, reactionary business leadership, in those sectors most affected by public regulation, saw this possibility and directed their lobbies—the K Street corridor—toward this goal. The Republican Party, notably in the House of Representatives under Newt Gingrich and later Tom DeLay, became the instrument of this form of corporate control. The administration, following the installation of George W. Bush, became little more than an alliance of representatives from the regulated sectors—mining, oil, media, pharmaceuticals, corporate agriculture—seeking to bring the regulatory system entirely to heel. And to this group was added another, overlapping to some degree, of equal importance: those who saw the economic activities of the government not in ideological terms but merely as opportunities for private profit on a continental scale. Jack Abramoff became, for a moment, the emblem of this class.

This is the Predator State. It is a coalition of relentless opponents of the regulatory framework on which public purpose depends, with enterprises whose major lines of business compete with or encroach on the principal public functions of the enduring New Deal. It is a coalition, in other words, that seeks to control the state partly in order to prevent the assertion of public purpose and partly to poach on the lines of activity that past public purpose has established. They are firms that have no intrinsic loyalty to any country. They operate as a rule on a transnational basis, and naturally come to view the goals and objectives of each society in which they work as just another set of business conditions, more or less inimical to the free pursuit of profit. They assuredly do not adopt any of society's goals as their own, and that includes the goals that may be decided on, from time to time, by their country of origin, the United States. As an ideological matter, it is fair to say that the very concept of public purpose is alien to, and denied by, the leaders and the operatives of this coalition.

The Predator State is different from the New Industrial State, and yet it grows directly from the decline of the economic system my father described in 1967. An economics of organizations and not of markets remains the only useful and pertinent way to describe it. Whereas in *The New Industrial State* the organization existed principally to master advanced technologies and complex manufacturing processes, in the Predator State the organization exists principally to master the state structure itself.

None of these enterprises has an interest in diminishing the size of the state, and this is what separates them from the principled conservatives. For without the state and its economic interventions, they would not themselves exist and could not enjoy the market power that they have come to wield. Their reason for being, rather, is to make money off the state—so long as they control it. And this requires the marriage of an economic and a political organization, which is what, in every single case, we actually observe.

The major battlegrounds of American domestic politics today emerge clearly once there is an understanding of the Predator State. They do not consist in the bipolar argument toward which so much thought and argument is directed—that of "government" versus "the market." They do not for the most part consist in a perpetual war, as many are led by their training in economics to suppose, over whether the frontiers of the state should expand or contract. Rather, they assume that over time, the role of the state *will* gradually grow. At some deep level, everyone with a serious role in the policy debates agrees on this. The politics consists in a continuing battle over who gets cut in on the deal—and a corresponding argument over who gets cut out, and how, for there is profit in both cutting in and cutting out.

Thus, health care. The politics of health care in our time does not revolve around any grand conservative scheme to return medical care to the private sector; it is immediately apparent that without state funding, both the medical sector *and the overall economy* would collapse. (Without Medicare, the life savings of many elderly would be quickly depleted, and their life expectancies would also fall.) Nor does any serious politician propose drafting American doctors and transforming American hospitals into a replica of Britain's National Health Service. Such a move, if it reduced American health care costs to British levels, would entail reducing total health care spending by nearly half. No less than complete privatization, that would also cause the medical sector to collapse and the economy to implode.

Instead, the health care battle is waged in ways that tend to expand the system; the issue is on what terms and with how many concessions to existing predators. A major liberal goal is to extend the coverage of health insurance, particularly to children. The private insurance companies are opposed to this. Why? Because they stand to lose part of their existing clientele: better-off families with small children. *Their* economic function is uncomplicated: it consists in marketing to people who are relatively unlikely to need health care, while also *not* selling it to those most likely to get sick. Reform would be less profitable, and the health insurance companies have both profits to defend and resources (those very profits) to defend them with. The political battle is over nothing else.

Does the country benefit in any way from having such families with children under private insurance? Does it benefit from having any families under private insurance? No. To insure the whole population without screening would be economically efficient. It would save the resources now devoted to screening, and this would be cheaper from both an economic and an administrative point of view. Among other things, more resources could then go to actual health care. Harvard medical economists David Himmelstein and Steffie Woolhandler estimate the bureaucratic waste from private medical insurance to be around $350 billion per year—just under 2 percent of gross domestic product, and more than half the cost of the defense budget.* They also point out that the popular liberal "solution" of employer mandates is ineffective, having been tried in numerous states without noticeable effect: "The 'mandate model' for reform rests on impeccable political logic: avoid challenging insurance firms' stranglehold on health care. But it is economic nonsense. The reliance on private insurers makes universal coverage unaffordable."

The struggle is epic precisely because it is zero sum. Here we see the immense power of the legitimating myth: by discussing it as though the issue had something to do with the efficiency of markets or the freedom of consumer choice, the defense of a functionless pool of profits can be made to seem a legitimate political position.

The expansion of Medicare to provide a drug benefit to senior citizens illustrates how the system works when a compromise is reached. In this case, a new benefit was delivered, meeting a need that had grown greater over the years as the composition of medical care shifted increasingly toward chemical and pharmaceutical therapies. But the program was done in such a way as to make payments to drug companies as large as possible. Notoriously, the U.S. government was prohibited

*David U. Himmelstein and Steffie Woolhandler, "I am NOT a Health Reform." *New York Times* op-ed page, December 15, 2007.

by law from negotiating bulk discounts on the drugs purchased for the program—discounts routinely exacted by other government agencies, such as the Veterans Administration. (Before the benefit was enacted, there had been developing a minor industry of exports and imports, as U.S.-made drugs were shipped to Canada, sold at the lower prices negotiated by Canadian public authorities, and reimported to the United States. Needless to say, although this arbitrage reflected one of the better moments for free trade, it did not win favor with the ostensible free traders then in power.) The Medicare drug benefit thus helped to ensure that a monopoly price on pharmaceuticals would be paid, while shifting the burden of paying it, in part, to the general taxpayer.

Schools have been a bastion of American public effort for nearly two centuries, and they are today on the front lines of the Predator State. Early in the Bush administration, policy toward the public schools took the form of advancing voucherization, a system that would have allowed a partial state subsidy for alternative schooling, encouraging middle-class parents to take their children to the private sector. (Such a system exists in Chile, having been created by the military regime of Augusto Pinochet.) The not very effectively disguised purpose was to get public funding into the hands of for-profit and religious entities, which would then set up voucher-eligible schools. The clients of this new system would have been middle-class parents unhappy with the public schools, able to spend something from their own pockets on their own children's schooling, but not willing to pay for private schools on top of the taxes that support their local school board. Vouchers would in effect permit those parents to pull their property tax payments from the public system.

The idea of vouchers, whose origins go back to Milton Friedman himself, once again rested on a rhetoric of markets, competition, freedom, and "school choice." But by and large, the public has not been persuaded: vouchers enjoy little public support, and the proportion of American children attending public school has so far not materially declined.* It developed that even most middle-class Americans were not sufficiently unhappy with the public schools their children were actu-

---

*According to a 2006 Phi Delta Kappa/Gallup poll, "The percentage favoring vouchers dropped from 38% a year ago to 36% this year, while opposition grew from 57% to 60%. Support for vouchers started at 24% in 1993, fluctuated up and down for years, and peaked at 46% in 2002. It is now at the mid-Nineties level." Accessed September 17, 2006, at http:www.pdkintl.org/kappan/k$609pol.htm.

ally in to risk confiding their children to schools not yet in existence, whether run by for-profit educational corporations or by churches. Nor were they willing, as a group, to desert the social and community networks that in many American communities are organized around the public school systems.

Taking stock, the Bush team switched its emphasis to No Child Left Behind, a program that *expanded* federal spending on public schools while imposing an intense testing regimen on them. Forms of predatory free enterprise in which certain Bush family members participated (selling test preparation programs to public school systems) quickly emerged. But the larger effect of NCLB was to foment middle-class discontent with public schools, for three reasons. First, the testing regimes cut deeply into the flexibility and creativity in the classroom, discouraging creative professionals from becoming teachers and demoralizing many who remained. Second, the emphasis on teaching to the test undermined educators' attention to and the resources available for untestable programs, including art, music, and athletics. And third, the harsh evaluation regime behind the tests themselves worked to label, and therefore to stigmatize, certain schools as failing. From the standpoint of both parents and teachers, schools that were judged to be failing by the test results sometimes were not. But this was beside the point: a bad test result could have serious, even catastrophic effects on reputation and funding, precipitating middle-class flight from the system. In this way, NCLB would feed the demand for vouchers later on.

At the university level, to take a minor but telling example, what had been a low-cost, publicly administered student loan program was devolved onto private companies, whose marketing programs quickly assimilated imaginative elements of bribery. The companies were offering a largely standard product in competition with one another; since the competing plans could barely be distinguished, advertising directly to students would have been largely pointless, an unnecessary business cost easily countered by other firms in the business. Instead the companies chose what was undoubtedly the rational economic strategy given the profits to be had, the market situation that they faced, and the ethical climate of the times. To succeed in this arena, all they had to do was persuade the student loan officers of universities to class the plans as approved by the university administration. The provision of convention holidays to those officers was a cheap, efficient, and no doubt agreeable way to build and maintain market share. Were the companies necessary at all? Was any efficiency gained? Was anything except private profit served by moving the provision of guaranteed student loans from the public to the private sector? Of course not.

Social Security presents a target for predators on a far larger scale, and for a straightforward reason: sharp private financial operators with good political connections have long seen the opportunity inherent in diverting the payroll tax—the Mississippi of cash flows—into private investment accounts. Such accounts would create, overnight, millions of inexperienced investors, needing advice and other services that could be sold to them for a fee. A new group of players—expensive private providers of what had been a cheap public service—would be cut in on the deal.

Correspondingly, a group of currently protected players would be cut out of the relatively stable retirement incomes that they can now rely on. These especially include those elderly who were unfortunate enough to make "wrong" investment choices, or simply to reach retirement age in a down market, for the privatization of Social Security would break the link that now exists between work and earnings and retirement, and substitute for it a system of benefits that would be largely dominated by the fluctuations of the capital markets. Losers would also include those who now receive survivors' and disability benefits, which account for about a third of Social Security benefits and support the upbringing of many children, because workers who die or are disabled young will not generally have accumulated sufficient assets, even in a strong market, to support their young children through to adulthood. The unpredictability and randomness that this would generate—all in the name of free markets and investment choice, naturally—would negate the contribution of Social Security to security itself.

The modern campaign against Social Security goes back to 1981, when Reagan's White House—led by budget director David Stockman—attempted to declare the program bankrupt. The result at that time was political disaster for the Republicans, who were unprepared for the stiff and skillful defense of Social Security mounted by Democrats in the 1982 midterm elections, led by the Speaker of the House, Thomas P. O'Neill. The upshot, in 1983, was the Greenspan Commission, whose political purpose from the Republican point of view was to bury the issue. In this, Greenspan succeeded by getting agreement on a major increase in payroll tax rates in lieu of significant benefit cuts. The intent and effect of this change was to put Social Security on a largely self-funded basis, at least for a generation. That is, a substantial surplus of payroll taxes over benefits paid out would be stored in the form of government bonds. The understanding was that these would be repaid with interest, presumably out of general revenues, when the time came for the baby boom generation to retire.

The Greenspan Commission had two deeply reactionary effects. First, it provided hundreds of billions of dollars from the Social Security payroll tax to support the government, thereby masking the revenue losses from the Reagan era cuts in the income tax. It was, in other words, the half-hidden part of a massive scheme to shift the burden of taxation from capital onto labor, and to do so in a way that could be sold as supporting the retirement, thirty years down the road, of the baby boom generation. And second, the Greenspan Commission created the artifice of the trust fund surplus—that excess of receipts over payments. In an artful financial maneuver, these were converted into U.S. government bonds, held by the trust fund, earning interest at the government rate. Now suddenly Social Security had an "asset"—and at the rate of interest on bonds, the return on that asset would not look very good. Thus, although there was no connection, direct or indirect, between the return on assets in the trust fund and the payment of benefits to actual retirees, it became possible to argue, for the first time, that Social Security's financial performance should be subjected to investment analysis—to a market test.

In the 1990s, as the stock market went up, the campaign to privatize Social Security naturally gathered force. (In a bubble, everything looks bad when compared to the bubble sector.) In the late 1990s, particularly in the wake of welfare reform, it appeared possible that even Bill Clinton's Democratic administration might capitulate to the mania. Mercifully, opposition among Democrats in Congress and perhaps Clinton's own impeachment troubles derailed that possibility. And then the equity market collapse of 2000 destroyed the general argument for placing basic retirement assets in the stock market. Partly in consequence, President Bush's 2002 Social Security "Reform" Commission, which was intended to open the way toward a privatization scheme, disappeared without a trace. Indeed the backlash was so strong that the campaign to privatize Social Security then went underground. The topic was barely heard of in the 2004 election. Following his victory, George Bush revived it in 2005, but faced with determined partisan opposition, his initiative went down to defeat in the Republican Congress.

Many observers regard that victory—of Social Security over the forces that would privatize it—as a turning point in the political wars of the Bush years. And the victory did show that most Americans do understand that Social Security is a good deal. A direct attack on the program itself is unlikely to be politically viable for some time. Moreover, the romantic appeal of a "market-friendly solution" to the Social Security "problem" has entirely disappeared; the rhetoric of choice and competition has no purchase in the case of an existing public program whose merits are as well understood as they are in this case.

There is therefore no popular enthusiasm for privatization of Social Security per se. And for this reason, we see again the pattern encountered with proposals to voucherize the public schools. The attack, in both cases, is on a public institution that many who know it directly, and who observe it closely, believe serves their interests reasonably well. Therefore, in order to make the move to a privatized and market system palatable, it is first necessary to persuade the public that the existing public system is failing and cannot be sustained. This is the broader public function of No Child Left Behind, and it is the intended function of claims, endlessly repeated in official dialogue on Social Security, that the system faces a long-term financial crisis.

The financial crisis argument rests on the large numbers of baby boomers set to start retiring—on the fact that eventually payroll tax receipts will start to fall short of benefits due and that at some point in the middle distance, the bonds accumulated in the trust fund will have to be retired. Yet the reality is that this was the bargain established by the 1983 Greenspan Commission. The baby boom was old news when that commission convened; it understood the demographics perfectly well, and nothing that has happened since has made the situation worse. On the contrary, the labor force has grown more rapidly in the years since 1983, thanks to higher levels of immigration than were foreseen and the recovery of productivity growth in the late 1990s, generating a larger economy from which projected benefits could be paid. If the Greenspan Commission, notwithstanding the reactionary deal it made, dealt effectively back in 1983 with the need to match payroll tax receipts to the stream of benefits due, then the finances of the system are actually better today than they were expected to be back then. And therefore if the Greenspan Commission resolved the crisis, there can be no crisis now. And there is not.

Seen this way, efforts to cut benefits to the impending baby boom retirees are a way, simply put, of taking back the 1983 bargain. If they were enacted, the very same people who overpaid their payroll taxes to "prefinance" their Social Security benefits would find that they had been given a dishonest bargain. Having paid a lifetime of higher payroll taxes, subsidizing the income tax cuts enjoyed by the investor classes of the 1980s and 1990s, they would come to the end of the rainbow and find the pot of gold empty. Or alternatively, a further rise in payroll taxes would fall on the *next* generation of workers, including the immigrants who would have to swell that generation's numbers, while exempting the *present* generation of the wealthy from any part in paying down the Social Security trust fund. If that doesn't sound fair, well—it isn't.* The issue however has nothing to do with any intrinsic crisis, except the ever-vigilant efforts of the influential to keep tax rates on themselves as low as possible.

Why then does the talk of an "impending Social Security crisis" never disappear? Because it is *instrumental*. It is not a candid assessment of facts and logic associated with demography and economics. It is, rather, a means to an end: toward the privatization of the Social Security system. It is perfectly predictable that once deep benefit cuts are on the table,† the "alternative" of private investment accounts will then resurface, in one form or another, to "ease the pain of the adjustment" for America's seniors. Crocodile tears will be freely shed at the doors of the "bipartisan commission" that will be convened to balance the needs of the bankers and fund managers, as against those of the elderly, in this matter.

This is, unfortunately, not a purely partisan matter, for the forces backing investor interests in the matter of Social Security have infiltrated and are strongly represented within the Democratic Party. This is not only smart but inevitable politics, for it is clear that so long as Social Security remains a partisan issue, the path to privatization will be blocked. It will therefore be necessary to take the Democratic opposi-

---

*If any tax measures were necessary, which they are not, a new "Social Security rate" on the income tax—say, 50 percent for incomes over $2 million—would be much better than another rise in income tax. A revived estate tax, set at say 80 percent for estates over $50 million and credited to Social Security, would be better still. The latter would have two especially good effects: projected earnings would help close any projected shortfall in Social Security funding and the threat of the tax would greatly stimulate philanthropy among the very rich.

†Large payroll tax increases on top of what are already at present very high rates are somewhat less likely.

tion down from the inside. To this end, some of the Social Security trimmers have regrouped, quite recently, behind former treasury secretary Robert Rubin's Hamilton Project, while outright privatizers throw themselves behind long-established "nonpartisan" operations like the Concord Coalition, and ostensibly nonpartisan projects such as the Fiscal Wake-Up Tour project of David Walker, lately the comptroller general of the United States.* This group of determined, patient insiders will now await the next administration.

Social Security offers perhaps the clearest, simplest, and most transparent large-scale example of the Predator State at work on a long-term project. But by all odds, the most complex and most damaging example, arising and persisting over several decades, has grown up in the financial sector itself, and particularly in the area of housing and consumer finance. Here we see today, in pure and unalloyed form, the consequences of market power, of asymmetric information, and of regulatory capture, leading to rampant predation against both a public system and the public itself, and on a colossal scale.

The housing finance system had been from the 1930s a protected sector offering low-rate, long-term mortgages to the middle class, funded largely by their own savings. The savings and loan institutions were able to pay slightly higher interest rates than commercial banks, in an era when the vast menu of investment vehicles giving the middle class direct access to stock and bond markets did not exist. In return, the S&Ls made standard mortgage loans on straightforward criteria for eligibility, held the resulting mortgages on their own books, and lived quietly prosperous lives on the difference between what they paid and what they earned, in an economy where home ownership was restricted to a broadly richer group than at present and defaults and foreclosures were rare.

The high interest rates of the 1970s and 1980s destroyed this stable, simple system. In its place grew a much more complicated system, pred-

---

*The Hamilton Project, which is housed at the Brookings Institution, melds its concerns over the "entitlement problem" with a liberal-leaning emphasis on inequality and public investment, combined with a firm commitment to free trade. The Concord Coalition, chaired by the longtime nemesis of Social Security, Peter G. Peterson, is devoted to budget balance as a larger social goal. Concord is closely allied with David Walker's Fiscal Wake-Up Tour, a traveling road show of dire long-term fiscal projections. An excellent recent summary of the broader campaign against Social Security is Joe Conason, *The Raw Deal* (Sausalito, CA: PoliPoint Press, 2005).

icated on managing the risks associated with an unstable economic environment and with high and volatile interest rates. Secondary markets grew up, guaranteed in whole or part by the government, permitting lending institutions to protect themselves by "securitizing" their mortgages and selling them to pools of investors. Standard, long-term, fixed-rate mortgages gave way to adjustable-rate mortgages, transferring interest rate risk back to the borrower. Meanwhile, complexity and instability bred corruption and fraud: the crisis of the S&Ls in the 1980s was due in part to a powerful, politically well-connected clique of criminals who discovered that these institutions could be looted, taking advantage of federal insurance to keep the funds flowing in while complex real-estate "flipping" and other transactions concealed the losses on the asset side from regulatory eyes.* Ultimately the S&L debacle required a massive congressional bailout, prosecutions that yielded over a thousand felony convictions, and reregulation of the industry. But the underlying temptation, and the possibility, to take advantage of the system would remain.

The 1986 Tax Reform Act removed the deductibility of nonmortgage interest, creating a powerful incentive for households to try to own their own homes. Now the channel for large-scale household borrowing would run almost exclusively through the collateral of home equity. Consequently the demand for homes would rise, prices would rise, and householders—particularly those living in the bubble regions—would borrow against their equity in order to finance ordinary consumption, education expenses, vacations, and the like. By the mid-1990s, the capacity to borrow for this purpose became unhinged from income, and (as we have seen) the unprecedented willingness of American households to "dissave"—that is, to finance their ordinary activities by borrowing against their houses—became a major motor of economic expansion. The housing finance system would eventually take on Ponzi characteristics, meaning that a continuing rise in home prices would become necessary in order to service the debts assumed following previous increases in the price of homes. Clearly, if it ever stopped, there would be trouble.

But it did not stop, for a long time. Indeed the home finance sector largely weathered both the tech bust in 2000 and the shock of September 11, 2001, in part because interest rates were cut sharply and the

---

*The best account is William K. Black, op. cit.

middle classes could and did cheaply refinance their debts. But in the early years of the new century, a new type of home lending took hold, eventually exploding to perhaps as much as a third of mortgage loan originations by the middle of the decade. This was the subprime sector: adjustable-rate mortgages made to borrowers who would never under previous standards have qualified for a mortgage loan. Subprime loans were abusive, if not fraudulent, on their face, for they typically involved a low teaser rate that would reset after two or three years to a rate determined by the then-prevailing short-term interest rates. Lenders knew, as borrowers did not, that in the wake of 9/11, short-term rates were unprecedentedly low, and these conditions would not endure. They therefore deliberately substituted adjustable-rate mortgages for fixed-rate mortgages—with the endorsement of then Federal Reserve chairman Alan Greenspan, to reassure the naive public that the exercise was sound. Interest rates then rose, the mortgages started to reset, and hundreds of thousands of borrowers found themselves unable to meet the required payments. Moreover, they had no prospect of rapidly increasing their incomes in order to meet their rapidly rising bills. By the late summer of 2007, new foreclosure mortgages were approaching the total number of persons permanently displaced from New Orleans by Hurricane Katrina every month.

The mortgages so originated (called "toxic waste" and "neutron loans" in the industry) were by then no longer in the hands of the banks or finance companies that had originated them. Taking advantage of the secondary markets, they had been repackaged and sold to pension funds, mutual funds, foreign funds, and "special investment vehicles" associated with the big banks. The riskiest elements were concentrated in some of the largest and most aggressive funds, including Bear Stearns in New York and the Union des Banques Suisses in Geneva. Here the market would show how little it could really do, for in fact these debt instruments were so complex, and so unstable, that they could not be priced; they had simply been accepted, among friends, at imaginary valuations. Ultimately, rising foreclosures would generate a panic, the imaginary valuations collapsed, and the funds would fail, thus forcing a massive public bailout in the United States and Europe in the fall of 2007 and another as this book went to press in the spring of 2008. As the losses and foreclosures compounded, housing prices would fall, and many with standard mortgages will find themselves also affected, perhaps for a long time. This is a topic to which we will return, as it threatens the stability of the system as a whole, and therefore the leading world financial position of the United States.

Interestingly, public interest regulation—health, safety, consumer protection, the environment—is not a major political battleground in these days of the Predator State. And why not? The answer is depressing: the organized forces that would defend and advance the regulatory process have been deeply, almost fatally, weakened. These are, first of all, public interest groups and trade unions, whose financial and political base has been eroded by the declining competitiveness of the industries in which they were formerly strongly organized. Perhaps more serious, the rise of advanced foreign competition in many industrial sectors weights the domestic political environment of American business toward the back end of the technological spectrum—the end that has the most to lose from aggressive regulation. Thus, the critical ingredient for the success of a regulatory regime, which is the potential for an alliance between the public groups that define the need for regulation and those parts of business that make it a success, is suddenly lacking. If the potentially progressive element of an industrial sector exists primarily in enterprises based overseas, it becomes that much more difficult to bring the political coalition to life that would use regulation effectively to solve the underlying social problem by spurring more rapid technological advances. (This is evident in the emerging battles over climate change, where practically all of the significant political pressure for action comes from foreign rather than domestic forces and through international rather than internal political negotiation.) Instead, the entire political weight of business becomes devoted to blocking effective regulation in every sphere.

The second Bush administration simply and systematically nominated the most aggressive antienvironment, antisafety, anti–consumer-protection advocates it could find—business lobbyists in most cases—to every regulatory position that it could not afford to leave unfilled. The pretense of neutrality, of weighing costs against benefits, let alone that of the original regulatory mission, was dropped. The result was an empowerment not of business in general, but of the reactionary wing—the predatory wing—within each branch of business. The political isolation into which the Bush administration eventually fell reflects the fact that considerable parts of business still oppose open government by its own most reactionary wing.

This brings us to the relationship of a corrupted and predatory corporate establishment to the American state and especially to the American welfare state. Under George W. Bush, a narrow coalition of the high plutocracy would rule, mainly from the resource industries (oil, mining, and agribusiness) and the surviving old-line industrial firms (notably automobiles, steel, and defense), combined with big media, insurance, and pharmaceuticals. For popular support, this alliance found itself entirely dependent on noneconomic issues: national security and the social issues directed at low-income working Americans through the one social institution that effectively reached most of them: their churches. National security dominated the elections of 2002 and 2004, but when circumstances neutralized that issue in 2006, it became clear that the ideological base of the Republican Party had shrunk, perhaps irreversibly, to the redoubts of Christian fundamentalism in the Deep South and parts of the Mountain West.

These developments—the placement of corporate men in charge of the state on the one hand, and the decline in their base of popular support on the other—have a profound effect on the character of the state itself. They bring on a tendency to run the state as though it were, in fact, just a corporation, with the rules that govern companies displacing the rules that govern republics. And so today we live in a *corporate republic*, where the methods, norms, culture, and corruption of government have become those of the corporation. This is evident in decision making, public relations, accountability, ownership, and the character and attributes of the desirable chief executive officer.

Republican (with a small "r") government, with its checks and balances, exists to limit the abuse of power. It is a matter of negotiation, compromise, the making of public arguments, and of listening to private dissent. Modern corporate decision-making structures exist, on the contrary, to permit senior executives to do what they want. This is the culture that Richard Cheney brought back into government from Halliburton, that George Bush imbibed at his minor perches at Harken Energy and the Texas Rangers. The operational result is a government by cliques operating in secret, indeed with their very membership unknown outside. Cheney's 2001 Energy Task Force is a characteristic example. The neoconservative capture of foreign policy inside the Bush administration is another. The drive by Karl Rove's political office to direct the U.S. attorneys into political prosecutions is a third. The advance and defense of torture as a method of interrogation in secret prisons run by the CIA is a fourth. The program of warrantless wiretapping, which evidently amounts to the blanket capture by the National Security Agency of all Internet communications, is a fifth. The list could go on, but the practice is clear: we live under a government that as a matter of principle does what it wants.

None of the actions just mentioned could survive serious external review, a system of checks and balances. But in the corporate republic, external review is suppressed. We have instead a governmental public relations apparatus whose purpose is not to persuade but to deflect, deter, and frustrate inquiry into the operations of the government. These are the distinct characteristics of a corporate propaganda machine, easily identified by the inability, or studied unwillingness, to tell a truthful story that is consistent from one day to the next. The operations of the White House press room are a daily case in point, as the most hapless flacks on the planet struggle to accommodate today's talking points to yesterday's lies and deceptions. The working press, employed by corporate entities to whom this sort of information flow is routine, struggles to cope; outside observers (now available to the world, thanks to blogs) observe the scene with incredulity and amazement. But there is no surprise to it: the press releases of a large corporation are meant for the business pages, and there they are generally treated with deference and respect. The bloggers are simply applying an out-of-date standard, that of an actually independent press, to the world they observe.

Republican government (in the small "r" meaning) places the executive under two broad checks: the legislative and investigative powers of the Congress and the imperative powers of the courts. Corporate democracy subverts both of these. It reduces Congress to impotence by depriving that body of independent staff and the practical authority to obtain sensitive information on executive actions. It fills the courts with functionaries who are prepared to act as enablers for the executive branch. This is precisely the way the board of directors, decorous, uninformed, and accommodating, works in the modern business firm and was so described in *The New Industrial State*. It is also the way major accounting firms, anxious for repeat business, approach the books of a complex corporation, which explains why no major corporate fraud has ever been brought to the attention of the authorities by an outside accountant.

In the corporate republic, elections likewise converge to their corporate counterpart. In the latter, the shareholders are nominal owners and can participate if they wish, but the outcome is predetermined: management does not lose. In the corporation, this is handled by the device of the proxy: management arrives at the election with an overwhelming majority of the votes precommitted to its program. In the corporate republic, matters are more complex. But it is evident that a common thread runs through the policies of voter intimidation, voter machine rationing, phony voter fraud investigations, purging of voter lists, caging of African American voters,* ex-felon disenfranchisement, and bottlenecks placed in the way of immigrant political rights. The common thread is to maintain political control for as long as possible in spite of an implacable demographic transition that is gradually sweeping the country out from under the control of the narrow political base of the GOP. The rebellion of 2006 may possibly have signaled the defeat of this strategy, but time will tell. In any event, the work was done: without it, Al Gore would have become President in 2000 or John Kerry in 2004.

And finally we have the peculiar manifestation of the CEO as a symbol or front man, a man who by virtue of his detachment from the culture and inner workings of the corporation cannot actually control much of anything in the organization over which he presides. So what is the function of this functionary? It is precisely to spend his time idly in order to advertise to the country that things are under control—or more precisely, to obscure the fact that they are not. The Bush White House, where all of the key information reaching the President was controlled by staff loyal to the Vice President, illustrates this method. In the first days of the regime, David Broder of the *Washington Post* described Cheney, a former chief executive of Halliburton, as "corporate cool." The description fit perfectly. The government has thus been remade in the image of the business firm. And in this way, it has become subject to all of the administrative and organizational pathologies that bring large private businesses to grief. It has come to absorb every great innovation in corporate mismanagement, deception, market manipulation, and fraud of the past forty years.

The Predator State is an economic system wherein entire sectors have been built up to feast on public systems built originally for public purposes and largely serving the middle class. The corporate republic simply administers the spoils system. On a day-to-day basis, the business of its leadership is to deliver favors to their clients. These range

---

*The term *caging* refers to the practice of using returned mail to challenge the validity of a voter's registration—a practice used by the Republican Party to impede voters in African American neighborhoods in Florida and elsewhere in 2004.

from coal companies to sweatshop operators to military contractors. They include the misanthropes who led the campaign to destroy the estate tax; Charles Schwab, who suggested the dividend tax cut of 2003; the "Benedict Arnold" companies that move their taxable income to Bermuda or the Isle of Jersey. They include the privatizers of Social Security and those who put the drug companies in position to profit from Medicare. Everywhere you look, regulatory functions have been turned over to lobbyists. Everywhere you look, public decisions yield gains to specific private persons. Everywhere you look, the public decision is made by the agent of a private party for the purpose of delivering private gain. This is not an accident: it is a system.

In the corporate republic that presides over the Predator State, nothing is done for the common good. Indeed, the men in charge do not recognize that public purposes exist. For this reason, the concept of competence has no relevance: to be incompetent, you must at least be trying. But the men in charge are not trying: they have friends, and enemies, and as for the rest—we are the prey. Hurricane Katrina illustrated this perfectly, as Bush gave contracts to Halliburton and at the same time tied up efforts to restore the city. The actual population of New Orleans was at best an afterthought; once dispersed, it was quickly forgotten. Several hundred thousand Democratic voters were scattered to the hinterlands of Texas and Georgia, where they would no longer hold the swing votes.

Is this class war? No. In a strict sense it is not, for not everyone who is successful under capitalism is a fan of the Predator State. Indeed the predatory model can help us understand why many rich and successful people came to hate the Bush administration and why major parts of business as a whole eventually swung into opposition against it.

Predation is the enemy of honest and independent and especially of sustainable business, of businesses that simply want to sell to the public and make a decent living over the long run. In a world where the winners are all connected, it is not only the prey (who by and large carry little political weight) who lose out. It is everyone who has not licked the appropriate boots. Predatory regimes are, more or less exactly, like protection rackets: powerful and feared but neither loved nor respected. They cannot reward everyone, and therefore they do not enjoy a broad political base. In addition, they are intrinsically unstable, something that does not trouble the predators but makes life for ordinary business enterprise exceptionally trying. Economic instability is in fact much more serious for small business operations than for large ones, and much harsher on the poor than on the rich.

It is reasonably obvious that to tolerate the Predator State is a formula for eventual national economic failure. It will lead, over time, to the crowding out of advanced, innovative, and useful businesses within each industrial line by their reactionary and backward counterparts. Where the reactionary branches of business—the worst polluters, the flagrant monopolists, the technological footdraggers—are given control over the system and capital markets reward them, their more progressive counterparts will eventually give up, disappear, or move away. Bad business practices will drive out good. Ultimately the country as a whole will become, in effect, a repository of the worst business practices and correspondingly unable to assert leadership in the world economy at large. This is the evolutionary opposite of the Scandinavian model. It is the race to the bottom, driven forward by government itself.

And equally: predators suck the capacity from government and deplete it of the ability to govern. In the short run, again, this looks like simple incompetence, but this is an illusion. Predators do not mind being thought incompetent: the accusation helps to obscure their actual agenda. But if the government is predatory, then it too will fail in every substantial way. Government will not cope with global warming, or Hurricane Katrina, or the occupation of Iraq, or Election Day chaos, or avian influenza, or the proliferation of nuclear weapons. Nothing will work, and nothing will be done about the fact that nothing works. Failure on that scale is not due to incompetence. Rather, it is intended. There is a willful indifference to the problem of competence. Inside government, no one cares. The attention of the people in charge is focused on other goals.

The end of the Predator State will come only when the more reasonable, more progressive part of the business community insists on it and is willing to make common cause with unions, consumers, environmentalists, and other mobilized social groups to bring the predators to heel. And the question is: What will it take? Will that "more reasonable" element ever be heard from? And will it be heard from, especially, while it remains important enough to matter? Or will action be delayed and blocked until such time as meaningful reform has no effective constituency left?

Dealing with this issue is, in other words, a race against time.

PART THREE

Dealing with Predators

CHAPTER ELEVEN

The Inadequacy
of Making Markets Work

M arxism used to be the hard-boiled left-wing dissident's creed, a doctrine founded on class conflict and the romance of working-class revolution. Unfortunately there were actual Marxist countries; "real existing socialism" took care of the romance. Meanwhile, Keynes and his allies in the progressive movement offered ways to reconcile the capitalists and the workers to avoid the calamity of revolution and the tyrannies that follow, through regulation and the management of total demand. But the price of progressive Keynesianism was big government: establishing countervailing power against the authority of private business. Free-market conservatives, once they recovered from the Great Depression, were inclined to reject that gift, preferring to take their chances with class conflict, and Keynesianism lost its leverage when the threat of Marxism disappeared.

Now we have a new liberalism, sometimes called the Third Way, which consists of hewing as closely as possible to market solutions. If the presumption of modern conservatives is simple—that markets work best when left alone—this new breed of domesticated liberals puts a simple gloss on it: government can help. But the well-brought-up modern liberal cautiously insists that in making this omelette, no eggs need be broken. The government should work unobtrusively, distorting as little as possible the outcomes that markets would otherwise achieve. Grand schemes for employment, distribution, infrastructure, or the environment are off the table; nothing is possible or permitted that would undermine the authority of the market in a fundamental way.

To concede the authority of the market is to affirm the legitimacy of the hierarchies that markets produce. Everyone in the system has a social role; there are no class enemies, no parasites, no leisure class, and not even anyone whose economic role is superfluous and unneeded. The market system is not open to fundamental reform; power relations cannot be changed. The system is already engineered for the best; new architects and new planners are not required. That is the starting point for the policy discussion. What is left for the Third Way is to tinker with the plumbing.

Having ceded this much ground, reputable liberals in modern America thus operate on a narrow ledge, differentiated from the conservatives by one basic premise. Both groups accept that policy must work through markets. They differ only on what it takes to make markets work.

Unlike conservatives, liberals permit themselves to admit that market mechanisms may fail from time to time. Prices and wages may be rigid, information may be asymmetric, and the costs of doing business may be too high. The policy game therefore becomes one of efficient market design. And yet, though well intentioned, it is largely a mug's game; in area after area, the pursuit of "market-friendly" policy solutions is the search for measures that have the virtue of being politically innocuous and moderately useful and have the defect of being ineffective. The perfectly functioning market is a will-o'-the-wisp in most areas to which this concept is applied, and in a good many of them the "market" itself barely exists. What does not exist cannot be perfected by minor adjustments. In many cases, the right policy requires limiting, restricting, regulating, disciplining, defeating, or bypassing markets, or even shutting them down. This is not the same as making them work.

Job training is a canonical example of the well-brought-up liberal's urge to make markets work. The policy follows from an argument about the nature of unemployment and low wages, and as with nearly all similar exercises, the argument begins by assuming the existence of a market. In this case, the market is known as the "labor market," and it supposedly matches demand for labor, which comes from businesses, to the supply offered by individuals. If individuals lack the minimal skills that business requires, they cannot compete for jobs. Unemployment must result. The purpose of job training therefore is to move individuals into a position from which they can effectively compete for available employment.

In this analysis every detail is correct: there are businesses that require labor, and there are individuals who would like jobs but do not qualify for them. It is true that a job-training program can help. Yet the sum of these details falls far short of the claim made for them as a whole. It does not follow that job-training programs reduce unemployment or poverty. It is not even clear that they foster the creation of a single additional job.

The problem is that poverty and unemployment are not much influenced by the qualities and qualifications of the workforce. They depend, rather, on the state of demand for labor. They depend on whether firms want to hire all the workers who may be available and at the pay rates that firms are willing, or required, to offer, especially to the lowest paid. Firms in the happy position of strongly expanding markets and bright profit prospects can almost always find the workers they need, either pulling directly from the pool of the unemployed or poaching qualified workers from other firms (or nations). For such firms, the costs of rudimentary job training for unskilled and semiskilled positions are secondary; if workers with appropriate training are not readily available, they can be trained in-house. Conversely, firms facing stagnant demand and bleak prospects do not add workers simply because trained candidates happen to be available.

Job training in most offices is extremely specific to that office: its systems, its bosses, its routines. Generic training programs, the only kind government can provide, cannot duplicate this function. Studies that evaluate job-training programs (and there are many) therefore generally focus on the effectiveness of a program in placing its graduates in jobs, and perhaps on their later success in holding those jobs and moving up a job ladder. But such studies confront a classic chicken-and-egg issue: Is the success of a particular individual due to the "value-added" of a training program, or is it the result of having chosen capable people for admission to the program in the first place? This is a difficult, perhaps even an unanswerable, question, which tends to absorb the energy of those concerned with program evaluation. But even assuming an answer is found, the only question that will have been answered is, Did the program effectively help its graduates compete for the available employment? This has nothing to do with the total amount of employment, unemployment, or the poverty rate.

There is nothing wrong with job training as a solution to the problem—if there were a problem—of a "skill mismatch." There is nothing wrong with job training as a form of affirmative action, assisting people to overcome physical or social disadvantages, and moving them up the applicant queue in the hiring game. But if companies are not hiring, job training is irrelevant. It is equally irrelevant, if they are hiring, to the numbers they plan to hire. Either way, it is no solution to unemployment and no substitute for programs that are solutions.

Conversely, if you really want to reduce unemployment and poverty, it is obvious from recent history that job training has nothing to do with it. Job training was not expanded dramatically in the early Clinton years, and the fall in unemployment that occurred after 1994 did not follow any increase in the general competence of the workforce. It was due to the great information technology boom, along with cheap credit, a boom in housing, and a general increase in state and local government spending. The prime beneficiaries of the boom were the nation's most fashionable technologists and engineers. But indirect benefits flowed massively down the chain of employment. Unemployment rates fell to 4 percent for the whole population; they reached 6.9 percent for black men, 6.2 percent for black women, and 13.1 percent for teenagers: in each case, they were the lowest values on record.* Poverty rates in the African American population fell to 22.5 percent in 2000, the lowest on record; in the Hispanic community, they fell to 21.4 percent by 2001, also the lowest on record. None of this had anything to with job training except to prove how little it matters when jobs are actually available.

There is a larger message in this tale. It is that the "labor market"—conceived as an interaction between forces of supply and those of demand—really does not exist, or to put it as Keynes did, in 1936, there is no supply curve for labor.† The total demand for labor determines employment, and that is essentially the entire story. "Plugging in the supply side," an obsession of many economists since the 1980s, counts for little in the real world of work, since it is employers, not workers, who control the scale of the workplace. Employers may like job training because it saves them some minor costs, or because it deflects attention from stronger medicine. They do not delude them-

*The value given for black men was reached in 1999; the others cited were reached in 2000.

†John Maynard Keynes, *The General Theory of Employment, Interest, and Money* (London: Macmillan, 1936).

selves that it is an actual cure for unemployment—and in many cases, they would oppose it if it were.

Here is another glass of liberal small beer: universal preschool. In a recent book, Clinton economic adviser Gene Sperling makes an impassioned case for placing universal preschool near the center of a liberal program. He cites, in detail, the track record of Head Start:

> The foundational study on the benefits of investing in preschool began forty-two years ago in Ypsilanti, Michigan. There, a group of researchers and educators began a remarkable experiment at the Perry Preschool. They split 123 African American kids into two groups. One was enrolled in a quality preschool program and the other was not. The study followed the two groups up through high school and recently published the findings through age forty. The results are striking. At age forty, 65 percent of the preschoolers had graduated from high school or received an equivalent degree, while only 45 percent of the non-preschoolers had progressed that far. The preschoolers had an average income of $20,800 . . . non-preschoolers' average incomes were $5,000 less.*

Let's grant that all of this is true, and perfectly typical of preschool programs everywhere. What does it demonstrate? At best, it shows that preschool is a good thing: it helped, in this case, to impart skills and capacity that made it easier to navigate the miserable economic climate of Michigan in the 1980s and 1990s. But Sperling's inference—that with universal preschool, everyone would enjoy these gains—is false. Without for a moment challenging the value of preschool programs to those who experience them, it takes only a moment's thought to demonstrate why the inference he would have us draw cannot be right.

Suppose every child in Michigan, beginning forty-two years ago, had enjoyed the same beneficial preschool experience as the fortunate sixty or so in the Ypsilanti study. Suppose further that the sequence of economic catastrophes visited on Michigan—and especially on its African American labor force—had been exactly the same: the rising challenge of Japanese competition in the automobile industry in the 1970s, the near collapse of the Chrysler Corporation in 1979, the devastating Rust Belt recessions of the early 1980s. How much would these eco-

*Gene Sperling, *The Pro-Growth Progressive: An Economic Strategy for Shared Prosperity* (New York: Simon & Schuster, 2005), p. 150.

nomic outcomes have been changed by universal preschool? Not at all—except to the tiny extent that the spending on preschool itself created new, publicly funded teaching jobs in the affected communities.

Under those conditions, what would the Ypsilanti study, capturing a fair sample of preschoolers, have shown? The answer is clear: economic outcomes for the African American community would have been exactly what they actually were. But now every job, every case of joblessness—and every prison cell—would be filled by someone who went through preschool. Thus, the perfect match of liberal puff and conservative rule: better-educated people, with no more hope for the future than they would have had without the education. Sperling's argument, in other words, is a simple logical fallacy. It is based on the false inference that because something works for an individual, it will also change outcomes for the entire population. To this fallacy one must add the mundane sin of wishful thinking. Sperling wants very badly to believe that preschool "causes" better economic outcomes. But in the large scheme of economics this is absurd on its face. Life experiences are not governed by what happens at the age of four; even the best prekindergarten experience is likely to be washed out by recession, depression, unemployment, and war.

Don't get me wrong: I *favor* universal preschool. In particular, it's a very good thing for *mothers*, for whom it makes balancing work and parenting much easier. Services aimed at young mothers are a seriously deficient area of social welfare policy in the United States by international standards.* But preschool is no solution for unemployment or poverty in the later lives of children. One may justifiably admire and happily support the full spectrum of human development ideas in Sperling's book, which cover future fathers, interventions against gangs, preparation for college, and help with college completion. All of this is good stuff, but it does not meet the skill demands of a future economy. In fact, no program could: those skill demands do not yet exist. We do not know what they are.

Training and even education are no substitute, in other words, for ensuring that good jobs at decent wages are actually available when needed. Yet in the work of many liberals, they are exactly that—a sub-

---

*This is partly because the United States did not experience serious population losses in either World War; such losses inspired strong pro-natalist and therefore child welfare policies in France and Germany as early as the 1920s.

stitute, not a complement, for policies aimed at full employment. The term *full employment* does not appear in Sperling's index. And that is a pity, since it was precisely the achievement of full employment, rather than new social policies, that made possible the great human gains of which veterans of the Clinton administration ought to be most proud.

But if labor is not bought or sold in a "market for skills," how about, say, health care? What is "health care," and is it bought and sold in a market? Obviously not: health care is not any specific thing, but a label covering a class of goods and services, an enormously diverse class, adapted to the specific health condition of each individual patient. There is no unit of health care; if you draw a supply-and-demand diagram, there is no quantity to put on the horizontal axis and no price to record on the vertical axis. Health care is therefore not a commodity that is bought and sold at a given price on an open market. Nor is any given medical procedure. In the overwhelming majority of cases, these are prescribed in one-on-one discussions between a medical professional following the norms and standards of the profession and a patient with extremely limited capacity to evaluate either the recommendations or the alternatives. The only issue in most instances is whether a particular doctor or clinic effectively represents the best available practice in terms of the judgments of the profession writ large. Decisions about the quality and character of health care are therefore organizational decisions; decisions about pricing do not flow from a negotiation between the patient and doctor but are based instead on norms established in negotiation among providers, insurance companies, and the government. There is not only no market in health care, there are no markets *within* health care either. The suggestion that "market forces" might be usefully deployed to regulate prices and quantities in this area runs into the basic difficulty that no such markets either do exist or could exist.

Of course, actual proposals to introduce market forces in health care are largely concerned not with the provision of health care itself but with the provision of insurance. The intrinsic costs of providing insurance are relatively low. There are no expensive inputs to purchase, no uncertainties of design or technology to be concerned with. The major inputs are personnel and computing capacity. There are few major issues of innovation; unlike the rapid changes characteristic of medical practice, the service of providing insurance to pay for them does not evolve rapidly. A successful private insurance company follows an ancient formula: it stratifies its clientele by risk class and charges premiums adapted to each class. The most successful companies are generally those that manage to exclude the riskiest clients.

Public universal health insurance schemes like Medicare do not evaluate risk. Since they are universal, they do not need to. Therefore, they save the major cost of providing private health insurance. They pay their personnel at civil service salary scales and are under no obligation to return a dividend to shareholders or meet a target rate of return. Insurance in general is therefore intrinsically a service that the public sector can competently provide at lower cost than the private sector, and from the standpoint of an entire population, selective private provision of health insurance is invariably inferior to universal public provision. Private health insurance companies would not exist except for their political capacity to forestall the creation of universal public systems, backed by their almost unlimited capacity to sow confusion among the general public over the basic economic facts. Liberals who support anything less than a common, public insurance pool have no argument. They are simply tugging their forelocks and bending their knee before this particular bastion of private power.

Thus, in jobs and health care, policies aimed at "making markets work" misconstrue the nature of the policy problem because they superimpose the artificial construction of supply and demand over a mass of phenomena that are in fact unified only by a label. When you hear someone speak of a market, the first question should be: Is it real? Is there a commodity, and can one really choose among competing suppliers? If not, there is no market, and an analysis based on supply and demand will not work.

The mania for markets where markets do not belong reached an absurd level with electricity in the 1990s. This is a "market" where there is a commodity—electricity is nothing if not that. But it is a market that cannot be made competitive on the supply side, at least for household users. Until the day of household windmills and universal solar panels, electricity inevitably pits a small number of major producers against millions of (politically) powerless consumers. Treating this as a "free market" is a formula for disaster. Yet deregulation of electricity markets swept the United States in the 1990s on the assumption—or, rather, the assertion—that competition between generating plants would lower costs and improve services. As the catastrophe of the California energy crisis showed, the opposite occurred: electricity prices could be readily manipulated by taking capacity off-line at times of peak demand, forcing the state to purchase power from sources beyond its boundaries. (Power could also be routed out of state and resold back to the state at enormous profit.) Consumers paid not the average cost of production but the spot price or marginal cost, with the result that their bills surged. Yet the technology (as well as the time and patience) available to them meant that they could not adjust their demand for power to the price peaks. The result was a predatory monopolist's dream world: pricing power in a market with nearly inelastic demand. Generators with relatively low costs did not cut prices but earned high profits, which should, in principle, have inspired them to expand capacity. They did not, and for a perfectly rational reason: it was precisely the shortage of capacity that led to monopoly pricing power in the first place.

The California fiasco is currently being replayed in slow motion in Texas, where it has been argued that a relatively self-contained power grid in a large state would generate better conditions for the successful development of competitive conditions. Once again, it is a farce. Deregulation and competition when consumers have no real power of choice will always lead to the abuse of power. It is a pure illusion to expect natural monopolies to transform into perfect competitors; calling something a "market" does not a competitive market make.

Unfortunately for the future of our blue planet, a similar mania has taken hold of the economic discussion of climate change. Here, schemes to create a "market" in greenhouse gases have come to the forefront, assiduously promoted by market economists who managed to have such a system written into the Kyoto Treaty.* A similar plan was advanced in 2006 in California by Governor Arnold Schwarzenegger, an outspoken admirer of Milton Friedman. Emissions trading is the centerpiece of the Stern Review Report on climate change, authored by Sir Nicholas Stern on behalf of the then chancellor of the Exchequer of the UK, Gordon Brown.† Stern's book is a particularly effective, grim, and foreboding account of the impending costs of cli-

---

*Article 17 of the Kyoto Protocol states, "The Conference of the Parties shall define the relevant principles, modalities, rules and guidelines, in particular for verification, reporting and accountability for emissions trading. The Parties included in Annex B may participate in emissions trading for the purposes of fulfilling their commitments under Article 3."

†Nicholas Stern, *The Economics of Climate Change: The Stern Review* (Cambridge: Cambridge University Press, 2006). Brown currently is prime minister of the UK.

mate change and of the need for action, which makes its advocacy of the "market solution" all the more credible in many eyes.

The economic logic of a "cap-and-trade" system is simple: government sets an overall level of pollution, and polluters buy and sell pieces of it. In this way, those who need most to pollute can do so, while those who can clean up most cheaply profit from doing that. It sounds logical, and it seems to have worked reasonably well in some local situations. In a single metropolitan airshed such as the Los Angeles basin, such a system can help polluters decide what type of plant to run, what types of pollutants to emit, at what hours of the day, and under what weather conditions. A cap-and-trade system is credited, by reputable observers,* with having helped reduce sulfur emissions that were a significant source of acid rain, and at a substantially lower cost than had been forecast by the Environmental Protection Agency in local and regional airsheds. So far, so good. But as a stand-alone device for dealing with global carbon dioxide emissions? That's another story.

Like all other market-based policies, cap-and-trade assumes that the sum of decentralized decisions, taken by thousands of businesses and millions of individuals, is the same as the best achievable result. But the existence of interdependence and externalities and asymmetric information and transactions costs is sufficient to show that there is no reason to believe this. As Joseph Schumpeter wrote of technological change, you may add up as many carriages as you please, but you will not get a railway thereby. Carbon dioxide is a global problem. The fact the Europeans emit about half, per capita, as do Americans for a similar quality of life is not a matter of market choices but of the way their lives are organized, of the housing patterns and transportation networks and power grids designed in part by the European states. Changing masses of individual driving decisions in America will not transform our systems into the efficiency equivalent of theirs, and the attempt to do so by prices alone could put the economy in such a slowdown that the ordinary course of progress toward more efficient patterns of energy use might stop.

An extreme version of the market solution to climate change was proposed recently by Princeton ethicist Peter Singer.† No one would

---

*Eban Goodstein, *The Trade-Off Myth: Fact and Fiction About Jobs and the Environment* (Washington, D.C.: Island Press, 1999).

†Peter Singer, "A Fair Deal on Climate Change," *Policy Innovations*, June 26, 2007.

accuse Singer of being a market fundamentalist; he is just an example of the extent to which markets are subsumed into the infrastructure of public discourse by people who do not spend much time thinking about how they work in practice. Singer's idea is to assign the property right in carbon emissions on an equal per capita basis worldwide, allowing each country to trade with the others for the right to emit. Thus India, with one-fifth the world's population, would receive rights to one-fifth of total emissions, even though India as a whole emits only one-fifteenth of world carbon dioxide. India could therefore sell two-thirds of its allocated quota, permitting the United States (say) to emit carbon dioxide at far above its per capita share. India would gain development resources and would be under no obligation to cut carbon dioxide emissions (so long as it did not increase them). The United States, meanwhile, would face a choice that would lead in principle to emissions reduction to the point where the marginal cost of abatement just equaled the marginal cost of emissions permits on the world market. It sounds eminently "fair and practical," which is what Singer claims.

But Singer is an expert on what is fair, not on what is practical. It is obvious—or ought to be—that the mechanism of global trading permits will work only if India, China, the United States, and other participants can actually regulate and control their internal carbon dioxide emissions. The trading system would only establish how much each country was entitled to emit. It would do nothing, by itself, to settle the question within each country of which technologies to foster, which power plants to close, how to design cities that are energy efficient and light on carbon dioxide emissions. Those decisions would remain entirely within the purview of national governments, which, in the cases of India and China, at least, are incompetent to execute them. The United States, as a buyer of permits, would therefore have on its hands the equivalent of an unenforceable contract. What recourse would the United States have when it emerged that India (say) was developing rapidly and emitting more than the contracts stipulated? The market mechanism provides nothing more than a lofty and elegant device for reaching decisions that can perfectly well be negotiated, and of which many aspects will have to be negotiated directly between national governments in any event. The solution to greenhouse gas emissions and

---

*The case of the large-scale payments called for under the Singer proposal also poses a puzzle. China presently holds more than a trillion dollars in U.S. bonds, and

to the climate crisis, similarly, cannot avoid passing through the hands of a competent public administration. Conversely, if there is no competent public administration, the problem will not be solved.

There are areas of the economy where wholly unregulated private markets are possible. This is the case in many instances of daily life, where the product transacted is transparent to both buyer and seller. The bookshop and especially the secondhand bookshop are nice examples, involving no hidden hazards and unit prices that are low in relation to customer incomes. Barbershops, landscaping services, bowling alleys, cinemas, and outdoor concerts are similar: what you see is what you get, potential losses are small, and there is little apparent need to validate that the service provided is in fact the one represented. (Even so, in rich countries regulation pervades these services anyway, from hygiene to fire codes—and a good thing too.)

There are also many areas of the economy where the regulatory hand of the state can work smoothly, efficiently, and unobtrusively—where problems with markets can be fixed. Clothing manufacturers, it seems, can generally be relied on to comply with the requirement that they disclose accurately the fabric content of the garments they sell. Though abuses and failures persist, grocery stores long ago came to terms, as a general matter, with the U.S. Department of Agriculture and the Food and Drug Administration. And even in a market as diverse and individuated as that for private housing, the broad similarities between houses and between households have made it possible for banks to provide standardized mortgage instruments, which can then be securitized and resold smoothly into a secondary market—that is, until the subprime operators came along and poisoned that particular well. The cost of buying or selling a house is not trivial, but it is not insurmountable either, and has not prevented the emergence of a robust and for the most part relatively liquid housing market. Markets,

India, though not so wealthy, is also a substantial holder of U.S. financial reserves. If either country wanted, or could use, more purchasing power in the global economy, they could deploy these reserves. It is therefore questionable that they would have any use for large additional cash transfers. The case of sub-Saharan Africa is somewhat different: there countries are cash-constrained and could use the sale of emissions rights to support development goals. But in many places serious questions of internal governance stand in the way; as a broad rule countries determined to reduce poverty (China, Venezuela, and Cuba are notable examples in today's world) do so without aid; countries dependent on aid do not manage to end poverty.

in other words, do exist, and there are policies that can make, and have made, many economic markets work. But that is not the issue.

The issue is whether, as a regulatory strategy, "making markets work" is a suitable universal metaphor for guiding the processes of policy design. And this, it plainly is not. It fails to capture the intrinsic possibilities for abuse of power. It fails to make easier the complex private decisions associated with technological challenges, and thus environmental policy. In all of these areas, markets have not evolved, and they have not arisen spontaneously where the opportunity presented itself, and they will not develop fully even if the rudiments of market structure are erected by regulatory fiat. There is a reason for that: where the metaphor of the market does work, it doesn't work. And it can't be made to work, so we need something else entirely—new metaphor, let's say, or at least an idea that has been down so long it has nowhere to go but up.

CHAPTER TWELVE

The Need for Planning

As liberals emerge from a protective crouch that has lasted three decades, the inadequacy of their policy vision must be faced. The various goals of expanded health insurance, universal preschool, job training, and cap-and-trade programs for carbon dioxide are assuredly well intended—except that once we have all those things, we will not yet have solved the fundamental problems to which they are addressed. Health care costs will still be uncontrolled. Jobs will still be in short supply. The rich will still have a big educational edge over the working poor. And climate change will still go on. The polite solutions to these problems have a common drawback: they do not do enough. To deal with them effectively—and to deal with them all together—requires the use of a dirty word: *planning*.

In the discourse inherited from the age of Reagan, syphilis, leprosy, and planning more or less rank together: they are all no longer frightening, slightly ridiculous, curable afflictions from another time. What Joseph Schumpeter thought drearily inevitable, what Friedrich von Hayek denounced as the greatest threat to freedom, a later generation has reduced to a sound bite. After all, the Soviet economy was planned, and it collapsed. Does anything more need to be said? (Instinctively, the epithet *central* is affixed to the word *planning* in order to discredit it.) No economic topic except price control is more easily pushed off the table; no declaration comes more easily than that one favors the market and opposes planning. This needs to change.

The experience of the wider world—even that of the most despised countries—provides no general case against economic planning and also none in favor of unfettered markets as a substitute for a planning system. On the contrary, it shows that in a properly designed system, planning and markets do not contradict each other. They are not mutually exclusive. Rather, the choice of one or another for any particular problem is a matter of what works best for the purpose: it's a question of a social and political division of labor, of what tools are needed for what goal.

Markets distribute today's production to consumers. This they do reasonably well: in ensuring that everyone eats, cash and also food stamps (an effective market-friendly solution to the problem of hunger) are less obtrusive and more efficient than rationing, soup lines, or the distribution of surplus cheese. Very few who live under rationing long regret its departure, and in a matter like food, individuals for the most part can be trusted to make their own choices.* Choices and variety are not only instrumental, a way of satisfying diverse preferences. They are also intrinsically desirable: they give people the satisfaction of making judgments, and therefore an element of genuine personal control, in the comparatively simple spheres of daily life.

Planning, properly conceived, deals with the use of today's resources to meet tomorrow's needs. It specifically tackles issues markets cannot solve: the choice of how much in the aggregate to invest (and therefore to save), the directions to be taken by new technology, the question of how much weight and urgency are to be given to environmental issues, the role of education, and of scientific knowledge, and culture. Decisions on these matters involve representing the interests of the future—interests that are poorly represented by markets. And in the modern world, planning happens: it is what corporations exist to do. The only issue, therefore, is whether the planning function is to be left entirely in the hands of private corporations—and therefore to a business and especially to a banking elite, some of them domestic and others foreign—or whether the government and the larger public are entitled to play a role.

Planning can be narrow-minded. It can be entirely corrupt. It can be misguided. In China, the planners can build the Three Gorges Dam, increase the electrical capacity of the entire country by 10 percent, and relocate millions of people in its path. Environmentalists warned that the lake would silt up within a few years and that it would turn into the world's greatest cesspool—and they were right. No market would have

---

*Unfortunately, here too predators are frequently at work, degrading the quality of prepared foods peddled to poor people and making it ever more difficult to secure a sound diet on a low income. But we will not go into that issue in further detail here.

built the Three Gorges Dam or have permitted it to be built. But then no market would have built the Hoover Dam either, and that one worked out reasonably well. Moreover, the market did not give the United States jet air travel while Europe built its trains: those were planning decisions, for better or worse in each case.

In real life, planning cannot be avoided. The questions are: Who will carry it out, according to what principles, and to what effect? In the case of the United States, state planning largely occurs inside the national security cocoons of the Defense and Energy departments. Here again the record is mixed. The history of atomic energy on the North American continent is a sad one of technological forcing, lax standards, and environmental poison. Likewise the history of jet air travel is one of dual-use technologies and subsidies to a firm of military importance. The same is true of the history of information technologies, perhaps most dramatically the Internet itself, which migrated from the military to the civilian sphere (giving us instant free communication at the price of universal surveillance). The history of compulsory planning cannot be purged of its warts; this is the conservative and the libertarian case, and it does no good to deny the force of their argument. But this does not make planning unnecessary or mean that one can do without it.

Again the issue is, In comparison to what? A state that does not plan does not, by default, turn this function over to the market. Even if the market is perfectly efficient, it still suffers from two ineradicable defects. The first relates to the distribution of income and power: the market conveys signals only in proportion to the purchasing power of the individuals transmitting them. The poor do not matter to the market. The second relates to representation: people not yet born do not turn up at the stores. They send no market signals at all.

Defenders of markets talk about futures markets, or long-term contracts, arguing that these serve the needs of the future and obviate the need for planning. This is a misunderstanding. Such markets and contracts serve only the needs of today's economic actors; they are a way of projecting the needs and interests of the present forward into the future, of managing risks for today's market actors. They have nothing to do with preparing for, protecting, or representing the needs of the future. (In theoretical models favored by academic economists, this problem is elided by assuming that economic agents live forever and enjoy perfect foresight over all future states of the economy.) In the market economy, no one speaks for those who will follow. Speaking for the interests of successor generations is a function that has to be imposed on the market by outside agency and regulatory power; it is an act of imagination. The great fallacy of the market myth lies simply in the belief, for which no foundation in economics exists, that markets can think ahead. But they cannot. The role of planning is to provide that voice, if necessary *against* the concerted interest and organized power of those alive today.

A country that does not have a public planning system simply turns that function over to a network of private enterprise—domestic or foreign—which then becomes the true seat of economic power. And that is why the struggle over planning is, and remains, such a sensitive issue: it is a struggle over power. It is a struggle not between democracy and the corporation, but between those—scientists, engineers, some economists, and public intellectuals—who attempt to represent the common and future interest and those—banks, companies, lobbyists, and the economists whom they employ—that represent only the tribal and current interest. It is an uneven struggle. It is a struggle in which, outside of wartime and the zone of permanent planning called the Pentagon, the planners have prevailed on only rare occasions, notably during the Great Depression. But it is an inescapable struggle. If the future is to be provided for, you must have a community of planners, and some way must be found to support them, to permit them to develop their plans and resolve their differences, and to give them access to the levers of public power. To walk away from this problem with a shrug about "markets" is to disenfranchise the future. To enable planning guarantees nothing. But to "rely on the market" is to guarantee that the interests of the future will never be provided for.

The American reality for the present is that state planning is for emergencies—for that protected category of public policy issues covered by the flag of national security. Here planning is accepted. It is even demanded—even or perhaps especially by conservatives—when clear and present danger warrants. World War II led, in this respect, to the cold war and the global war on terror: each served to justify—with a diminishing degree of authenticity as time went on—the reservation of a sphere of American economic activity to a planning process. But now all of that is to be superseded by a global state of emergency that will not go away.

On August 29, 2005, as Hurricane Katrina tore through the levees that had protected New Orleans, it exposed exactly what markets cannot do: it focused attention, albeit too briefly, on the most massive failing of American government in the twenty-first century, which is its incapacity to plan effectively in advance of great dangers or in response to them. The catastrophe that hit the population of New Orleans, southern Louisiana, and the Mississippi Gulf Coast on the days that followed stemmed from the wilful neglect, decline, and disintegration of coherent public forethought, carried out deliberately by a political class that has used the metaphor and myth of markets to abandon the responsibility to plan.

About 500,000 people lived in New Orleans on August 29, 2005. It was well known, to those who had responsibility for them, that a hurricane of level three or higher on the Saffir-Simpson scale would, if it came ashore below New Orleans, destroy the system of levees that kept the city from complete destruction in a flood. It was known that sooner or later, this disaster would happen. Three years earlier, the *New Orleans Times-Picayune* had printed a precise account of how the disaster would occur, as the counterclockwise winds of a north-bound hurricane delivered a storm surge over the levees separating the city from Lake Borgne, to the east, and from the canals that ran into Lake Pontchartrain, to the North.*

Given those facts, the public obligation was clear: either the levees should have been reinforced until they could cope with an event substantially less probable than a Force Three hurricane, or the low-lying areas of the city should have been abandoned and the levees rebuilt around the areas that could be protected. As a conceptual matter, plans actually existed; this was not a case where the underlying technologies were unknown. The Army Corps of Engineers knew what the levees required. But the will, the ability, and the compulsory authority—in one word, the public power—to carry out the plan did not exist. Moreover, owing to the demands on the army budget of the war in Iraq, funds for even basic levee maintenance had been cut. Levees subside when they are not maintained, and the city was in a deep state of vulnerability when Katrina struck its glancing but fatal blow.

New Orleans did have an evacuation "plan"—or the elements of one. That plan was quite simple: people were to get into their personal cars and drive out of town; the interstate highways would be turned into one-

---

*Mark Schleifstein and John McQuaid, "The Big One," *Times-Picayune*, June 24, 2002, p. 1.

way escape routes. And this plan (known as contraflow) worked. But it worked only for those for whom it had been designed: the car-owning part of the population. In any large city many people do not have private cars or could not drive them if they did: the elderly, the disabled, the poor, and those who, for whatever reason, simply prefer to live without the expense and trouble. In New Orleans, as would be the case in any other substantial city in America, their numbers ran into many thousands. No provision had been made for them; they had no places to gather, no buses were dispatched to pick them up, and if there had been, there would have been no places for them to go. For the survivors, these details were worked out after the fact. The price of failing to plan properly was, in the first place, unnecessary death, and in the second, a vast and costly improvisation after the fact. And as with the levees, the main issue was not a failure to think: it was the absence of public authority, will, and money to turn thought into execution.

In the months following the hurricane, once again the failure to have a plan—or, more precisely, to have a credible planning mechanism with compulsory authority—remains the central obstacle to recovery in New Orleans. A master plan would have told exiled and returning residents alike what to expect and when, by way of reconstruction, services, and security. In this way, it would have tried to overcome the collective-action problem inherent in all such situations: the fact that no one will rationally invest in rebuilding a destroyed neighborhood until they can be reasonably sure that their neighbors will do the same. A plan would have provided credit and commenced clearance of neighborhoods that could not be resettled or rebuilt, whether because of long-term inability to provide for their security or simply because of low population densities. None of this has happened, and even though the levees are largely repaired, the City of New Orleans is today largely a ruin.

New Orleans encapsulates the dilemma of planning writ small. Global warming raises the same issues writ large. The publication in 2007 of the Fourth Assessment Report of the Intergovernmental Panel on Climate Change (IPCC) makes clear, in a way that cannot be gainsaid, that the problem of technological planning and disaster management will soon enough become the central security issue facing every part of the planet.* And it will become so in a way that must necessarily remove a central ele-

*"Climate Change 2007: Synthesis Report," Intergovernmental Panel on Climate Change Fourth Assessment Report, November 17, 2007.

ment of economic life—control over the sources and uses of energy—from the purview of private corporations and place it under public administration. Indefinitely. That is the reality of climate change if we are going to manage climate change and not simply succumb to it. Taken in its essentials, the impending climate catastrophe is a phenomenon for which the basic evidence is clear and well within the understanding of the ordinary educated person. We know the relationship between global temperature and carbon dioxide concentrations in the atmosphere. We know that rapid growth in carbon burning places the current concentration of carbon dioxide in the atmosphere outside all historical limits. We know that there will be severe consequences for drought, flood, agricultural productivity, and storm damage in much of the world.

Ultimately we know that if this process is not controlled, the West Antarctic ice sheet and parts of the ice sheet covering Greenland will start to collapse. We do not know when this will happen, but the possibility is there that it could be within the lifetimes of children now being born, or within the lifetimes of their children. We know that when half the ice in these two places is gone, sea levels will rise by twenty feet. We know that the consequence will be the loss, through flooding, of every beach, every low-lying island, every coastal marsh, and nearly every coastal city on the face of the globe, as well as the ports, airports, power plants, refineries, and other seaside infrastructure that has been built up over three hundred years. We know that carbon concentrations sufficient to begin an irreversible process of ice-sheet melting could be reached in this century. And we know that the process of averting this must begin quite soon if this prospect is to be avoided.

Suppose we do not act. Ultimately in the United States, New York City, Boston, South Florida, Houston, and much of the Bay Area will flood. In Great Britain, London will be lost. The Netherlands will largely disappear. So will large parts of Bangladesh and the city of Shanghai. On the hotter, drier land, about half of the existing global biodiversity will be lost. The implications for farming, manufacturing, and the trade that delivers goods from their producers to their consumers remain to be determined. There is little doubt so far that the human species will ultimately survive. But its numbers will be greatly diminished, its patterns of industrial society disrupted, if not destroyed. This will happen unless, within a few decades, greenhouse emissions are reduced by at least half, and possibly much more—to within the capacity of the biosphere to absorb them.

What can be done? What should be done? At this moment, we do not yet know in detail. In the IPCC, we can come as close as humanity has ever come to a trusted voice on a scientific matter. Yet politically we have not advanced beyond setting broad targets and timetables for the reduction of carbon emissions, and we are not meeting the targets.

For the purposes of argument, let's stipulate a concrete technical goal: to get gasoline out of automobiles and coal out of power plants within thirty years. To achieve that we will need a plan, set by an authority with public credibility as the IPCC, and a far greater amount of public power than that organization has. The power must be sufficient to bring the auto companies into the forefront of a technical transformation and to quell the inevitable rebellion of the oil companies. It must also be sufficient, on the international front, to prevent the oil and coal not burned in the United States from being burned somewhere else. In other words, it must have a national dimension, aimed at conservation and technical transformation inside the United States, and a global dimension, aimed at capping the worldwide emission of greenhouse gases. A first task—the urgent, immediate task—will be to bring the entity necessary for this purpose into existence. The requirement for economic planning on this scale—essentially a global effort to delay and ultimately avert the collapse of organized civilization on this planet—brings us squarely into conflict with certain economic freedoms and certain classes of personal choice. Large parts of the current consumption pattern of the rich countries will be changed, and those of the developing countries cannot be allowed to evolve toward the present consumption patterns of the rich.

It is true that until the day the emergency arrives, the forms of coercion required to make the essential changes on a crash basis are likely to be unacceptable, and the attempt to apply them risks provoking the political collapse of the entire project. But if the emergency is allowed to arrive, then, as with New Orleans, the emergency itself will cripple the capacity to respond. The fate of New Orleans will become the fate of the country as a whole—and even more so that of the wider world. The path to survival of the existing human way of life requires acting now, in ways that the political system can support, to achieve goals within three or four decades that can avert a catastrophe that is, at a reasonable guess, somewhere between six decades and two centuries off. Nothing quite like it has ever been attempted.

Achieving the goal will require something far more than compulsion. It will require the agreement and the cooperation, plus the active insistence, of a mobilized population—a population that must be not only willing to change its patterns of economic life, but also willing to demand that the choices offered to it by the planning system comport, practically above all other priorities, with the larger goal of reducing greenhouse gas emissions. In other words, it must be a population that is aware of the danger, conscious of the need to act, and mobilized to act in ways that promote rather than obstruct the objective.

What are the elements of such a plan? A rough template can be drawn from the only major example of successful planning in the history of the United States: the economic mobilization for World War II. That mobilization doubled GDP within four years, reduced unemployment to zero, placed an army of 11 million men and women in the field, controlled inflation, and established both the technical and financial foundation for a generation of stable prosperity and social progress—albeit founded on ever-increasing use of fossil fuels. Unraveling fifty years of burning will require economic transformation on a similar scale, begun with an almost similar intensity of effort, but designed to be carried forward on a sustained basis for a longer time. It will be, for all of these reasons, substantially more difficult to pull off. The major elements are, however, just as they were before.

A first one is education. The job of alerting the broad public—in America and around the rest of the world—to the consequences of climate change and the means of its prevention cannot be left, in the end, to the initiative of Hollywood and Al Gore. It must become part of the fabric of public education in the United States, just as art, music, math, civics, evolution, and racial tolerance are all part of that fabric today. It must also become a part of the fabric of higher education, deeply incorporated not only into special programs of natural science but also into undergraduate and graduate instruction in engineering, business, economics, and public policy. For the moment, courses, curricula, and teachers in these areas barely exist. They must become mainstream, and universal, in time for this generation of American children to grow up understanding their own responsibilities in this matter.

Second, there is science. The United States has a distinguished world leadership in funding scientific research in universities and government facilities, including the nuclear laboratories at Los Alamos, Livermore, and Sandia; the health research centers at the National Institutes of Health and the Centers for Disease Control; and the

National Aeronautics and Space Administration. Where is the Center for Climate Change and Energy Transformation? It does not yet exist. But it could be brought into being within months if the will and the money were put into place.

Third, there is engineering. World War II posed for the United States specific problems of industrial mobilization: capital resources and labor had to be found to meet incredible targets for the production of aircraft, tanks, and ships within a very short period of time. In part, this was a matter of making technical choices on the basis of scientific judgments—for instance, in deciding, within the Manhattan Project, the efficient path toward the atomic bomb. But in substantial part it was also a matter of finding resources within the civilian economy that could be most efficiently transformed to military use. The great economist Simon Kuznets here played a vital role, showing how labor utilization could be increased—it was doubled, at least—without incurring increases in hourly labor costs, through a combination of increasing shifts and cutting out time-and-a-half payments for extra hours. Beyond this, civilian production in critical areas—rubber tires, private automobiles—had to be forcibly curtailed so as to free essential resources for the most rapid expansion of weapons production. Something similar will ultimately be required to make the technical transformation from gasoline engines and coal-fired power plants to successor technologies based, no doubt in part, on storable electricity and solar power. A role for economists comes in managing the price and income effects of the transition. It lies in keeping inflation at bay while making sure that appropriate prices help to structure the many private choices that will remain. Gasoline and heating oil will not, after all, disappear. But how much should they cost? That is a complex question that cannot be answered properly by the market. It depends not merely on supply and demand, but also on the costs that never surface in market calculations: the increasing scarcity of petroleum required for future generations and the environmental damage associated with burning too much of it at any one time. The price of fossil fuels needs to reflect both the consequences of their use and the interests of the future in having a residual supply on hand for purposes that cannot be easily replaced.

Yet having decided the valuations best associated with environmental necessity, you cannot simply fix the price of gas at (say) ten dollars a gallon and expect the larger economy to adjust. There are inescapable questions of fairness: people who cannot make the switch from gasoline to some other transportation technology will suffer. Up to a point they deserve—and they will certainly demand—a measure of compensation for their loss. One key is to keep the loss, and any required compensation, small by ensuring that feasible technical alternatives—for transportation, heating, and other basic needs—come into existence as they are needed. That is a matter of engineering, of the investment plan. Another key is to deliver compensation in deferred form—in effect, as an illiquid bond that generates purchasing power not in the present while the available technologies remain destructive, but in the future when they will have become more sustainable. This job—controlling the time flow of purchasing power to match the pace of technical transformation—is the economists' job. Inevitably the present-day economy will have to shrink as we all get busy creating the new one that must come to be born. The success or the failure of the enterprise will depend on timing perhaps more than anything else. People must be persuaded not only of the necessity of action but of the possibility that a better life can be created through action. And they must be assured that they themselves—personally and their heirs—will emerge from the crisis as well as one may reasonably expect.

The final task of the planner is to manage the markets that will in part help to implement the transition. Markets will have a role. Properly designed and rigorously enforced cap-and-trade systems can (for instance) encourage private holders of diversely efficient carbon sources, from power plants to feedlots to landfills, to seek the least costly means of reducing total emissions. In this way, the efficiencies achievable by the mere reduction of waste can be most effectively exploited. Simple higher prices for fuel, imposed and kept in place by a fuel tax or a carbon tax, will encourage transportation economies, and in a society like the United States, which is built on a vast waste of available energy, this alone can make a measurable impact. Corresponding subsidies for (say) home weatherization and the purchase of hybrid vehicles can magnify the effect, accelerating the transition to efficient use of known technologies. These are market mechanisms, price mechanisms, and they exploit the virtues of decentralization and choice in two important respects: they permit individuals to substitute against carbon-emitting products and processes in whatever way they see fit (thus, the way likely, under the circumstances, to do the least damage to happiness), and they permit producers to choose the least costly approach to emissions reduction. Within the limits of its capabilities, the market is useful.

But the limits are severe, and what the market cannot do is replace the planning system. Either the problem of climate change will be planned out, by a public authority acting with public power, or it will be planned away, by private corporations whose priorities lie in selling coal, oil, and gas-burning cars. If the latter happens, then within a century or two, the industrial and developed world as we have come to know it may no longer be around. Nor will many of the people whose lives that world has showed itself, uniquely, capable of supporting. The transition will inevitably be ugly.

Climate change is not the only area of public policy requiring a planning process; it is merely the most cosmic and most pressing among a considerable number. The United States has many public investment needs—in the areas of transportation infrastructure, environmental systems, water resources management—that have been severely neglected for thirty years. Energy security remains an important concern. The complexities of fiscal federalism, in which vital needs depend on the errant and fluctuating fiscal fortunes of state and local governments, is a major obstacle to rational planning. These issues too need to be thought through—which is to say, planned out—in any process under which the broader issue of climate change is confronted.

The avatars of the Predator State have understood very well what is at stake. That is why climate change denial and free-market ideology now go together. The right wing realizes that dealing with climate change must empower the scientific and the educational estate and the government, that it must involve a mobilization of the community at large, and that it will impose standards of conduct and behavior and performance on large corporate enterprises that the leaders of such enterprises would greatly prefer to avoid. In this view, they are entirely correct. For those who take the challenge of climate change seriously, it does no good to pretend that these issues can somehow be avoided.

CHAPTER THIRTEEN

The Case for Standards

On his first day in office, Ronald Reagan abolished the Council on Wage and Price Stability. There was no protest and no weeping. The council was worn out, and even Democrats were not unhappy to see it go. But in its way, its end marked a watershed, the end of an era. The last vestige of direct government interference in wage-and-price setting for the purposes of inflation control was now gone. Ever since, Americans have lived in an economy where one principle has been accepted, in principle, above all others: the setting of prices and wages belongs to the market. And as time went on, the principle spread. Deregulation in transportation, telecommunications, banking, energy, and other areas reinforced it, creating new worlds of flexible pricing where once prices were fixed by government, settled in collective bargains, or subject to public review.

By accepting this principle, liberals as well as conservatives conceded the triumph of the market idea. Flexibility in prices and wages became associated as such with efficiency, so long as average prices did not rise. The idea that "getting prices right" was the essential step in public policy spread through the economics of employment in advanced countries, justifying (as we have seen) the rise of inequalities in pay. It also flowed into development economics, where it underpinned an assault on subsidies, for instance, in agricultural production and in the distribution of food. It was part and parcel of the radical reform movement in post-Soviet Russia, which started by enacting a complete abolition of price control. That move was described at the time, inevitably, as the "freeing of prices."

Over the generation since, that prices and wages should be "free" and "flexible" has come to seem not only ideal but also historically normal—something that it definitely is not. We have largely forgotten how much price regulation and control we used to have; no one anymore considers why we used to have it. The medieval concept of a "just price," that the American colonies practiced price control, that transportation and utility rates were (and to some degree still are) regulated in the public interest—all this is treated as premodern if it is thought of at all. Rent control and rent stabilization persist only as relics, a bit of middle-class special pleading, in defiance of textbook wisdom. The periods of comprehensive price and wage control in World War II, the Korean War, and under Richard Nixon are dismissed as either anomalies or mistakes. That price caps were required, even under George W. Bush, to end the California energy crisis is passed over. Economists who mention these matters tend to do so with distaste.*

Equally, the persistence of controlled prices elsewhere in the world—up to the very recent past and sometimes into the present—is rarely noticed, whether one speaks of natural gas in Russia, gasoline in Iran or Venezuela, tortillas in Mexico, rice and beans in Cuba, or rents in much of China. When such things are noticed, the economist's assumption and the advisers' prescription is that these phenomena are merely transient, sources of inefficiency, to be abolished as soon as circumstances and enlightenment permit. Academic economics even has a terminology—the phrase is *distortions*—to describe any price not set by the "market." "Computable general equilibrium" models assess the efficiency gains achievable when distortions are removed (and prices adjust, presumably to match those set in existing market economies). When economic crisis hits, international advisers insist that subsidies and controls be removed as a condition of aid and assistance. In this way, creditors shove "reform" down debtors' evidently unwilling throats; any resistance is treated as in part a measure of ignorance, in part a measure of corruption.

But is this correct? Is the evident popularity, and past pervasiveness, of selective price control really evidence of benighted self-delusion and ancient economic error? Or does it represent, in certain respects and under certain conditions, a rational alternative to government by the powers that hide behind the "free market"?

What was (and is) the function of the form of business regulation

---

*Indeed, the last concerted effort to defend price control *in principle* to an audience of economists may have been my father's book *The Theory of Price Control*, published in 1952.

known as selective price control? A first answer is simple and obvious: in most cases, price controls are put in place in order to reduce economic inequalities—that is, inequalities in real living standards. They are by far the simplest, most direct, most effective way of achieving this objective. This is true of subsidies for tortillas in Mexico, fertilizer in Malawi, and milk historically in the United States. Likewise the provision, not so long ago, of tuition-free enrollment in major state universities, and still of the provision of tuition-free public schools. Likewise the cost-free provision of medical care in more expansive social democracies than ours. Likewise many laws and other means of regulating interest rates. The benefit in each case lay in ensuring that key components of a civilized life—including electricity, communications, energy, banking, education, and health care—were available to all, regardless of their money income. This fact placed a floor under the real incomes of working, retired, and disabled people so far as the most basic consumption goods were concerned. It placed a ceiling on profits that could be extracted from certain markets by virtue of monopoly power. It is therefore no accident that rising inequality almost always follows the deregulation of wages, prices, rents, and utility rates.

The critique of regulation and price control, shared by conservatives and liberals, rests on a comparison of controlled prices with the ostensible market alternative. There are three possibilities. One is that price controls work but induce too much consumption of the controlled good. A low price for gasoline, for example, encourages the use of gas-guzzling cars, and (in a producing country) reduces the fuel available for export. A second is that the regulators have been captured by monopolists and that regulation works mainly to control entry and protect existing businesses. If this is true, then prices are set too high, giving insiders a guaranteed return and an easy life. In that case, introducing competition—free entry and deregulated prices—should drive prices and profits down, while driving the introduction of new technologies up, and the effect of liberalizing prices and allowing markets to work should therefore be to decrease inequalities. A third—again, not altogether consistent with the other two—is that controls and regulations are cumbersome and outmoded, that increasingly sophisticated business strategies have rendered them moot. In that case, removing controls will not change much, but it will save the resources spent on controls.

What the critiques all share is the frame of reference. For every good, there is, in principle, a competitive market price. The actual price under regulation can be above, below, or (in rare cases) just at the competitive norm. But why control things if competition will give you the right result without the controls?

The problem with this argument lies in the presumption of the existence of a competitive market price. As economic theorists know, the real world is necessarily devoid of any such thing. If there is just one administered, or controlled, or monopolistic price in the system—an oil price or an interest rate—then even if all the other markets are perfectly competitive, all of them will be "distorted" by the presence of that one monopolistic price. Deregulating all of the other markets does not help. The idea that social welfare is enhanced by moving individual markets from controlled or monopolized toward a competitive position is simply wrong; for the theory to work, even in principle, you have to go all the way. All of the markets have to be competitive, as well as free of externalities and public goods.

But in the real world of complex organizations and advanced technologies, we have seen, this is never the case. The fact is that monopoly and market power are not only pervasive; they are at the center of economic life. The very purpose of a new technology is of course to create a monopoly where none previously existed. If a product is new, it is—for a time at least—by definition monopolistic. And if a product is well established, it is largely, if not in every single case, produced by a limited number of large organizations that coordinate with one another in multiple ways: they emulate one another's products, plan their investment decisions with the investment decisions of the others in view, mimic one another's advertising, and so forth. In such a world, there is no competitive price because there is no configuration of "perfectly competitive" firms that could bring forth the same or similar products.

That being so, prices and wages would serve a quite different function in the real world than the market model assigns to them. Instead of being set so as to maximize efficiency in production, they are set essentially by social relations between groups of workers and by the pattern of prices that are explicitly controlled. They express, in other words, the preexisting matrix of relative wages, materials costs, capital costs, and technology costs that firms face when they undertake a process of production or distribution. Firms do, from time to time, attempt to change this structure of costs within a single country directly—for example, by attacking a union pay settlement. But this is always highly conflictual and often deeply damaging to the firm's organizational efficiency (since workers faced with pay cuts will often leave, if they can, rather than accept them). It is usually far easier to accept the given structure of wage rates and prices and to reduce costs by changing technology or outsourcing to a foreign land.

Seen in this light, deregulation of wages and prices in the great move toward competitive market pricing is nothing more than a rearrangement of social power relations. And the consequences have little or nothing to do with the efficiency whereby a good or service is produced. Rather, they have to do mainly with whether the regulated entity is being supported and assisted by the controls, or whether it has elements of monopoly power of which the controls and regulations have inhibited the exploitation.

What actually happened in the great wave of deregulation? The fairest appraisal is that there were indeed some cases where the regulatory apparatus supported wages in an industry that was generally competitive in nature. In these cases, the effects of deregulation were mainly to force those wages to fall.

But in most cases regulation had served mainly to keep monopoly pricing power under control. And where regulation served that cause, the effects of deregulation were bound to be adverse. The actual balance of effect depended on the potential in three directions: the potential of new entry and competition to reduce wages and profit margins, the potential gains from faster technological change, and the potential for monopoly control and the exercise of monopoly pricing power.

The deregulation of trucking rates in 1979 was a singularly atypical case of the first type. In trucking, workers really did enjoy, through their Teamsters union and regulations which reinforced the union by restricting entry into the business, a degree of market power, and so the first potential was important while the other two were relatively minor. Deregulation above all undermined the union, and thus the pay of the drivers. With greater competition, the relative wages of truckers fell; truck drivers largely ceased to be the labor elite that they had become in the 1950s and 1960s. Although deregulators promised that free entry and competition would generate important efficiencies in the delivery of trucking services, the reality was that there were few of these to be had.

In airlines, deregulation similarly led to the rise of nonunion, low-cost carriers—again largely a straightforward attack on unions and transfer from workers to consumers. But here the technological potential was greater. Lower prices facilitated large increases in air travel, which spurred technological change in the airline industry, including the adoption of hub-and-spoke routing, and sped the purchase of more efficient planes. At the same time, airlines got very good (through frequent flyer programs and complex pricing schemes) at exploiting the differences among their consumers, an exercise in monopoly pricing power. But this third effect was arguably small compared to the other two; overall the cost of air travel fell, and the volume increased dramatically.

In telecommunications, a capital- and technology-intensive business, the potential for savings at the expense of workers was relatively small. Deregulation therefore led mainly to a contest between the cost-reducing potentials of technological advance and the profit-increasing potential of monopolistic consolidation. Both happened—especially the number of major media firms fell sharply from around fifty in 1983 to just six by 2005—but the industry continues to evolve as digital technologies blend formerly distinct industries (television, telephone service, and the Internet) into one. As this happened, despite the trend toward monopoly, the cost to the consumer of information services has seen a marked tendency to decline.

And then there were sectors like banking and energy, where the potential gains from either cost reduction or technical improvement were (and remain) comparatively small and where regulation had fostered and protected large numbers of substantially competitive firms, keeping down the profit prospects of each. Here we observe, with deregulation, mainly the consolidation of ownership and the quasi-monopolistic tactics of product differentiation, market segmentation, and price discrimination. These were (and are) devices for extracting more money from those who can afford to pay—and sometimes from those who cannot. In these cases, what had been relatively simple and standardized pricing of relatively simple and standardized products was replaced within a short time by price-and-product schedules of massive complexity. This was true even where the underlying goods (such as electricity or telephone service) remained fairly simple and standard so far as the consumer is concerned. Generally the cost of the basic service to low-income people went up. So did the cost of the supposedly more sophisticated services to all who could be persuaded to buy them.

Information is, as ever, asymmetric. When new complexities are introduced to a market, the effect is always to the advantage of those better equipped to navigate them. For some consumers—those willing and able to seek out the best deals in a complex array of generally bad ones, those with flexible and adaptable needs, and those with enough market power—the product diversity brought by deregulation could prove an authentic blessing. But low-income people were rarely in this position, and they became major victims of new forms of price discrimination made possible by deregulation. In some cases, new technical developments came faster under deregulation than they otherwise might have—but not always. And in all cases, the newly complex market structures opened the way to darker forces: sharp practice, price manipulation, and fraud.

In banking and energy especially, deregulation was driven by forces within the Predator State. The deregulation of the savings and loans was the work, in substantial part, of a task force in the early 1980s headed by Vice President George H. W. Bush; the beneficiaries were people like Charles Keating, head of Lincoln Savings and Loan, the largest fraudulent S&L, who could hire Alan Greenspan, then in private consulting practice, to shill for his company with federal regulators. The deregulation of electricity in California, which so favored Enron (a company headed by George W. Bush's largest campaign contributor), was facilitated by an energy task force in the early 2000s headed by Vice President Richard W. Cheney. The mode of operation, and the results, were entirely parallel in the two cases.

Thus, the economic world of "flexible" wages and prices is a world where a manufactured form of complexity is a major implement of private power. The ability for a consumer to prosper in this world depends to a large degree on one's ability and willingness to search—to find the needles of good value hidden in the very large haystacks of dross, scam, and flummery. Without reliable standards, without clear guidelines as to what is safe and reasonable and what is not, the overall efficiency of the market declines because search and transaction costs rise beyond all reasonable limits. The efficiency of the market becomes limited by the fear of fraud. Shopping, far from being the exercise of market freedom, becomes itself an endless absorber of time and attention, whether one is discussing clothes, electronics, cell phone contracts, a mortgage application, or airline seats from New York to Pittsburgh.

Meanwhile, the capacities to manipulate, change, innovate, differentiate, discriminate, and exploit become in their turn the defining characteristics of corporate success. And those who pursue such strategies the most aggressively are, naturally, the heroes of the corporate world. It is not that there is a thin line between meeting consumers' needs and presenting them with complex choices intended to make them easier to fleece. It is that there is no line at all: one practice bleeds over into the other. Success in meeting needs and success in screwing the vulnerable cannot be readily distinguished, except perhaps by prosecutors and juries much later. Thus, the CEO who is initially celebrated for brilliant innovation is later exposed as a crook. The interaction of complexity and deregulation transforms and actually criminalizes the market; where the environment is criminogenic, prosecution alone cannot bring down the crime rate.

This is a systematic problem, but it is one to which the liberal political community, committed inflexibly to the principle of flexible and responsive wages and prices, has no systematic response, and this is particularly true where one considers the incentive effects of excess pay or the already very rich. Few liberals want to suggest that corporate titans are simply paid too much, for the good of the companies that they operate under public charter. The abuses are noted, to be sure. But the pattern linking them together is not, and the role of the state, which is basically one of solving the information problem, is not placed front and center. When a crisis erupts, as happens with mind-numbing regularity, an enthralling moral tale of greed and hubris can be told and retold. The message is that occasionally large corporations fall under the leadership of bad people. Bad people should, of course, be punished. The issue is therefore punted to the legal system; it stays off the docket of social reform.

At the other end of the income scale, the older ethical attitudes are stronger. Throughout the era of market fundamentalism, basic notions of what is a fair wage have remained broadly popular and widely shared. Proposals to raise the minimum wage invariably command widespread support in the general population, and citywide referenda favoring much more aggressive "living wage" standards have to be fought off, case by case, with expensive corporate smear and disinformation campaigns. Economists who oppose the minimum wage on the grounds that it causes unemployment are considered purists, even by their professional colleagues. Even under Reagan, the earned income tax credit emerged as a broadly acceptable intervention on behalf of low-wage workers (its initial purpose being to offset the impact of Social Security payroll taxes). Wage subsidy schemes have been proposed by free-market economists such as the 2006 Nobel Prize winner Edmund Phelps. So there is wide agreement that, at the bottom, work in America should be paid at some acceptable minimum standard. The issue is not one of deep principle. The arguments are only over how high the standard should be set and on whom the burden of a standard should fall.

Between the case of minimum wages (where there is a consensus in principle) and that of CEO pay (where there is no organized effort), there should be an area of truly contested terrain—of dispute within the mainstream of policy debates. What should the wage for this or that occupation actually be? And we find this especially in the battles over free trade, for it is concern about fair wages—and opposition to competition from workers paid far less than oneself—that most strongly animates the populist opposition to the doctrines of free trade. Certainly that opposition has almost nothing to do with the case for, or against, the obscure doctrine of comparative advantage.

It is because it has to do with wages, and with the erosion of wage standards or norms, that the reaction against free trade is potent. In a time of (ironically) low overall unemployment, it is perhaps the only economic question that has proven capable recently of turning elections in the battleground states. Here the transformation of Ohio in 2006 stands out: a state carried by George W. Bush on culture issues in 2000 and 2004 fell decisively to the Democrats, particularly in a Senate race marked by a mobilization against the ravages of deindustrialization, linked to trade.

So it is worthwhile to examine the ideas behind this position. In an essay in the *Washington Post* shortly after the election, the newly elected senator from Ohio, Sherrod Brown, and veteran senator Byron Dorgan (D, N.D.) gave voice to the anger that had fueled both Brown's election and the Democratic takeover of the Senate. Under the headline "How Free Trade Hurts," the senators wrote:

> Fewer and fewer Americans support our government's trade policy. They see a shrinking middle class, lost jobs and exploding trade deficits. Yet supporters of free trade continue to push for more of the same— more job-killing trade agreements, greater tax breaks for large corporations that export jobs and larger government incentives for outsourcing.*

*Sherrod Brown and Byron Dorgan, "How Free Trade Hurts," *Washington Post*, December 23, 2006, p. A21.

This statement puts the issues bluntly: trade works to destroy the middle class. Senators Dorgan and Brown define the problem: it lies in "free trade agreements," in the export of jobs through outsourcing, and in the action of large American corporations that will not renovate and renew their factories in the United States. Moreover, as the senators go on to say explicitly, the specific problem of trade agreements is their failure to incorporate effective "standards"—in other words, rules and regulations—for fair wages, decent working conditions, and environmental protection in the countries with which the United States trades. The absence of standards is what makes foreign countries attractive to large corporations. The solution therefore is to impose them. The drive for such standards has, in this way, become the centerpiece of the liberal position on trade.

There is, moreover, a broad consensus around "international labor standards," reflected in the fact that codes exist: they have been developed by the International Labor Organization (ILO) and based on universal social principles, such as bans on trade in products made with child labor or in prisons. They are largely uncontroversial, at least in principle: no one favors child or slave labor except the companies that actually profit from it, and they tend not to speak in public. Moreover, the focus is not pointless: flagrant abuses in labor practices can be and have been targeted and sometimes even ended by such means. This is especially possible if the perpetrator happens to be a well-known multinational corporation with a reputation to lose.

But there is a problem. *As a trade strategy*, the potential of the ILO's universal codes and standards is minor. The proscribed products are not major items in trade. They almost never compete seriously with what American workers do. Child labor remains pervasive in many developing countries, but except possibly in the garment trades (where the news occasionally shocks), children are not widely used anywhere to produce advanced consumer goods for export markets. Nor are prisoners suited to the task, and for a simple reason: they are not up to the job at any price. As long ago as 1993, the Chinese agreed quite readily to block the use of prison labor in goods destined for export. There is no evidence that they did this in bad faith; the only serious obstacle to implementing that ban lies in the sprawling scale of the Chinese economy and the weak capacity of the government to police the agreement.

Similarly, environmental standards will never have a major protective effect on American wages, for two basic reasons. The first is that when we restrict the discussion to the production of consumer goods, regulatory differences have relatively little to do with environmental impact. Firms installing new plant and equipment to produce manufactures aimed at advanced markets, even in a low-wage setting, usually use the latest technologies. They do this not because they are addicted to novelty or virtue, but because new technology usually provides the cheapest way to produce. But newer technologies also tend to be cleaner. It is therefore quite possible for a firm to cost American jobs while improving environmental quality—replacing an old and dirtier American factory with a new and cleaner Asian one. Indeed such events are not rare.

To be sure, and to take a notorious example, China has lots of dirty, dangerous factories, but they generally do not produce for the export trade. Getting rid of them, if it could be done, would have little to no effect on American imports of Chinese goods. And in any event, the major environmental problems in Third World production are not in manufacturing at all, but in mining, oil exploration, deforestation, and plantation agriculture. These are not going to be controlled by standards imposed at the port of entry to the United States: oil is fungible, and a refusal to import (say) oil produced in the Ecuadorean Amazon would only lead to that oil being used somewhere else in the world. Ecuador is the only country that can solve that problem.

The second problem with environmental standards as an implement of American trade policy is that the United States hardly comes to this table with clean hands. Genetically modified organisms—frankenfoods—are a major issue in Europe, which Europeans consider to be an entirely proper environmental concern. If the United States were to impose environmental standards on its imports, how could it object to their imposition on its exports? And if the world got the idea that carbon dioxide emissions should be the basis of environmental trade standards, it would be hard to see what exactly the United States could continue to export to the rest of the world. Jet aircraft, industrial agriculture, and oil field equipment are all major carbon dioxide offenders. Viewed from the perspective of global warming, the idea that United States workers would benefit from restricting trade for environmental reasons is plainly absurd.

Many who support strong trade standards through the environment or human rights or any other avenue (and many who oppose them) believe that they are simply code for measures that would stem an undesirable flood of imports from low-wage countries. They seem, to some supporters and many opponents, to be primarily an instrument for achieving by stealth and indirection what the commitment to free trade prevents from being done directly. So here is the hard question: Leaving aside whether standards work "as advertised," leaving aside the merits of arguments over pay, working conditions, and the environment, are standards a good tool for "getting the job done"? In other words, would it be a good idea to impede or block (say) Chinese exports to the United States? Brief consideration is sufficient to dispose of this idea.

First, blocking trade with China would not bring a single job back to the United States. It would only cause Japanese, or Taiwanese, or Korean, or American multinationals to shift their outsourcing from China to some other low-wage country, such as Vietnam, Malaysia, or Indonesia. No American jobs would be saved, and none would return.

Second, if blocking Chinese exports to the United States really did cut into our imports overall, that would raise prices and lower real wages here. It would hit especially hard at the lowest-wage Americans, who rely most on cheap imports to meet their budgets. The higher prices would show up as inflation, prompting higher interest rates from the Federal Reserve. Blocking low-wage imports creates a transfer, in other words, from low-wage working Americans to bankers and investors. This is not a progressive redistribution.

Third, there would be retaliation. China is a large market, especially for advanced United States products such as aircraft. Those sales could, and very likely would, shift to Europe. The losers in that case would be high-paid American workers at firms like Boeing, whose jobs would shift to Airbus. This is where the United States has real competitive strength, which would be needlessly put at risk, and not just temporarily. Competitive advantage in high technology is a cumulative process, and once lost, it is very hard to get it back.

China's increasing dominance of the world market for low-wage manufactured exports *is* a problem. But it is a problem for Malaysia, Thailand, the Philippines, and other low-wage countries—even for India, whose handicraft workers are increasingly undercut and overwhelmed by the sheer quantity of very cheap Chinese substitutes for their products. There is a case for dividing up our import markets, as we once did under the Multi-Fiber Agreements—a case in favor of spreading economic development around. But the concentration of certain types of manufacturing in China is not a big problem for American workers. And trade-related standards are therefore not a solution to the issues normally associated with competition from China. Nor of course would the international labor standards solve our trade woes with Europe, Canada, and Japan—where in any event labor standards are higher than in the United States and environmental protections are at least as good.

It is therefore useful to ask again: Where did the nationalist-populist emphasis on standards in trade agreements actually come from? The answer is that it is an outgrowth of the NAFTA debate, from 1992 to 1994, and of the side agreements for labor and the environment that some Democrats insisted on as the price of a pro-NAFTA vote. Those agreements, of course, did little. Some believe they were always a sham. But those who backed them in 1994 invested a lot of political capital in them. They sold them—and continue to sell them—as a cure for the deficiencies of the larger trade regime. But the results have been poor because the issues were largely symbolic.

NAFTA could in principle, and in practice, have had little effect on American manufacturing jobs and wages, for a basic reason: it made almost no difference to the tariff treatment of Mexican goods entering the United States, many of which had been entering duty free since 1965, when the old *maquiladora* program got under way. Did some jobs leave the United States to take advantage of cheaper Mexican labor? Of course, some did. Were American workers pressured to cut wages because of Mexican competition? Yes, many no doubt were. But that happened because of Mexico, not because of NAFTA. It was happening before NAFTA and would have continued to happen if NAFTA had been defeated. Mexico would not disappear if NAFTA did. From the standpoint of American workers, NAFTA and its successors are just scapegoats. And the fact is, China has long since passed Mexico as the prime outsourcing threat, even though we have no "free trade" agreement with China.

CAFTA—the Central American Free Trade Agreement—contains numerous innovative and predatory provisions, including one abusing the power of North American monopolies (especially in drugs) to maintain and extend their patent protections in these small and low-income markets. It contains the same disruptive provisions in agriculture as NAFTA, which will result in more exports from the United States and more immigrants coming back. But the manufacturing provisions are trivial, and the same is true of free trade agreements with

Singapore, Bahrain, Jordan, Peru, Colombia, and other actual and possible agreements. It would be good policy to stop making these agreements; they have become a playground for pressure groups seeking small extensions of their monopoly powers over some of the world's poorest people. But they have little or nothing to do with the future of employment and wages in the United States. In short, the fight over NAFTA, like the international labor standards of the ILO and the new "trade agreements" with isolated developing countries, is a poor template for the struggle over standards that should occur.

On the other hand, the idea of standards as such is a very good one. The problem with the concentration of populist effort on standards in trade is not with the focus on standards but with their application to trade. And this is particularly true of the one type of standard that everyone would like in principle, but that everyone agrees is not practical for trade policy: a standard for the actual level of wages. You cannot impose a wage standard on China or Vietnam. But as the long experience of the minimum wage and of union pay scales generally in this and other countries establishes very clearly, you can certainly impose wage standards for workers in these United States. And you could impose maximum pay standards for corporate executive officers too if you chose to do so and felt that corporate governance would thereby be improved.

Indeed, rather than being spooked by the supposed effect of trade on wages, let us consider how that relationship works when you take it the other way around. *What, in other words, is the effect of wages on trade?* Suppose that instead of building a trade policy to help with wages, we built a wages policy to help with trade? Does that sound far-fetched? It is not. If you did that, you would have something that has been tested and proven in the real world: a reasonable facsimile of what economists have long referred to as the Scandinavian Model.*

The Scandinavian countries are the most egalitarian capitalist economies on earth. They have nearly universal unions, high minimum wages, and a strong welfare state. But as trade campaigners often neglect to acknowledge, they also are highly open. They practice free trade. Business there is free to import, export, and outsource. Business there is free to hire and fire, change lines of business, and otherwise

---

*The model is due to two Swedish labor union economists, Gösta Rehn and Rudolf Meidner, who developed it in detail in the 1950s.

conduct itself as it sees fit. And yet the Scandinavians enjoy, most of the time, the lowest unemployment rates in Europe.

How can this be so, if markets are always pressing for wages to be cut? The secret in this policy mix is not, as many imagine, industrial policy or job retraining, though these have some role. The true secret lies in the aggressive regulation of wages. If you are a business in Sweden or Norway, you are free to import, export, and outsource as you like. There is, however, one thing you are not free to do: you are not free to cut your wages. You are not free to compete by going after cut-rate workers, either native or immigrant. You are not free to undercut the union rate. You have to pay your workers at the established scale, and if you cannot do that and earn a profit, too bad for your business.

The effect of this on business discipline is quite wonderful. To succeed, businesses must find ways to compete that do not involve running down the wage standards of their workforces. They do it by keeping productivity high and investing in the search for technological improvement. This means that advanced industries thrive in Scandinavia, while backward ones die out. (Progressive businessmen prosper, while reactionaries fade away.) As a result, the economies as a whole stay competitive: the Scandinavian countries started the twentieth century poor and ended it at the top of the world's distribution of income and wealth. The tax and welfare systems then make sure that everyone has enough to live on.

The United States is not Sweden or Norway. It is much larger, in particular, and for this reason it cannot move ahead as far or as fast as smaller countries. But the economic principles do not change when they cross the North Atlantic. And we have, in fact, applied them in the past. As Dorgan and Brown correctly state in their essay, this is how the American middle class got built in the first place. It was done not by "free markets" but through unions, laws, regulations, and, yes, standards. But the standards were not imposed on other people. They were imposed at home—where they can be enforced—and the rest of the world adjusted to what we did here. The problem, in short, *is not* foreigners and trade. The big problem is that unions, laws, regulations, and standards have been undercut by conservative policies right here at home. And the foundation stone of those policies is the idea that wages and prices should be set by the market, and not interfered with by the political process.

Even today, the problem is not universal. In certain industries, with advanced technologies and strong unions (think aircraft, information technology, the oil sector), high wages persist. Yet those sectors remain competitive. How does this happen? The answer is that this is how the model works! High wages, enforced by strong unions, help ensure that business has no alternative but to stay on its competitive toes. Information technology firms in particular have to hire the best people, at the highest wages, or they will not succeed in competition with other information technology firms. If Boeing ever ceased to pay top dollar in aerospace, it would eventually become a technical laggard as well.

If we concentrate on improving standards here in the United States, will we lose some jobs to trade? Sure. But unlike the Scandinavians, we do not have to balance our current account. We have not done so, practically speaking, for over thirty years. So long as the dollar's global position lasts, we can improve our living standards, productivity, and competitive position and still run a substantial trade deficit. Or, to put it less optimistically, we have been able to do this up to now. *The big question is, How long will this last?*

This is a financial question. It is not a question about trade and has almost nothing to do with trade policy. Senators Brown and Dorgan, along with many others, see trade policy as though it were intimately connected to the imbalance in America's external accounts.

> The results of such trade agreements are skyrocketing trade deficits—more than $800 billion this year alone—and downward pressure on income and benefits for American workers. Why? Because these agreements enable countries to ship what their low-wage workers produce to the United States while blocking many U.S. products from entering their countries.*

On even the most friendly reading, it is not very easy to make sense of this statement. How exactly do trade agreements affect the trade deficit? The big changes wrought by NAFTA were a reduction of Mexican trade barriers in manufacturing and in agriculture. Before NAFTA, there were practically no barriers to Mexican products entering the United States. As a result of NAFTA, it is surely difficult to

---

*Brown and Dorgan, "How Free Trade Hurts," p. A21.

think of a single American product that NAFTA prevents from entering Mexico. The implied idea that the United States lets itself get taken in negotiations with countries much smaller, much poorer, and much weaker than itself is absurd.

The United States does have a trade deficit with Mexico, but it is only about a tenth of our total trade deficit. We run bigger deficits with Canada and Japan, which are not low-wage countries. We run a deficit about four times as big with China, with which we have no free-trade agreement. The trade deficit overall has practically nothing to do with trade agreements, and not all that much to do with low-wage countries.

Is the system that permits us to run a trade deficit of $800 billion per year risky? Yes, it is. Could our bond holders, notably China, panic? Could they act to cut us off for political reasons, such as a crisis over Taiwan? Or even Iran? Yes, they could. Could our currency collapse? Yes, those things are possible. The system is fragile, and it is dangerous.

But those are financial risks. They have nothing to do with trade agreements. No trade policy aimed at any one country is going to reduce the financial risks. A policy aimed at hurting China could, on the other hand, increase them. Buying euros and dumping dollars is an easy Chinese reply to a decision on our part to squeeze their exports to us.

In short, one may not like the acute state of mutual dependence that currently exists between the United States and China and our other big creditors, such as Japan. But it's too late: the condition exists. In the world economy, the Middle East will produce oil, because that is where it is. The Chinese will produce labor-intensive consumer goods, because they have the labor and know how to use it. We will produce bonds so long as everyone else is willing to take them. The question before us is not whether this situation can be cured, but how best to cope with it—how to keep it going—and how to be prepared if it collapses. This is a topic for the next chapter.

How would wage standards affect the position of American business in global competition? The notion held by market economists as a rule is that there must be a link between wage rates and the productivity (at the margin) of the workers paid those wages. Otherwise, the economist reasons, the worker would not be profitable to employ and could not be hired. The logical error lies in thinking that productivity is a concept given from the outside, objectively, by technology and other circumstances not controlled by the firm. In the world as it actually is, wage structures are, by and large, fixed by the society; they are what the business firm sees and adjusts to. Technology and business methods are invented and adapted within the firm, to conform to the pay structures that society imposes *on* the firm. And more egalitarian structures are more demanding and therefore, as a rule and up to a point, more productive.

This is a very general principle, closely related to the political economy of regulation in the United States explored in Chapter Ten. Important though they were, it is not possible that activists like Ralph Nader and Rachel Carson could have created the National Transportation Safety Administration, or the Occupational Safety and Health Administration, or the Environmental Protection Agency entirely on their own. What actually happened, and what must happen in a democracy substantially dominated by corporate interests, is in some sense a coalition of the (relatively) progressive forces, including labor and some elements of business, against the reactionary business powers. That is, for a standard to work, firms that are capable of meeting standards must be found, and they must be prepared to accept them or anyway to acquiesce, more or less in alliance with labor and environmental or consumer interests that formulate and advance the ideas. For such firms, once they put their minds to it, the standards are a competitive weapon. They work to expand the market share of those who comply against those other firms that cannot or will not do so. The standards are then met, the reactionaries must either adapt or be forced out of business, and the best practice becomes the norm. Wage standards, which push the whole of industry toward best practices, are simply the general version of what can be done with environmental, health, and occupational and consumer safety issues.

Imposing standards, and enforcing them, is thus the general policy response to the rise of the Predator State, which is just a coalition of the reactionary forces within business who seek to maintain competitiveness and profitability without technological improvement, without environmental control, without attending to product or workplace safety. They are the forces behind deregulation, behind tort reform, and behind the assault on unions. If they will not adapt—and the experience of the past three decades demonstrates that powerful parts of present American corporate leadership have no intention of adapting—then they must be defeated politically. And following their political defeat, they should be pushed, by aggressive implementation of new standards, to the economic wall. Where the need is pressing and the technologies exist, companies that cannot adapt really should be let go. New and better ones can be created.

Seen this way, the fact that other advanced countries now compete for world leadership creates opportunities. The imposition of rigorous standards will affect the behavior of those companies as well, so long as they wish access to the American market; it thus opens cracks in the political armor against standards that can be assembled by domestic firms. If the Japanese automakers are more effective than General Motors or Ford at raising corporate fuel economy, if they are willing to build hybrids and electric cars and market them in the United States, if the French can build high-speed trains or the Danes efficient windmills, why should we not take advantage of those capabilities? If the way is cleared, at least some of that production will come over, as Japanese automakers long ago proved. Indeed, where would American carmaking be today if Toyota, Nissan, and Honda had not moved years ago to these shores? Is there anything wrong, in retrospect, with the combination of better cars and lower prices that the Japanese carmakers brought to the American mix? Of course not.

Wage standards would have an important effect in one other area: immigration. Here a conventional narrative holds that the presence of undocumented migrants "pushes" wages down, and thus that immigrants "take" jobs from native and documented workers by being "willing to work for less." So long as the story is told in this way, the onus is on the migrants for having come where they do not belong, and the remedy is to try to keep them out. This is the logic behind tighter visa restrictions, more rigorous border controls, registration requirements, and walls along the Rio Grande.

But in many cases the conventional narrative is misleading. In many cases, the active agent in the migration process is not the immigrant. Rather it is the employer who seeks migrant labor in order to pay less for labor and to minimize the risks of unionization or other agitation from the workforce. Employers or their labor contractors send recruiters to Mexico and to San Salvador and Guatemala for this very purpose. They do so because they can get away with it. And so long as they can get away with it, the undocumented immigrant is preferable to native labor, and more immigrant labor will be employed at the substandard rate. Undocumented immigrants cannot, of course, complain very loudly.

In a world where all workers had to be advised, in plain language, of the wages and conditions to which they were entitled—whether they were documented or not—what would happen? Plainly, the advantage to hiring undocumented workers, which is a combination of a wage discount and intimidation, would disappear. Migrants would still be hired where they were needed, but the numbers would be fewer, the displacement of native workers would be much less, and the treatment of both types of worker would be significantly fairer. From an economic point of view, enforcement of fair labor standards is the easy way out of our immigration troubles. Why do we not hear this stated more often? Because it runs against predatory business interest, and because immigrants do not vote.

In short, the populist objective is to raise American wages, create American jobs, and increase the fairness and security of our economic system, especially for citizens and legal residents but also for all who seek work within our borders. Is there a better way to achieve this than by manipulating the trading system? Of course there is—and that is to do it directly. You want higher wages? Raise them. You want more and better jobs? Create them. You want safer food, cleaner air, fewer carbon emissions? Pass laws and establish agencies to achieve this. Enforce the laws, staff the agencies, give them budgets and the mandates that they require to make the changes that we need. Politics may stand in the way, but economics does not. And there is nothing really to lose, except "free-market" illusions.

CHAPTER FOURTEEN

Paying for It

We turn to a final set of questions. How to pay?

Does the United States face a financial limit on its ability to implement a plan? Can it afford to deal with the core deficiencies of infrastructure, social development, and the environment? Could it set and enforce standards to raise pay and incomes at the bottom while limiting them at the top? Can it, by these and other measures, should it choose to do so, bring the Predator State to heel? Or does the market, in some deep exercise of a cosmic power, effectively rule these things out? If the markets command that we must privatize Social Security, or cut Medicare, or deregulate banking (and bail out the perpetrators of every resulting bubble), or accept every trade agreement, must we do so? Is it true, as President William Jefferson Clinton exclaimed in frustration in 1993, that the world and the country are actually run by the "fucking bond market"? More deeply, is the U.S. government "bankrupt," in the precise sense that its economic affairs are, for some deep technical reason, no longer in its own hands?

This is an analytical question. It's useful to take it in two parts: the case of an economy closed to international trade and finance, and the case of an economy seeking to maintain open borders to the flow of goods and capital and finance.

At a fundamental level, a closed economy can never be bankrupt in the sense described. A closed economy—say, China until 1979—is one that engages in trade mainly on a cash basis and therefore essentially has no financial intercourse with the outside world. Such a country is subject only to the pressures and forces arising from the inside. It may be poor, but markets cannot constrain it. Any country can, in principle, mobilize its population and distribute its resources—those it commands at home—in any way it likes. The limitations on what can be achieved are limits of knowledge, productivity, organization, and political capacity. Finance, in other words, is merely a mechanism whereby resources are placed in motion to achieve particular ends or empower particular people. Where financial problems occur in a closed-economy setting—inflation, deflation, banking crises, and the problems of debt—they are merely expressions of the weakness of the state. The state may be ineffective, incompetent, or unstable; the state's rulers may be tyrants or kleptocrats or mere puppets of oligarchs whose power rests on their control of land or mines or oil. But if there are no external financial agreements, no credit contracts that have to be honored, no currency traded internationally whose external value is of any concern, then clearly there can be no objective outside constraint on what a country can do.

In an open economy, the reverse holds. A fully open economy is one that trades in an unbalanced way—sometimes running a surplus and sometimes a deficit—and that therefore borrows or lends on the world stage. A country that wishes to borrow on world markets must conform to the rules, standards. and expectations of those markets. If it does, then presumably capital will flow in at reasonable interest rates, business will boom, and government will enjoy the tax revenues required to fund at least measured expansions of infrastructure and public services. If it does not, the markets will sell the currency, interest rates will rise, tax revenues will fall, capital will flee, and the government will face impossible difficulties even in raising funds for day-to-day operations, let alone for major new investments. That is the theory.

Now consider the actual situation of the United States. Is the United States a fully open economy? Well, of course it is: it is certainly fully open to trade and capital, it certainly trades in a highly unbalanced way, and it certainly borrows on a phenomenal scale. And yet precisely because the United States operates in global capital markets in a way open to no other country, the rules as they apply to the United States are different from what they are for anyone else. To put it crudely, the United States is not subject to the normal rules of the world system. It does not have to accept the terms and the discipline of the capital markets. Rather, it is in a position, up to a point, to make the rules, impose them on others, and exempt itself from their harshest implementation. This is hardly fair, to be sure. But it is the way the system has worked.

How did the United States get into this position?

The answer goes back to the dominant financial role the United

States played in both world wars and in the construction of the postwar financial order and the cold war. In World Wars I and II, the United States was far more than a military ally: it was also the "arsenal of democracy," and in addition to that, democracy's banker. Both wars strengthened America's financial position, moving the world's stock of gold to our shores and ultimately permitting us to dictate the terms of the postwar monetary order. As agreed at Bretton Woods in 1944, that order would be centered on the dollar as the anchor currency, to which the value of all the others would be pegged.

Underlying that agreement, there was an implicit bargain between the United States and the anticommunist, democratic governments of Europe and (eventually) Japan. We provided and would continue to provide military security, including the nuclear umbrella represented by U.S. strategic forces. (At the beginning, we would also supply steel, machinery, and credit to get European and Japanese recovery under way.) Those countries in turn accepted a subordinate diplomatic *and* financial role, and continued to accept it long after their own economies had fully recovered from the war. Indeed, they continued to accept it long after they had gone on to create new areas of industrial and technological advantage, even dominance on world markets, and despite the fact that in the 1970s, their currencies, especially the yen and the mark, were in increasing demand on world markets. In much of the developing world as well, particularly through Latin America, Africa, and Southeast Asia, friendly governments—anticommunist but not always democratic—put themselves under American protection. And the United States assisted them in repressing both external subversion and internal dissent, whether real or imagined, legitimate or otherwise. This bargain—security for seigniorage, defense for dollars, in effect—defined the global economics of the cold war.

Thus, for a half-century the United States led a world community centered on a common defense of managed capitalism. American policy set limits on what lesser members of the alliance, from Guatemala to Italy, could get away with. Our senior allies advised and participated; occasionally they dissented (as over Vietnam), and occasionally we agreed to differ (as over Cuba). But at the end of the day, the preeminence of the American role had to be accepted. Margaret Thatcher's catchphrase "There is no alternative" was invented for a different proposition, but it applied to this one.

The American trade deficit is nothing more, or less, than the normal consequence of that system, and particularly of what emerged *after* the formal mechanisms of international financial management and exchange rate stabilization were abandoned between 1971 and 1973.

Bretton Woods still partook of the idea, rooted in ancient practice and folk wisdom, that every country in the world had to run a balanced current account—a rough parity of imports and exports—over time. Under the discipline of the gold standard, foreign accounts before 1913 had to be settled in precious metal. If you ran a deficit for too long, gold would drain away. Eventually your domestic prices would fall (because there was not enough gold in the system to support the economy at current prices), or your domestic output would collapse (because credit could not be had at any cost), or you would find that you could not pay your import bills on your contractual debts (often, if you were a small country in debt to a larger one, a cause for war). Bretton Woods created a peaceful and orderly means for easing those trade adjustments that might be necessary from time to time, but it did not obviate the need to adjust. Faced with a deficit, a country could in the first instance borrow from the IMF. If the deficit proved intractable, it could devalue—adjusting the parities of the world currency system. Eventually, the theory had it, a general pattern of trade balance would return.

By putting the dollar at the center of the system, Bretton Woods had removed the possibility that the dollar could devalue, and at the same time insulated the United States alone from the need to adjust to a deficit in our trade. But not entirely. As noted, central banks retained the option of demanding trade settlement in gold. And as tensions within the system built in the 1960s, notably over Vietnam, they increasingly did so.

The contradiction in the system for the United States was that unlike other countries, it could not adjust its trade deficit using devaluation; devaluation by the currency to which other currencies were tied was a system-breaking move. Thus, if other countries were not prepared to tolerate U.S. deficits at high employment, the United States could either retreat from full employment at home or break the system. In 1969–1970, Richard Nixon had tried the first course of action, to near political disaster. In 1971–1972, he took the second course, ensuring his own reelection at the expense of plunging the world economy into turmoil. For a time, in consequence, the future of the world financial system was very uncertain; many thought that the dollar might fail and be replaced by some combination of currencies, including the German deutsche mark, the Japanese yen, the British pound, and the Swiss franc. The entire decade from that point forward was financially unstable, and the United States itself paid part of the price in the form of inflation and periodic recessions.

Reagan's macroeconomics ended the uncertainty—and resolved the contradiction. And although monetarism and supply-side economics wrecked major sectors of American industry, drove up the rate of unemployment, and made the nation far more unequal, they also fundamentally reestablished American financial power. The same high interest rates that did so much damage to Ohio and Michigan were even more devastating outside the country than within. And in the relations between the United States and the rest of the world, they turned the financial tide, creating a new dollar-based system that became the foundation of the world economy. From a purely national perspective, this would lead to huge benefits to the United States, at everyone else's expense. For now, most countries came to protect themselves against the worldwide financial instability, itself often generated from within the United States, by holding financial reserves, which consisted mainly of U.S. Treasury bonds.

Now the Prometheus was truly unbound; even the largely self-imposed macroeconomic and trade discipline of the Bretton Woods period became a thing of the past. The post-1981 position of the dollar meant not only that Americans could import much more than we export; actually, it meant that we *must* import more than we export. We routinely cover the difference with nothing more than a note and a promise to pay interest down the road. The extent to which we can do this—the extent that we *must* do this—is determined, entirely and exactly, by the willingness and the desire of other countries to hold the bonds. And as the world economy grew, and particularly as China emerged as a global financial player with reasons of its own for holding dollar bonds, that extent appeared to have few practical limits.

As a result, the United States has been running trade deficits continuously. And every year as the world economy grows, they grow larger. At this writing, they are greater than 6 percent of annual GDP, more than $800 billion. To repeat, the main reason for this is that other countries, *for reasons of their own*, have wanted to anchor their financial portfolios in U.S. Treasury bonds. We could not do it otherwise, and we cannot avoid doing it, given those desires.

The bonds are costly to hold. They represent a real use of resources that could otherwise be put to buying imports and helping developing economies to grow. But the decision to hold them is the decision of other countries, not ours; at most we can influence that decision, at the margin, by altering our short-term rate of interest.

Why do other countries do it? For three reasons—in some sense, all of them "safety" reasons. First, the U.S. bond market is the most liquid in the world. There is no chance that the U.S. government will fail to repay a loan drawn on that market, no chance that debt will not be refinanced, no chance that a bond might have to be dumped at a deep discount, measured in dollars. (This is not yet completely true of the euro. The reason is that there is no such thing as a "European" bond issued and backed by the same central authority that issues the European currency itself. Rather, to hold bonds in euro, one must hold the euro-denominated bonds of a particular national government, such as Italy—and while the risk of default on an Italian bond is low, under European arrangements it is not actually zero.)

Second, so long as most of the rest of the world holds their reserves in dollars, the currency or exchange rate risks of any one country doing the same thing are also low. There is safety in numbers; the currency that everyone holds is the one least likely to collapse. And this herd psychology is self-reinforcing: if no one expects the dollar to collapse because everyone else is holding it, then it will not collapse, almost no matter how many dollars are issued on world markets.

Third, other countries rightly sensed that in the final analysis, the United States would continue to provide a source of steadily growing demand for their goods simply because the political cost inside the United States of failing to do this would be too high. Therefore, export earnings would continue to be substantially in dollars, and dollar profits will continue to be available on the U.S. market. It would be imprudent to disturb this system, generating inflation and perhaps an unpredictable, defensive economic policy response from the United States, simply for the theoretical benefit of a better balance of financial holdings.

It is worth repeating: despite the entire panoply of conservative economic ideas on which it was based, the fundamental long-term contribution of the Reagan revolution played out on a different stage, little noted and only weakly understood at home. As we have seen, the Reaganite policies were apparently designed mainly in terms of domestic economic policy: to fight inflation, stimulate growth, promote the supposedly efficient working of private markets. As we have also seen, each of the policies employed—monetarism, supply-side tax cuts, deregulation—soon substantially disappeared under the weight of its costs. Monetarism was abandoned when it led to the 1982 recession, the supply-side tax cuts were largely recaptured in waves of tax reform and tax increases from 1982 through 1993, and deregulation in the most critical sector—banking—had to be undone after the savings and loan crisis unfolded in the late 1980s.

But in the one area it never advertised or sought to defend, the Reagan revolution not only achieved its purposes but endured: the domain of imperial finance. The radical monetary policies of the early 1980s engendered a new international financial system. The difference from what had followed the collapse of Bretton Woods was this: whereas the 1973 system opened the possibility that the yen or deutsche mark would come to coanchor the world system, the Volcker ascendancy from 1979 to 1982 made it clear that the United States would not tolerate any close competition to the dollar. And until the creation of the euro in 2001 the power of the dollar went unchallenged for nearly two decades. And so the United States could run unchecked, *whatever* trade deficit the demand for dollar balances in the world system prescribed. The ultimate triumph of the era came at the end of the 1990s, when the technology boom brought full employment, yet with low interest rates and a rock-steady international dollar. In this sense, one annoying claim that late 1990s conservatives made was actually true: by restoring the hegemony of the dollar, Reaganism was responsible for—it did enable—the Clinton boom.

Then in 1989 the cold war ended. And in addition, Europe consolidated itself into an economic and ultimately into a currency union, setting the stage for fundamental change.

When the cold war ended, one pillar of the dollar was weakened, for now the need for an American-led security umbrella came into question. The aftermath of 9/11 briefly restored this belief, but with the Iraq invasion, confidence in U.S. foreign policy further eroded, and so did the dollar.* This has partly to do with distrust of American motives, partly with the perception that the global war on terror is a fraud. And it has partly to do with the understanding, which prevails everywhere outside

*At this writing, the decline is by roughly a third against the euro.

the United States, that the solution to the threat of terror is political, diplomatic—and a matter of police work. It is not primarily military, and there is not very much that military means can contribute to it.

In addition, there is a growing awareness that U.S. military power—indeed, that all military power—has reached its demonstrated limits in Iraq. The United States, acting largely alone, could from the 1950s through the 1980s provide a perimeter defense against the Soviet Union. To hold that perimeter in most of the world, after all, did not require actual fighting. (And one can reasonably question, in retrospect, how aggressive the Soviet Union was, especially toward Western Europe and Japan.) But the United States is not capable of providing security to an empire, even a small one, against the determined fighting opposition of those who live there. This is not a limitation of American forces, but simply a fundamental fact about the limits of military power in the modern world.

Without a persuasive security justification, what then held the dollar in place? In the late 1990s, financial crises in Asia and Russia were complemented by the extraordinary rise of the American stock market, particularly the NASDAQ, which made the U.S. economy once again the favored destination for profit-seeking capital. There was no difficulty, under those conditions, sustaining a growing trade deficit and a strong dollar. But when the technology boom collapsed, that second pillar weakened, for now American growth became unsure. And yet this pillar too was restored, beginning in 2003, by economic recovery in the United States, fueled by a combination of government spending for the Iraq war and other purposes and by the continuing apparent strength of the housing sector.

As we now know, the strength of housing after 2003 was built on the subprime mortgage market. It was yet another bubble, which has turned, and continues to turn, into yet another bust. And so the question must be raised: What will happen next?

The domestic implications of the unfolding mortgage crisis include the personal effects on hundreds of thousands of displaced people, most of them quite poor, many elderly, all under conditions of extreme distress. It includes the neighborhood effects, as those who are not foreclosed suffer the consequences of boarded-up houses in decaying cul-de-sacs nearby. It includes the banking effects, as the credit that has fueled the home equity borrowing explosion dries up. And it includes the downstream effects on economic activity, which historically is largely driven, both up and down, by the ebb and flow of investment in residential housing. These effects could drag on, and impede full economic recovery, for years.

The international consequences of a crisis in the U.S. credit markets could be, under these conditions, even more severe. In this grim environment, it is to be expected that foreign investors and foreign central banks will begin to look for other ways to ensure their financial stability. The possibility is certainly there, and some will certainly take it, of shifting into euro or at the least a more balanced and diversified portfolio of dollars, euro, pounds, and yen. From this point of view, the days of the hegemonic dollar system may be numbered.

But while this is possible, it is not certain. The dollar reserve system still is not dead. It is not even necessarily dying nor its fate sealed. Like the Ottoman Empire it may endure for a time—perhaps a very long time—simply because it would be costly and dangerous to let it fail. The dollar could fall in value for a while, reach a value at which those who hold dollars cease to expect further falls, and then stop falling. It could be restored for a time by another round of global monetary shock therapy, in the Reagan-Volcker style—though the consequences for the rest of the world of that would be cataclysmic. Alternatively, we could perhaps see something prepared—a new system toward which the global monetary arrangements might evolve without disaster. Each of these alternatives is possible. None of them is certain. That is the condition of the world in which we live. We simply do not know.

The question for policymakers is this: Given that we do not know, what should we do? If the analysis above is correct, it has three essential lessons.

First, so long as the dollar reserve system holds, the rules really are different for the United States. The United States is not Argentina; it holds a position in the world economy that Argentina does not. Any statement or claim that the United States cannot, or must not, act to make investments or set standards must explain why such actions would erode or destroy the dollar reserve system. If they would not do that, there is no financial argument against taking those actions. The statement that the financial markets would treat the United States as they treat Argentina is simply unfounded, because the United States has never been in Argentina's position of dependence on the international financial markets, operating in the currency of some other country.

Second, if my argument about the relationship between financial and military security is correct, then it would be very useful for the United States to reconsider how best to re-create a global framework for collective security in which other countries would be willing to place their trust. A system based mainly on military power, financed through the dollar reserve system, provides neither comprehensive security nor a compelling case for preserving the reserve system. It particularly provides no clear argument for a creditor like China, a geopolitically independent country outside the U.S. security perimeter, whose external economic relations may as easily be threatened as protected by American military power. A system based on U.S. investment and leadership in a system of collective security might—and here the word *might* is carefully chosen—have a stronger argument for the continuing financial support of the wider world.

Third, the experience of the late 1990s showed plainly that it is not necessarily dangerous to be doing things. The flow of capital depends on the flow of profits, and a rising market, fueled by the underlying activity of the technology boom, brought money in, supporting the dollar even as the trade deficit grew. The rest of the world will invest in America, in other words, if they are given a reason to do so.

Why not give them that reason? This argument, if it is correct, suggests that the way to protect the dollar reserve system is *not* to play the cautious card of inaction and of placing "fiscal responsibility" before other goals. It is, rather, to focus the dynamism of the underlying economy. A program of planning and of standards, particularly if it is aimed at providing a new generation of investment goods to the world and especially if that generation of goods is itself directed at meeting the challenge of climate change, could in fact move the world back toward a dollar-centric system, preserving the leadership position of the United States and thus the country's capacity to lead effectively.

Here is the key question: What would be the impact on the dollar of a major change in American policy, away from predation and toward collective international security, toward domestic full employment and infrastructure renewal, and toward renewed technological leadership in the areas most needed by the world, such as climate change? Could and would the world react to this by extending to this country the financial backing required to pull off the transition?

We do not know for sure. The world might turn against us. Perhaps it has already done so. In that case, the option—perhaps under those conditions, the only viable option—of closing the U.S. economy until our underlying technological and competitive position has been restored would have to be considered. But it is also possible, and perhaps more likely, that the world has not turned against us yet. And in that case, there is the vastly easier, infinitely more promising path of asking the world, once again, to hold our bonds while we launch ourselves on the path of internal reconstruction and renewal.

And that brings us to the final, decisive issue: What would be the consequence of such an initiative for the policy posture of Europe, China, Japan, and other financial powers? What would they think about it, and what would they do?

The answer can only depend on the difference between a world ruled by fear and one ruled by hope. The existing system has been held together by military power and by a shared perception of threat. The rationale for that system has disappeared, and the cynical effort to replace it with a facsimile, the global war on terror, has failed. Meanwhile, the fear of (or respect for) U.S. power as such has also lost its hold, as the limits to that power are increasingly apparent. So, plainly, the effort to continue with a world financial system based on the *perception* of U.S. power risks coming to an end sooner or later.

For this reason, if there are other ways to make the financial bargain with the rest of the world, then they must be chosen. And in principle, such ways do exist. The world needs a financial anchor: the United States provides one. The world needs a scientific and technological leader: the United States has been, is, and can continue to be that leader. The world needs a country with the capacity to innovate, change, define the course of economic development going forward. That has been the historical American role.

And despite the wrecking efforts of the conservative economic worldview, despite the rise of the Predator State, these strengths to a large extent remain. The conservatives, when in power, were not fully effective. The ideology of free markets behind which they hid is bankrupt, but the country is not. The underlying stability and versatility of the quasi-public institutions in the United States have not disappeared. Our universities and research centers remain the leading technical and scientific institutions that the world has. Our government can be repaired. Mechanisms for creating new institutions as they are needed, and for forging new directions for those that we already have, exist. The way forward is to use them. At the same time we must come to grips with the need for effective and enforced regulation and break the power of the predatory elements—of the culture of predation—over the government and major corporations.

Should this be done, with commitment, energy, competence, and good faith, there is no reason that the rest of the world should not be willing, indeed eager, to allow the United States the financial leeway that it requires in order to forge the tools and make the investments that alone can overcome the climate crisis, set the direction of a new, energy-sane economy, and secure the survival of human civilization at large. There may be other ways to achieve this objective, and perhaps sooner or later they will have to be called on. But this one can be implemented, or at least attempted, from the current point of departure. It can be done without first demanding worldwide political changes, without first rebuilding the existing financial structure, and quickly enough to make a material difference in a short time. It is clearly the path of least resistance and therefore the right first line of attack.

From that point of view, and so long as this opportunity may exist, then—to borrow once again from Margaret Thatcher—is there any alternative?

ACKNOWLEDGMENTS

On Wednesday, April 26, 2006, I visited my father in his room at Cambridge's Mount Auburn Hospital for what would prove to be the last time. I told him a little bit of what I'd been working on, and he said, "You should write a short book on *corporate* predation. It will make you the leading economic voice of your generation." Then he paused and added, with his usual modesty, "If I could do it, I would put you in the shade."

I told this story a month later at his memorial, held on a glorious traditional Memorial Day in Harvard's Memorial Church. Shortly there came a message from Bruce Nichols, my editor at the Free Press on *Created Unequal*, suggesting that I actually write the book. And though I could not commit at that moment, some months later, when relations with another editor turned sour, Bruce came through to rescue and guide this project. So my most important immediate debt is surely to him. I have also a deep obligation to my talented agent, Wendy Strothman, and to Bruce's successor at the Free Press, Martin Beiser, who took over in the late stages and brought the manuscript home.

At the LBJ School of Public Affairs, I am ever grateful to my assistant, Paula Bickham, for keeping me stable and organized over the past ten years. I thank my dean, Jim Steinberg, for letting me go on leave on short notice in the fall of 2006; ultimately the first draft of this book started to take shape at the end of the year in an apartment in the city of Fuzhou, in southern China. My young collaborators in the University of Texas Inequality Project have done much of the hard technical work that underlies the argument in these pages even though that is, by design, only described lightly here. Every UTIP team member has helped in one way or another, but I have specifically relied here on work done with Enrique Garcilazo, Olivier Giovannoni, and Travis Hale. I am indebted to Dimitri Papadimitriou and the Levy Econom-

209

ics Institute, who over many years have supported my writing on macroeconomics. Finally I have profited from constant interaction with my friends and colleagues in Economists for Peace and Security, the economist's home for the analysis of the costs of war and the benefits of stable collective security arrangements. A year as a Carnegie Scholar was not originally justified by this project, but it helped, and the support of the Carnegie Corporation is gratefully acknowledged.

Certain parts of this book have been adapted—in all cases extensively—from essays published elsewhere. Chapter Four was first sketched in the *Journal of Post Keynesian Economics*. Chapter Seven is broadly based on an essay originally prepared for *Social Policy and Philosophy*. Chapter Eight has its origins in an argument published in *Industrial and Corporate Change*, while Chapter Nine builds on an argument that first appeared in my Foreword to the 2007 reprinting, by Princeton University Press, of my father's classic work, *The New Industrial State*. Chapter Thirteen has some roots in a debate with Jeff Faux in *The American Prospect* online. Chapter Ten takes up an argument that I tried to develop, perhaps with more flair than coherence, in lectures at the New School University, the University of Southern Maine, and the European Association for Evolutionary Political Economy at various times in the past several years. I have appreciated and learned from the audiences on each occasion.

This book has not had the benefit of as many outside readings and conversations with colleagues as I would have liked. But I especially thank Bob Auerbach, Bruce Bartlett, Norman Birnbaum, Bill Black, Jack Blum, Ping Chen, Sandy Darity, Susan Feiner, Tom Ferguson, Wynne Godley, Michael Lind, Douglas Massey, Stanislav Menshikov, Warren Mosler, Alain Parguez, Luigi Pasinetti, Erik Reinert, my dear friend the late Elspeth Rostow, Ajit Singh, Bat Sparrow, Pan Yotopoulos, and Janine Wedel for general or specific inspiration at various times and places. Karel von Wolferen holds a special place on this list for having discussed over several days in Amsterdam the core ideas and presentation at an early stage. I also thank Wiliam Forbath and the participants in the colloquium on neoliberalism at the University of Texas Law School for an inspired afternoon's discussion of the manuscript.

Finally I thank my older children, Doug and Eliza, for occasional companionship; my young daughters, Eve and Emma, especially for inspiring good humor; and my wife, Ying, for just about everything else: love, support, patience. Especially patience.

Errors, of course, remain my own responsibility.

INDEX

211

ABOUT THE AUTHOR

James K. Galbraith is an economist whose previous books include *Created Unequal: The Crisis in American Pay* (Free Press, 1998) and *Balancing Acts: Technology, Finance and the American Future* (Basic Books, 1989). His columns and articles appear frequently in *Mother Jones*, *The American Prospect*, *The Nation*, and *The Texas Observer*, among others, and in many academic journals.

Galbraith holds the Lloyd M. Bentsen, Jr. Chair in Government/ Business Relations at the Lyndon B. Johnson School of Public Affairs, the University of Texas at Austin. He is a senior scholar with the Levy Economics Institute and chair of the Board of Economists for Peace and Security, a nonprofit professional organization. In the early 1980s, he served as executive director of the Joint Economic Committee of the U.S. Congress.